CARIBBEAN TEARS

By
Emiliya Ahmadova
A PSYCHOLOGICAL thriller

Library of Congress Control Number:2019919971
Copyright © 2019 by Emiliya Ahmadova.
 All Rights Reserved.
ISBN: 978-1-7336982-9-0
Illustrations inside of the book by IMarts
Illustrations copyright@ Emiliya Ahmadova
Publisher: Women's Voice Publishing House

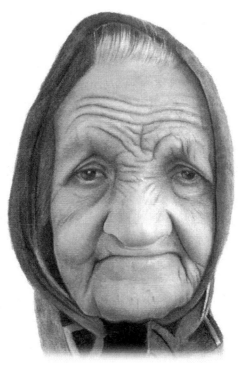

In loving memory of my dear granny, Aliya Mehtieva, daughter of Sanan. Sunrise 1939, 15th October and Sunset 8th August 2018. She was an angel who devoted her life to raising me and my three siblings up by herself. She was my protector, mother, father, and granny at the same time. For us she faced many tribulations and sacrificed her happiness. On cold winter days, in her old age, she used to leave the house at 3 p.m., and travel to the city. There, she would stand outside in the snow and rain till 8 p.m., selling plastic bags in order to buy food for us. Sometimes, on the way home in the dark, she would fall because of bad eyesight. There were times when she only made money enough to buy one loaf. She would come home and divide it between her four grandchildren but would not eat anything herself. At other times, whatever little change she made she would give to the poor. Despite the fact that she had a very difficult life and faced many tribulations, she stood strong on her feet. She never accepted any help from anyone. I will always remember you, Granny.

In memory of my brother Ruslan Ahmadov. Sunrise 28th July, 1978- Sunset 25th May 2019. He was a man who sacrificed his happiness for the sake of his granny! He spent the last ten years of his life taking care of her. Twenty-four hours a day he had to deal with the effects of dementia that Granny had. Because of this he was unable to create his own family. Looking after her affected his life, sleep pattern, and health in negatives ways, but he stood behind her until the end of his life. Unfortunately, his life was cut short at the age of 39 because of a heart attack. Rest in Peace, my brother.

Please say a prayer for both of them and light a candle.

***

This story is also dedicated to those who became victims of kidnapping and trafficking, were killed or raped, or who have lost loved ones by violent death. It is also dedicated to those whose lives have been affected by evil's presence, which keeps causing chaos and destruction in this world.

It is time to break the bonds of evil and welcome goodness into society. The change must start within you and spread to your surroundings. Let love blossom in your heart, nurturing kindness, righteousness, and patience towards others.

ACKNOWLEDGEMENT

All glory goes to God for allowing me to write this and other books. Without God there would be a void in my soul. He is our hope, protector, and the one who is always there for us. Having Him in our lives nurtures our souls and makes us better persons. He plants seeds of hope and goodness in our hearts and minds.

Demons may distract and mislead us with their lies and hatefulness towards humanity, but God listens to our prayers and continues performing miracles.

My gratitude extends to my editor, Kathy Ree, and to my family, especially Granny. She always used to tell me that my gift of writing came from Jesus and kept encouraging me with her words of wisdom and kindness. She was everything for me.

Thanks also to my illustrator, Imarts, for the drawings of my granny and Candice, plus the title drawing. She has done a wonderful job, and can be found on https://www.fiverr.com

TABLE OF CONTENTS

PROLOGUE

The evil forces under the command of Satan roam the earth to destroy and take away every chance that humans might have to enter Paradise.

Resentful, filled with jealousy, and doomed, they cause chaos and destruction everywhere. Their only goal is to throw mankind into the pit of burning fire by planting anger, depression, lust, and every type of sin into humans' hearts and minds.

People are being killed, raped, used, and abused. Marriages are broken. Human life has no value anymore. Women and children are being trafficked for sex or free labor, and sometimes even for organs. Prostitution, drugs, corruption, and gang war is widespread, and faith in God is being diminished. Satan has corrupted the world with greed, power, and false promises!

These evil forces are always on guard, attaching themselves to the weak, especially those who do not lead a life of prayer. However, not everything is lost. God is far greater and more powerful than Satan.

ABDUCTED

17th December, 7 p.m.

The wild wind swirled the dust from the ground and swayed the branches of the trees. Rain showers followed soon after, making the roads muddy and dangerous. The thunder that accompanied it roared like a hungry lion in search of prey.

Father Piero sat in his living room, his attention fixed on the TV screen before him. What was on the news was a lot more important than the wild weather raging outside.

The reporter was saying, "There are only a few days left before New Year's, and the rate of murders still keeps rising, promising to make this year one of the worst this island has seen. Yesterday, another life was taken away.

"The partially-burnt body of a man of African descent was discovered near the Poreto forest by a farmer. This latest victim was tied to a tree. He was wearing jeans and a blue t-shirt. No identification was found on him. The police have yet to identify the man, who has become the 491st victim of murder for this year. WCB police station is requesting information from anyone who might know his identity."

"There is yet another case of domestic violence. The mother of two children was rushed to the hospital after her drunken husband chopped into her hands with a cutlass. The woman is in stable condition but might never be able to use her hands again due to deep tissue damage."

A sudden rush of wind found its way into Father Piero's humble dwelling; without warning, the rain was slashing through his living room. Lightning streaked across the firmament and lit up his surroundings for a moment, especially the part of the wall where a huge cross hung. Father focused his attention on it and made the Sign of the Cross.

"Lord Jesus Christ, Son of God, have mercy on me, a sinner. Have mercy on our nation."

Then he rushed to the window and shut it. He looked at the empty street, and at his friend Miguel's two-story white house across from him. Miguel had to leave his family alone when working night shifts, so Father Piero always watched his house, like a loyal watchdog making sure that his owners are safe.

Hmm. Miguel isn't at home yet. I told him to change his night shifts to daytime ones. But then he would have to stop his night adventures! Which he refuses to do. Lord, please put some sense into him.

A lightning strike illuminated the sky once more. Father Piero's keen eyes noticed dark shadows flying in the sky. His forehead wrinkled as he struggled to figure out what those dark masses might be. His body was suddenly overcome by shivers.

Why am I feeling as if something weird is going to happen? I do not like this peculiar sensation at all! Lord Jesus Christ ,have mercy on us sinners.

He flinched nervously, crossed himself again, and closed the curtains. Then he sank back into his armchair.

Sheila, Miguel's wife, sat on the bed while her two children snuggled under the sheet in her spacious, cream-colored bedroom. She was reading 'The Brave Mouse' to them.

"And the courageous mouse lived blissfully ever after," she said, and put the book on the bedside table.

Thunder clapped and echoed in her bedroom, sending shudders into six-year-old Nadia's body. She seized her brother's hand.

"Mummy, I'm afraid. Please come and lie next to me," said Nadia, as her body flinched.

"Princess, what are you afraid of?" asked Sheila, a smile forming on her face.

"Thunder. It makes a frightening and eerie noise."

Her mother caressed the child's head.

"There's nothing scary about it. It's just a hollow sound."

"Mummy, why is Daddy taking so long to come home?" asked 10-year-old Ronnel. With his short height and slim figure, he could pass for a child of seven.

Sheila glanced at her watch. "His night shift isn't over yet."

She picked up her cell phone from the bedside table and tried to call him, but his phone just kept ringing.

Why isn't he answering? He sure has been behaving oddly lately.

Her thoughts were interrupted by Ronnel's voice.

"But he never worked so late before. Now he comes home after we fall asleep."

She leaned towards him and tousled his short black hair.

"Nosy parker. He used to have morning shifts, but now he works evenings."

She turned off the ceiling light, leaving the wall light over the bed on. Then she lay down on the bed between her children.

"It's late now. So please close your eyes and try to sleep."

Nadia hugged Sheila and put her head on her chest. Then she lifted it up and looked at her mother.

"Mummy, can you please read another story?"

"No, no, no. Put your head down and sleep."

Nadia lay back and closed her eyes. Sheila hugged her and they lay quietly together until they all fell asleep.

At 4 a.m., feeling unwell, Miguel left the police station

and slowly drove his Mercedes-Benz home. While he was in the police station, he managed to run to the toilet a few times. He had hoped to stop by his usual place after work, but the stomach bug halted his plans. As he drove, he rubbed his belly with one hand.

No boy I can't go there like this.

His eyes kept closing, and he fought to stay awake, trying to focus on the road ahead of him.

I shouldn't have eaten peppery doubles.[1]

He glanced in his rear-view mirror and saw a speeding jet-black cargo van drive up behind him. Its windows were heavily tinted, hiding the driver as well as the passengers.

Miguel pressed the lock button on the door. Then he touched his pistol, which was lying in the storage compartment.

I should stop that car and issue a speeding ticket.

The cargo van tried to overtake him from the left side of the road. Miguel pressed his foot on the accelerator and drove to the left lane, ending up right in front of the van. The driver of the other car reduced speed and changed lanes. Both vehicles stopped in front of the traffic light.

"Hey, man! Are you rushing for a date with a hot chick?" shouted Miguel, trying to get a glimpse of the driver.

As soon as the light changed to green, Miguel turned his car to the left, drove between some houses, and then parked his car in front of his gate. When he got out of the driver's seat, his cell phone fell on the wet asphalt and rolled under the car.

"Oh, shit!"

He stooped down and reached under the Benz.

The van came to a halt five houses away from Miguel's. The driver and one of the two passengers got out of the van and cautiously observed the area. They wore black gloves and masks.

One of them was a woman named Candice, or Candy, and the other was a man by the name of Leroy. He had lost an eye

---

[1] Trini doubles are chickpea sandwiches-made of bread called bara and filled with a spiced chickpea filling -channa.

and now wore an artificial one, so he was better known as Cyclops. They were armed with Beretta pistols loaded with 14 rounds of 9mm ammunition.

The tall and thin Cyclops pointed at Miguel.

"Let's go and get him before anyone sees us," he said.

Errol, whose nickname was Kingpin, stayed inside the van. He touched his beard and then rolled down the window.

"Remember, we need her alive and unharmed!" he said.

"What about Miguel and his little bastards?" Cyclops inquired.

"You gonna kill dem all. It's payback time.[2]"

"No! You gave me your word that you wouldn't touch Miguel," said Candy, as she adjusted the mask on her face.

"Because of him my brother locked up and we lost millions. Police should know that they can't push their noses into our business."

Kingpin hit the steering wheel, and when he did, a white plated-gold skull ring, encrusted with diamonds, caught Candy's attention.

"*No bossman[3], buh yuh..,*" protested Candy.

Kingpin seized her hand and squeezed it tightly.

"Whey yuh say?"[4]

"Aye-yah-yie dat huttin![5]" said Candy.

"I will not tolerate the slackness. You had better use some brain. It became rusty!"

He let go of her hand.

"It won't happen again!" she blurted out.

Kingpin paused for a second, his hand on his chin.

"Leave him alive but slaughter his children in front of him and burn down his house. Let him stand outside and see his

---

[2] You going to kill them all. It is payback time.
[3] Boss man is a male leader. No boss man but you…
[4] What did you say?
[5] Ouch that's hurts.

house being destroyed. After that, his life will be worthless."

I will exterminate him myself, like a cockroach, at a later time.

"Hey, don't forget this!"

Kingpin pulled out a plastic bag with a soaking-wet rag in it and handed it to Cyclops.

Miguel pulled his cell phone out from underneath the car. Soaked to the skin, he pushed open his gate and ran towards the door. He searched his pants pockets for his bunch of keys, but they weren't there.

They might have fallen out when I looked for the cell phone.

He rang the doorbell nonstop.

"He's by the door now. Get him!" ordered Kingpin.

Cyclops ran toward Miguel's house and stepped into his yard.

Kingpin lifted a black bag from the passenger's seat and handed it through the window to Candy.

"Take it and go! Don't do anything stupid."

Candy grabbed the black bag and ran. Kingpin rolled up the window and leaned back in his seat.

These two chupidy 6 have no brains at all. When all of this done, I will get rid of them as well, especially her. She's getting too soft.

As Cyclops ran, he pulled the rag out of the plastic bag. He stopped out of sight of the gate, climbed over it, and crept up behind Miguel. He wrapped his right hand around Miguel's throat and tried to put the rag on his nose.

Miguel pushed Cyclops' left hand away from his face, at the same time hitting him with his elbow and trying to turn

---

6 Stupid person

around. However, as Cyclops' grip tightened around his throat, he began choking. With both hands, Miguel clutched at the hand that was taking the life out of him, which allowed Cyclops to put the chloroform-soaked rag over Miguel's nose. With all his might, Miguel kept trying to pull Cyclops' hand away from his throat.

Miguel blacked out. The thug dropped him on the ground by the door.

Candy ran up to them, out of breath.

"Is he okay?"

"Stop worrying about dat, gyul, and focus on finishing de work or dey guh kill we."[7]

Cyclops rang the doorbell as his accomplice's eyes darted over at the neighbors' windows.

"Damn it, I'm soaking!" she said loudly.

"Yuh dotish owwa?[8] Someone might hear you," whispered Cyclops. Candy noticed that his hands were shaking.

The doorbell chimed impatiently, filling the whole house with its disturbing noise. Ronnel opened his eyes and lay staring at the ceiling for a moment. Nadia sat up and looked over at the bedroom's door, her eyebrows raised. Then her attention shifted to her mother.

"Mummy, Mummy, wake up! Daddy came!" Nadia cried, as she shook her mother.

Sheila opened her eyes as Ronnel got out of the bed.

"What happened?"

"The doorbell is ringing," said Ronnel.

Sheila rose and rushed out of the bedroom. As she got to the stairs, she noticed her children following her.

"Go back to your own rooms!" she said.

She left them standing on top of the staircase, and hurried to let her husband in.

Why can't he open the door himself? Is he drunk again?

---

[7] Stop worrying about him, girl, and focus on finishing the work or they will kill us."[7]
[8] Are you stupid or what?

Ronnel glanced at his sister.

"Go to your room!" he told her.

"I don't want to stay alone. The lightning might enter my room and burn me," said Nadia, as she grasped her brother's hand.

"Don't be silly. Lightning can't burn you."

Nadia pulled Ronnel's hand. "Let's go," she said.

The children returned to their parents' bedroom instead of their own. They lay on the bed under the sheet in hopes that their mom and dad wouldn't make them leave.

Sheila opened the front door without looking through the peephole. Before she could react, Cyclops rushed inside. Sheila screamed and ran for the stairs.

"Help!"

She had gripped the rails of the staircase and was taking the first step when he caught at her hair.

"Help me!" she screamed again. The lightning struck again.

"Ah chut nah!"[9]

Her plea for help echoed in the children's ears. They quickly jumped off the bed but found themselves frozen in fear. It felt as if they were glued to the floor. Their eyes swept the room, looking for a place to hide. Then, at the same time, both ran to hide behind the curtain.

Cyclops pulled back on Sheila's hair, forcing her to come down a few steps.

"If one more word come out of your mouth, I will buss[10] your brain to the pieces," he said, pointing the Beretta at her head. He glanced briefly at the kitchen's entry.

His partner in crime entered the corridor, carrying a black duffel bag. She dropped it on the floor.

"What to do with Miguel?" she asked in a shaky voice. "Someone might notice him."

---

[9] Shut up
[10] Burst

"Drag him in and tie his hands!"

"Hull yuh ass[11] to de kitchen!" he ordered his captive, pushing her roughly. She dragged her legs to the kitchen, shaking like a leaf and ready to collapse at any moment.

"Sit on dat[12] stool!" he ordered.

She turned to face him and, with pleading eyes, touched his hand.

"Please take whatever you wish and go," she said.

He pushed her hand away, avoiding eye contact. She could smell the odor of alcohol emanating from him. The scent was so strong that she felt dizzy.

"Listen, you woman. Doh make dis ting hard fuh yuhself. Glue yuhself to dat stool and hush yuh mouth!"

Quivering, Sheila quietly dropped down on the stool.

Upstairs behind the curtain, Nadia wet herself. Her knees quivered uncontrollably. She embraced her brother tightly.

"Why is Mummy shouting?" whispered Nadia. Her teeth chattered.

"Shh. They're going to hear you," he whispered back.

The boy took his sister's wrist and pulled her to the closet. He pushed her deep inside, behind the clothes. Shaking, he tiptoed to the door.

"Don't leave me alone here," she pleaded.

Ronnel looked back at the closet and put his finger on his lips. Beads of sweat rolled down his forehead.

"Shut up nah, dey guh fund we.[13] "

Candy dragged Miguel through the door and left him lying in the corridor. Her hands shook as she stared at him, and her heart skipped several beats. She shook her head and turned to shut the door.

---

[11] Move over, keep going.
[12] That
[13] Shut up, they will find us.

9

She took out some ropes from the bag and tied Miguel's hands behind his back, then tied his legs together. When that was done, she stood and silently observed his chest going up and down. She blinked back tears.

"I know you don't deserve this. But I must follow orders, or they'll kill me," she whispered.

Cyclops walked to the window and gazed outside. Then his attention shifted to Sheila. He strolled towards her while his pistol pointed at her head.

"No! Please, no! Let us go!" Sheila implored him, staring into his red eyes.

"Allyuh women doh[14] understand de simple instructions."

"My husband will pay you handsomely."

"Shut yuh mouth gyul15!"

"Why is this happening to us?" she whispered, her face wet with tears. Her gaze shifted around the room.

What to do? The kids are still upstairs. Think, girl! They gonna kill us all if I don't do something!

The knife on the counter caught her attention. The rain continued drumming on the window, making it hard to hear inside the kitchen.

Get up, gyul, and get dat knife. Either dem or yuh family.

The neighbor's dogs began barking loudly. Cyclops dashed to the window. His curious eyes darted from side to side as he gazed into the darkness.

"Damn it. These dogs will wake the people up."

Sheila rose, feeling every beat of her racing heart. Everything seemed to be spinning around her. Slowly, she tiptoed to the counter, biting her lower lip. She picked up the knife and dashed toward the intruder, the knife in the air. With

---

[14] Do not
[15] Shut up

all her strength, she slashed the weapon down.

The sudden pain in his upper arm made Cyclops spin around. Sheila let go of the knife and moved backwards, her eyes glued on him. With a painful grimace, he pulled the knife out of his arm. He stared at his t-shirt, which was now splashed with blood. Some of it dripped onto the tiled floor.

Sheila's eyes widened as cold sweats ran over her body. She found herself backed up against the cupboard with nowhere to go.

"I... I... sorry. I didn't mean..."

Cyclops flew across the room like a tornado, pointing the bloody knife at her. She shut her eyes, ready to scream.

"Damn you. You gonna pay for this!"

He grabbed her hair and pulled her away from the cupboard.

"I doh like harden[16] women."

"Please, no, no, no!" she pleaded.

He put the knife to her neck and cut off the fistful of hair he held. It dropped to the floor. Sheila's limbs shook, and her legs became so weak that she slowly slid down.

He pulled her up, causing her to cry out in pain.

"Please don't do this! Have mercy on my kids," she cried out.

"Allyuh women only causing bacchanal with allyuh ole talk[17]. Hush yuh mouth."

Suddenly Sheila felt a blinding flash of pain as a pistol butt hit her on the head. She collapsed on the floor, yellow lights flashing before her eyes.

Candy stooped down and pointed a handgun to Sheila's head.

"Boy, you cyah[18] even handle one woman. I guh[19] shoot

---

[16] I do not like disobedient women.
[17] All you women only causing confusion with your old talk.
[18] Cannot
[19] Gonna

she," she said.

"Buh wait nah gyul!20 Bossman want she alive," said Cyclops.

"Fuh real?21" Me'en know."

Candy spat on Sheila and walked into the hallway. Then she took out another rope from the bag and came back.

Sheila opened her eyes. "Oh, oh! God, please help us!" she prayed aloud.

"Tie she with the rope and make she shut up. Otherwise I'll end she life," Candy said, staring at Sheila's pretty face.

"You want she dead. So yuh cah have she....22"

Candy gazed coldly at his face.

"Hey Cyclops, mind your own damn business," she interrupted him.

"Who are you? What do you need from us?" groaned Sheila.

Candy slapped Sheila in the face.

Cyclops pulled Sheila's hands behind her back and tied them. He took out a roll of masking tape from his pocket and taped her mouth as she kept whispering, "No. no, no..."

Miguel opened his eyes slightly and raised his head. He gazed around, his body stiff.

"What's happening?"

Out of the corner of his eye, he caught a glimpse of his wife, sobbing as she stood in the kitchen surrounded by intruders. Her husband's face reddened.

I will kill them all if a hair falls from her head.

He turned his hands from side to side, loosening the rope enough to pull out his left hand, thus freeing himself. Then he kicked the rope from his legs. The vein in his temple throbbed.

He shot his gaze up the stairs. His son stood by the

---

[20] But wait a minute.
[21] Really? I did not know.
[22] You want her dead. So, you can have her...

slightly open door, staring at his father and shaking uncontrollably. Miguel waved his hand as if trying to push something away.

"Go and hide," he whispered.

Ronnel's eyes teared up. He looked back at his dad as he tiptoed away from the door.

His vision became blurry from tears as he crept to the closet, and his foot inadvertently kicked a toy fire truck. It began moving, and its loud siren spread through the house. Ronnel stood for a moment, motionless, watching his toy cross the floor. His heart jumped, as if trying to escape his chest.

They're going to find us!

He pulled himself together and dashed into the closet. His sister clutched him tightly.

"I heard Mummy. Why is she crying?"

"Tish! They're going to come here now."

Ronnel's knees shook as he looked out at his toy car.

"Please stop making noise," he pleaded, unable to take his eyes from it.

"I want to go to Mummy," whispered his sister.

"No, you can't go. They'll hurt you."

Nadia hugged her brother tightly and closed her eyes as her teeth chattered.

Hearing the siren, Miguel began running upstairs. Candy ran out of the kitchen and shot at him, hitting his leg. Miguel lost his balance and fell on his knee. Candy grabbed onto Miguel's shirt and pulled him back to the door, leaving a trail of blood on the steps. Then she kicked his injured leg.

"Go upstairs and get dem!" shouted Cyclops from the kitchen.

As she started toward the stairs, Miguel struggled onto his feet and threw himself on her. She in turn lost her balance and fell on the steps. Miguel shot past her and up a few steps, as fast as his aching knee would let him.

Candy caught his leg and pulled it. Miguel collapsed on the step, hitting his face.

She stood up, rubbing her aching chin. "Yuh look fuh dat,[23]" she whispered, afraid that he might recognize her voice.

Her companion in crime joined them. He directed a pistol to Miguel's head.

"Don't move!" he ordered.

Tremors shook Ronnel's hands when he heard Cyclops's voice.

"They're going to shoot Daddy, and then come for us," he said.

He pushed his sister under a shelf full of shoes and covered her with clothes. Then he left the closet and crawled under the bed.

Miguel's face and eyes reddened as Candy climbed the steps, a gun in her hand.

"You're not going to get away with this. The police will hunt you down if anything happens to us."

***

The rain kept overflowing the drains and flooding the farmers' crops.

Father Piero fell asleep in front of his TV. However, his slumber was interrupted when his phone began ringing nonstop. Irritated, he glanced at his watch and walked to the phone stand.

"Hmm. It's 4.40. a.m. Oh Lord, sometimes I do feel overwhelmed with all these late-night or early-morning calls. Don't they know that I need to sleep too?"

He picked up the phone. "Father Piero's residence."

---

[23] It's your own fault

At first, Father could only hear heavy breathing.

"Are you there?"

"Father Piero, I need your help."

Anil walked from one side of his bedroom to the other as he spoke to the priest. His eyes stopped on the TV, which was showing a video, paused at the moment. The scene was frozen on a man who was with two naked women. One of them sat on top of him while he was kissing the other.

"Who is it?" Father Piero's tired voice brought his attention back to the conversation.

"I tried, but I couldn't stop it!" Anil said.

His eyes ran around the room and stopped on a picture of his wife and stepdaughter, which sat on the bedside table.

Father Piero went to the window and gazed outside. He noticed a van parked by the neighbor's house.

What...? I don't recognize that car.

"She's pregnant now," whispered Anil.

"Pardon me. What are you talking about?"

Anil tried to light his cigarette with a match but dropped it on the floor. He put the cigarette in an ashtray and sat on the bed, rubbing his neck.

"The feelings towards my 14-year-old stepdaughter grew day by day. She blossomed into a beautiful young gyul. I couldn't control my desire for she. I drugged she and then had sex with she."

"What?"

"Yesterday, I heard she talking to someone over the phone. She carries my child. If dem find out it's mine, she mudda guh report de police. Me'eh know what to do."[24]

Father Piero squinted as he stared at the car. He noticed a silhouette of someone in the front seat.

---

[24] Her mother will report to the police. I don't know what to do.

Who would that be?

"Sorry, what did you say?"

Anil rubbed his head.

"I raped my stepdaughter!"

"This is a very grievous act. You should be calling the police, not me."

"No, jail is not fuh meh nah."[25]

Lightning lit Anil's bedroom.

"She's a sexy ting with big tot tots[26]. Oh boy, I tried to stay away from she. God is my witness. But whenever I try to conquer my desire, my thirst for she grows stronger."

Father Piero stared at Miguel's house. His eyes fixed on the kitchen window. Through the curtains he saw silhouettes of two people.

He isn't at home. Who is there?

"Fadda[27] are you there? I am little bit tipsi[28]. Aint thinking clearly."

Anil lifted a glass of rum from the bedside table and took a sip. As he stretched his leg, it touched an empty liquor bottle that had been left on the floor. It rolled to the wall.

Father Piero noticed a shadow in Miguel's bedroom window. He squinted his eyes, trying to get a clear picture.

The silhouette of someone holding a pistol went across the window. Seeing the gun, Father Piero quickly moved away from his own window. He disconnected the phone call and began dialing Miguel's number.

In Sheila's bedroom, Candy stared at the king-sized bed, with its maroon-colored silky bedding. She sat on it and rested her forearm on the edge of the bed, passing her hand over the

---

[25] No, jail is not for me
[26] Breasts
[27] Father
[28] Drunk

smooth sheet. Then Candy spread herself on the bed and crossed her legs.

In his hiding place under the bed, Ronnel closed his eyes and breathed slowly, careful not to move a muscle.

Nadia peeked out at Candy through the little space between the closet door's louvers. Her muscles tightened, and she could barely suppress a scream for help.

"Hurry up, gyul!" shouted Cyclops.

Candy sat up and retrieved her pistol. When she got off the bed, her foot hit the truck and the siren came on again. She picked the toy up from the tiled floor and turned off the sound. Then she tossed it onto the bed.

"I doh know why dey doz make these cheap toys fuh children nah!"

She turned and walked toward the closet. Nadia covered her face with her hands. Her heart raced.

"Did you find anyone?" shouted her partner in crime.

"Nah,[29] just a stupid truck that makes noise."

She walked towards the dressing table and touched Sheila's perfume. She sprayed herself with it, then dabbed some shiny lipstick on the part of her lips that weren't covered by the mask. Satisfied with her look, she then pulled out the drawers and searched inside of them. There were gold rings, bracelets, chains, and earrings. She put them all in her pocket except for the earrings, which she decided to wear.

These earrings will look better on me than she.

As she tried to put one on, it fell to the floor.

She bent and picked it up, and Ronnel noticed a tattoo of a snake on her hand.

The phone on the bedside table began to ring. She whirled and stared at it, motionless, eyes wide.

---

[29] No

Cyclops heard the phone, but he was too busy wrapping a rope around Miguel's legs to stop its ringing. He rose and glared toward the upstairs.

"Do something about the phone!" he shouted.

Even though Miguel's lips were sealed with a strip of tape, he kept trying to shout.

Sheila's gaze jumped from Cyclops to the phone that was on the kitchen's counter. She got up and dashed toward the instrument.

Leaving Miguel on the floor, Cyclops ran towards her.

"Hey, go back to your seat! Yuh harden thing,30 but dey guh tame you," he said.

The phone stopped ringing and the answering machine came on.

"This is Miguel and Sheila Siglobeen's residence. We're unavailable now. Please leave a voice message and we will return your call."

"Miguel, this is Father Piero. I saw some movements in your house. Since you aren't answering, I'm going to call the police."

"Oh shit," Cyclops murmured. Then he ran to the bottom of the stairs. "Hey! Come downstairs right now!" shouted Cyclops.

Candy quickly ran down the stairs and into the kitchen. Cyclops stood by the window gazing outside.

"The police will be here soon. We have to leave," said Cyclops, turning towards Candy.

He dialed his cell phone with shaky hands.

"Someone has seen us. Drive up to the doorway. We're coming," he spoke.

He wrapped his hand around the back of Sheila's neck.

"Walk outside!"

They marched towards the hallway. As they passed

---

30 Disobedient

Miguel, prone on the floor, Cyclops suddenly stopped, turned, and pointed his pistol toward Miguel's head.

Candy moved his hand away.

"What the hell are you doing? Leave he[31] alone!"

Cyclops punched Miguel in the mouth and nose, making him spit blood. Candy swore at him, and then ran to the kitchen to get a rag.

Sheila's eyes became moist as they passed over her wounded husband. Her knees shook with each step, and weakness took over her body.

A cargo van was parked by her gate. Sheila stopped and tried to look back, but Cyclops pushed her forward.

"Shif' yuh ass, woman![32]

As they got closer to the van, Kingpin got out and opened the side door.

"What have you been doing so long, sleeping?" he asked.

Cyclops let go of Sheila's hand and glanced at his boss.

"Woman gave some trouble."

Sheila punched Cyclops, hitting his artificial eye. It dropped out of its socket. She looked at his empty socket and then at the eye that had fallen at her feet.

Cyclops froze for a moment, which Sheila used to her advantage.

"Help me!" she screamed and ran towards the house.

Cyclops quickly retrieved his eye and chased after her. He got hold of her blouse, and she pulled herself forward to get away. Unfortunately, she overbalanced and fell face down. Cyclops hurriedly put his foot on her back.

Kingpin stood by the car, silently watching Cyclops's every action.

Just a dotish fool.

"Where do you think you're going?" said Cyclops.

---

[31] Him
[32] Keep going

He pulled her up and gave her a slap. Then he forced her into the van and made her lie down on the floor.

"How could you let her run away from you?" asked Kingpin.

Cyclops did not dare to look at him.

"She knocked my eye out, and I got confused."

Kingpin shook his head and then opened the driver-side door. He sat in the seat and took out a syringe from a storage compartment.

Cyclops pulled down the car seat and sat not far from Sheila, pointing his firearm at her. Sheila bent her knees towards her belly and lay silently, afraid to make any noise.

Kingpin stared at her over the back of his seat. "Inject she with this."

Cyclops took the syringe from Kingpin. He stooped down and grabbed her hand. She kicked him, and he dropped the syringe. Before she could make another move, Cyclops picked up the syringe and pressed harder on her hand, pinning it to her body. Then he injected her and freed her hand.

Almost immediately, Sheila began to feel drowsy and nauseous. Then she blacked out.

Kingpin's attention shifted to Cyclops' wound.

"What happened to your arm?" he asked.

"She stabbed me," said Cyclops.

"Why are you always running into chupidness? Is chupidness your middle name? Stay with she and don't mess my car with your blood."

Candy came up to the van, but didn't get in.

"Where's the first-aid kit?" Kingpin asked.

"It's in the bag, and I forgot it in the house," she said.

"Yuh rass chupid or wah?[33] You want to put police on our trail? Go and get it," said Kingpin.

She ran back to the house.

---

[33] Are you stupid or what?

Once inside, she found Miguel standing on the stairs and trying to walk up. She pushed him and he fell on the staircase. She picked the bag up and left the house.

Father Piero's hands trembled as he stood by the window witnessing Sheila being kidnapped. He kept trying to call the police but was getting a busy tone. He watched as Candy got into the van and shut the door. It sped off.

Finally, a woman answered. "Lestra police station."

"I saw three people kidnapping my neighbor!" shouted the priest, his forehead sweating. "There are children in the house, and possibly a man!"

"Please calm down. Where are you calling from?"

"Lestra, 23 Pentecost street. Please, hurry up!"

"Right now, we have no cars. As soon as we get one, we will send someone."

"Are you kidding? By the time the police show up, they'll be far away!"

Father Piero hung up the phone and paced nervously from one side of the room to the next, his hands behind his back.

What should I do? They could be bleeding to death.

He ran out of his house in his pajamas.

Nadia, still hiding under the shelf, burst into tears.

"Daddy, where are you? Help me! It's hot in here."

Hearing her cries, Miguel pulled the masking tape off his mouth and clutched the rails of the stairs.

"Oh, boy, that's hurts!"

Grimacing, he slowly pulled himself into a standing position. He tried to push forward but stumbled and hit his knee on the step. He pulled himself up again, leaving a trail of blood on the stair.

"Nadia! Ronnel! Are you okay?" he shouted.

Nadia's sobs became louder. Ronnel came out from under the bed and rushed to the closet to get his sister. He moved aside the clothes and took his sister's hand.

"Come out. They gone."

"No! Naughty people going to take me away!"

Ronnel pulled her out. He hugged her and patted her back.

"They aren't here anymore."

Her tears kept falling like a waterfall. She was shivering, and her teeth chattered.

"Where's Mummy?"

"I don't know."

"Son, pick up the phone and call Granny!" shouted Miguel.

Ronnel glanced at the door.

"Okay, okay. Don't cry." He hugged Nadia again. "We'll call Granny, okay?"

Ronnel walked towards the phone, his sister behind him. He dialed Granny's phone number.

"Daddy, come upstairs!" Nadia cried.

"Tish! I'm on the phone." Ronnel gave her an annoyed look.

Father Piero hurried into Miguel's house. As he dashed in, he found Miguel standing on the steps. Father ran towards him, then stooped down and began untying him.

"Thank you, Father," Miguel gasped.

"Oh, my God! You've been wounded! You must go to the hospital," he said.

He freed Miguel's legs and hands.

"Who did this to you?"

"I have no idea."

Miguel hurried upstairs. He opened the bedroom door and dashed in. Ronnel dropped the phone receiver, and both children ran towards him. Nadia embraced her father, burying her face into him.

"Where's Mummy?" asked Nadia through her sobs.

"She's..."

"Did they harm the children?" inquired the priest as he entered the bedroom.

Miguel looked at his children and sighed with relief. They didn't have even one scratch.

"They're shaken by this, but they're unhurt."

"I've called the police. They should arrive soon," said Father Piero.

Ronnel grabbed his father's hand.

"Daddy, did they take her away?"

Miguel caressed his son's head.

"We'll talk about it later," he said.

Nadia noticed the blood on her father's leg.

"Daddy, you have a cut."

Miguel squeezed out a smile. He lifted Nadia up and put her on the bed.

"You sit here. I have to take care of my wound."

She stared at his leg and then turned away.

Miguel rushed into the bathroom. He took out a first-aid kit from the corner stand and inspected his wound. The bullet was still there. He got a pair of tweezers and wet it with medical alcohol. He pulled out the bullet.

"Oh, shit."

Then he poured the alcohol on his wound and dressed it, all the time grimacing in pain.

Once the pain had receded a bit, he came out of the bathroom.

"I'm done."

"You had better take care of it as soon as possible."

"Father Piero, I will. As soon as I drop the children off at my mother's."

The priest patted Nadia's head.

"Keep them away from here till you find out who did this," he suggested.

"Father Piero, can you please stay and wait for the police? As soon as I take care of my wound, I'll be back," said Miguel.

"Yes, I'll stay and wait."

Miguel lifted Nadia. He grasped Ronnel's hand.

"Let's go, son."

He limped away, carrying his daughter and followed by his son. As they headed to the car, Ronnel spoke up.

"Daddy, she came upstairs and stole Mummy's jewelries."

Miguel opened the Benz's door, and the children clambered inside. He got in behind the steering wheel, then turned around to face them.

"Son, did you see her face?"

"No, Daddy. But I saw a snake drawing on her hand."

"Anything else?"

Ronnel looked up, trying to recall what he had seen.

"No, Daddy. She had a mask on. When she lay on your bed, I was afraid that she would see me underneath the bed."

Pearls of tears rolled down his face. He shook his head.

"I heard Mummy pleading for help, but I was too afraid to help her."

Nadia sat silently, looking at her brother. Then suddenly she burst crying.

"I want my Mummy! Why did they take her?"

Miguel got into the back seat and sat there hugging his children.

"Come on, calm down. You'll see Mummy soon. I promise you."

The day became lighter as the night left, and the rain stopped falling. The three of them, feeling the pain and remembering the night's events, sat silently as Miguel drove to his mother's. He then rushed to the hospital's emergency room. The wound was cleaned and stitched up.

Now came the hard part—returning to the scene of the crime.

THE BITTERNESS OF THE BROTHEL

Sheila opened her eyes and found herself lying on a dingy mattress. She sat up and looked around.

She was in an abandoned house. The room was dilapidated - rotten wooden walls and no furniture. The window had a dirty and thin curtain hanging across it.

She rubbed her head, which felt as if she had been hit by a sledgehammer or slammed into the wall.

"Uggh. Where am I? Miguel, where are you? My children..."

She forced herself to stand up, and immediately felt light-headed. The walls spun.

Sheila made a step towards the door, but a sudden pain in her ankle made her stop. She looked down and was horrified to see that she was chained down. There were scratches on her legs, caked with dried spatters. She noticed blood spots on her blouse.

How did I get them?

She grimaced at the pain behind her eyes. She dropped down and frantically twisted the leather cuff around her ankle, in an attempt to free herself.

After several unsuccessful tries, she walked towards the wall to which the chain was attached. She grabbed it and yanked on it. But the chain was firmly bolted to the wall.

I can't shift it. What to do!?

She trembled, and her eyes darted around as she dragged herself to the window. The chain ran out when she was two feet from it. She stretched out her hands towards the window.

I cannot reach it!

Her sobs echoed through the room. She dropped down on the floor.

They had Miguel. Ronnel and Nadia were upstairs.

She recalled waking up after the effects of the drug that she had been injected with wore off. As she opened her eyes, she found herself lying in the van. The front windows of the van were down. Outside were voices; it was a conversation between Candy and Cyclops. Sheila got up and peeked outside, trying not to be seen. When Candy turned around and looked at the van, Sheila quickly dropped back down. After a few minutes she peeked outside again. Seeing that her kidnappers were occupied with arguing about something, she slid the door open as quietly as possible. Noiselessly, she got out and crept away from the van.

"Why are these two idiots taking so long?" Candy asked.

"They probably stopped in the rum shop for a drink," Cyclops answered.

"No wonder why dey can't function properly."

Sheila began running away from the van. Candy turned around at that moment and noticed Sheila's escape.

"She's getting away! Get she!" she shouted and ran after her.

"You have nowhere to run!" she yelled at Sheila.

As she ran, Sheila kept searching desperately for a means to escape.

Suddenly she stumbled on a root. She fell but got to her knees and crawled as she tried to get her legs back under her.

Her pursuer caught up to her. She grasped Sheila's hair and forced her into a standing position.

"What did I ever do to you?" Sheila had asked, in tears.

Candy spat her gum out on the sand.

"Practically nothing. However, you should have left

Miguel a long time ago. You and he don't make a good match."

Sheila stared into Candy's eyes, then gave her one hard slap.

"Leave my husband alone!"

The unexpected blow made Candy bite her tongue. She felt a metallic taste in her mouth. With a snarl, Candy spat saliva mixed with blood into Sheila's face, and then pulled her hair. Sheila grasped Candy's hair. They began walking in circles.

"While you're gone, making money for us as a prostitute, your children will grow up without you. I will become their new mother."

With a cry, Sheila leapt at Candy, and dug her nails into Candy's neck.

As they struggled, Cyclops got behind Sheila and stuck her with a syringe. Sheila's grasp weakened, and everything before her eyes went blurry.

"Cowards! You won't get away with this," she slurred, as she fell to the ground.

Candice came up to her and kicked her until Cyclops pulled her away. Sheila blacked out completely.

Sheila's attention returned to her present predicament. She stared at her leg.

I need to pull myself together. I can't afford to lose my mind. My children need me.

She pulled the chain over and over, harder and harder. The skin on her palms became scratched and red from the effort.

"Ouch! Come on, get out! Damn you!" she said loudly.

Finally, she gave up, and let go the chain. As she quietly stared at it, thoughts of her family passed through her mind. She recalled her wedding day, and the birth of the children. She saw herself holding her newborn daughter as Miguel and Ronnel stood nearby, gazing at them.

As her aching heart worried for her family and her own plight, she heard distant voices. She jumped up and walked back to the window.

Her ear caught the distant roar of waves crashing on the beach. Then she heard footsteps. Two dark-skinned, shirtless, muscular men stopped outside the door.

The taller man, who wore a gold chain around his neck, turned to address his companion. "Bossman said you must ship her tonight on James' pirogue. They'll be waiting on the other side. Keep her quiet--the guards will be around."

"It won't be easy to silence her, Jaiden. She might try to escape as well," said Caleb who is called Toothless because of the gap between his teeth.

Jaiden sucked air through his teeth and stared silently at him.

"Toothless, are you bobolee34? I don't know why I always have to tell you what to do. Inject she with a drug. Tie she hands and legs, and tape she mouth. Anyway, where can she run?"

"Oh, yeah! It slipped my mind," said Toothless, hitting his forehead.

"For once, think with your brain, boy!"

As they approached the door, both put stocking masks over their heads. Sheila quickly moved away from the window and continued trying to free herself from the chain.

The door flew open, and the men came inside with weapons in their hands.

"Don't even think about it," said Jaiden.

Sheila let go of the chain and stared at him, her eyes wide.

"Let me go! If anything happens to me, my husband will hunt all of you down and kill you, one by one."

Toothless shot a penetrating look at Sheila.

"Your husband is a helpless man," he said, with a grin that showed his yellowed, gap-toothed teeth.

---

34 A Stupid Person.

Jaiden walked over to Sheila and pointed a pistol at her temple.

"Hush, woman. You are not in a position to threaten anyone," he said.

"Please free me. We'll pay you handsomely," she pleaded. Her eyes became teary and red.

Just then she noticed Toothless staring at her blouse. She looked down and, to her alarm, saw that part of her breast was exposed. Her eyes shot back up to meet his, and she pulled her blouse closed.

He walked over to her, licking his lips, as she tried to move away from him. With one sudden move, he yanked her hands away and burst her blouse wide open.

Sheila moved backwards.

"No, please! Don't you have a sister or mother?"

He pinned her to the wall and began kissing her as Jaiden watched silently.

"Damn it. She too hot," he mumbled.

"Help!" she screamed, pushing him away. She turned pleading eyes to Jaiden.

"Please! Have a heart!"

Jaiden pulled Toothless away and threw a fist into his face. He fell back, his mouth bloodied.

"You idiot! How many times do I have to tell you not to force yourself on women? This time, I must report you to the bossman."

Toothless spat out blood.

"What's the difference? She'll be a puppet for many as a prostitute. Why can't I have a taste of she first?"

Sheila's whole body shook, and her teeth chattered.

"It's only a dream. It'll pass soon," she whispered, her eyes closed.

Toothless put his finger on her lips. "Shh! Shh, gyul. This is only the beginning of your nightmares!"

Jaiden touched his shoulder. "I said, leave she alone. Let's go!"

Toothless turned around and pointed a handgun to Jaiden's head.

"I don't need a watchdog here. Get the hell out of my sight!" he said.

"Calm down, Toothless. I'm just trying to keep you from trouble. You're like a brother to me."

Toothless dropped his hand, and Jaiden moved away from him.

Toothless put the pistol in his pocket and grabbed Sheila's breasts with both hands. His laughter echoed in the room.

"Round and firm. Just the way I like them," he said with a leer.

Sheila shot her leg up and kneed him in his groin. He screeched in pain, then bent double, holding himself.

Jaiden laughed. "Too rough for you!"

Toothless stood up and grabbed her hand. He twisted it, making her to scream.

"Stop it!" Jaiden said.

A ring on her finger caught Toothless' eye. He removed it from her finger and inspected the ring carefully.

It was a 5-karat-gold diamond ring. As he turned it around, he saw writing engraved on the inside of it. He brought it close to his eyes and read it.

R+S=L.

With a sneer, he put it in his pocket. "You won't need this anymore."

Sheila spat in his face. "Moron."

"Come on. Let's leave, boy!" said Jaiden.

Toothless grasped her neck with both hands and began choking her. Sheila, her eyes wide, pulled against his hands, trying to release his hold. Her face paled.

Jaiden quickly pulled Toothless' gun from his pocket and aimed it at his head.

"Let go she neck," he ordered.

With a snarl, Toothless followed his instructions.

"Now move away from she! If you ever touch she again, I will shoot you myself."

"Why are you care for she? We could have good fun with she but you're too softy."

"Go outside!" ordered Jaiden, still pointing a pistol at his friend.

Toothless glared at Sheila.

"Today is your lucky day," he said, and walked out, followed by Jaiden.

I will deal with she later.

Sheila sat down on the floor, shaking like a leaf.

At 8.30 a.m., the street in front of Miguel's house was crowded with police cars. A few neighbors stood in their own yards, gaping at what was going on.

Policeman Clyde, a short, stout man, evenly distributed powder on the front door handle, using magnetic force. He continued the same procedure with the door, his gloved hands working quickly and efficiently.

In the kitchen, Police Officer Dale spread powder on the window. He put his face close to it, and inspected the powdered piece of glass. His eyes caught fingerprints.

"Inspector Miguel, I've found something!" he shouted, looking at Miguel through the kitchen window.

Then he walked to the kitchen counter and opened his briefcase.

Miguel was standing outside with his partner, Sameer, discussing what had happened. As soon as he heard his name, he limped into the kitchen.

"What did you find?"

"Fingerprints on the window."

"Hopefully we'll catch these bastards soon," said Miguel.

He walked to the window and tried to see the prints. Dale took out a camera from his briefcase and joined him.

"Don't worry. We'll get your wife back."

He took pictures of the prints, then put the camera back in the briefcase. Next, he picked up some rubber tape with an adhesive surface and returned to the window.

Miguel looked down at the bloody spots on the tile.

"Did you take blood samples?" he asked.

"Yes, I did."

Dale applied the rubber tape to the fingerprints and slowly peeled them off the surface. Then he placed the tape in a plastic container.

"By evening we should have some answers," he said.

Just then, Father Piero walked into the kitchen. There was a mixture of pain, shock, and sympathy on his face.

"Miguel, is there anything I can do?" he asked.

"No, thank you, Father. No offense, but I do have to ask you to please leave this area. We want nothing tampering with the evidence."

"Miguel, if you need me you know where to find me. Don't lose faith. You'll find her soon. God is with you!"

Another police officer appeared in the kitchen doorway.

"Father Piero, can I have a word with you?"

"Sure. How can I help you?"

"Can you describe the vehicle you saw?"

"It was so gloomy and drizzly. I'm not sure. Maybe it was either a black or grey van."

"Did you see anyone?"

"I saw silhouettes of people through the shutters. But I can't tell if they were women or men."

"Kavish, let Father go. He did enough for today," Miguel suggested.

"I'm sorry that I wasn't any use. If I think of anything else, I will come to the station."

"Thank you."

Father left Miguel's house.

The glittering stars covered the sky as the pirogue sailed through the darkness. Inside the boat, Sheila was sprawled, unconscious, under a canvas.

Toothless sat on a bench next to her, unable to take his gaze from Sheila's exposed legs. He kept biting his lips as his lust for her rose.

At the age of thirteen, he had caught his dad watching porn and having sex with other women many times when his mother and uncle were away. During those occasions, he would stand at his father's closed door and peer through a hole in the lock. Eventually he himself looked at porn while his papa was at work. By the time he reached age fourteen he was sexually active, thanks to his uncle, who had abused him. His zeal for women increased, as well as his anger—towards them and towards his uncle. Sometimes it was hard to tell what got him angry.

A wave struck the pirogue, rocking it from side to side. Sheila opened her eyes and peered uncomprehendingly into complete blackness. She knew that her body was wrapped in something, and she felt the sensation of being swayed. The smell of the sea and the rocking made her nauseous.

"Where am I?" she whispered. She lifted her hands to take the canvas off her face but realized with a shock that they were tied together.

Seeing her movements, Toothless pulled the canvas away from her. She blinked in surprise as her eyes met the sight of the many stars in the sky.

Sheila raised her head and looked around, trying to see

her abductor. When she saw Toothless, she let out a small scream and moved backwards to the edge of the pirogue, breathing erratically. She sat up quickly, and her eyes darted around, trying to find a way to escape. However, it soon dawned on her that she was alone with a monster, and there was nowhere to go.

With a sneer, Toothless picked up his pistol from the bench and aimed it at her.

"One bullet and you dead. So lay back and stay still," he instructed.

She slipped back down onto the deck, trembling, her eyes watching his every move.

He leaned over her and slid the pistol over her body, and her teeth chattered at the coldness of the gun. She closed her eyes, feeling a tightness in her throat.

"You're a naughty girl. It makes me horny."

"Please don't do it," she pleaded, turning her head to the side.

"Hush, woman, or you will never see your family again!" he said, pushing the weapon into her mouth.

The pistol almost gagged her, making her cough. He took the gun out of her mouth and forced her arms over her head. As he caressed her face, her sobs got lost in the sea, and tears fell on the deck.

"You have soft skin and beautiful blue eyes. Very unusual color for Caribbean woman."

He stretched out next to her, taking a deep breath as he gazed into her eyes.

"I loved a woman once, stubborn as you. But a few months before our wedding she caught me with two hot chicks, right in the middle of the action. She got so enraged that she tried to cut me up with a cutlass. Then she run out the house. The next day police found she walking naked in distress and saying nonsense."

He suddenly got up and pointed the gun at her again. The

sudden anger in his eyes made her cower.

"A few months later she hooked up with next man. You just remind me of she."

"No, please, no!" she pleaded through chattering teeth. Her heart felt like it was going to burst from her chest.

He sat on the bench and lit a cigarette. As he exhaled the smoke, he gazed silently at her.

"After she, I met ah dougla. I fall for she, but when I find out that she horn me with white man, I strangle she with my bare hands and buried she ass in the forest. Up to now de police can't find she corpse."

He gestured wildly with his gun hand as he ranted, and Sheila froze in fright. She was sure that he was going to accidently shoot her.

"Maybe I should do the same thing to you and throw you in the sea."

Toothless accidently pressed the trigger. The sound of gunfire went through Sheila's head as a bullet flew over her

"Oh, my God you almost killed me," she cried. Then, louder, although she knew it was useless: "Help me, please! I beg you! Please!"

Her sobs irritated his ears.

"Shut up, woman! No one will hear you between the sea and sky."

As he turned away to pick up his bag, Sheila scrambled to her feet and tried to throw herself overboard. He quickly got up and pulled Sheila by her blouse and wrestled her back down to a prone position. He glared at her and dug in his black bag. After a quick search, he took out a syringe and a vial. He broke off the end of the vial with his teeth, spat it out, and began to draw the liquid into the syringe.

"What are you going to do?" she asked in a low voice.

"Ah want yuh to shut yuh damn mouth, and if yuh say a

single word ah go murda[35] ya."

He sat down by her, and she froze. She felt her hair standing on end.

"Good gyul."

He pinned her hands to her belly with his left hand and injected the drug into her right arm. Then he let go.

"What did you inject me with?" she asked, her lips trembling.

"Something that will help you relax."

He sat back on the bench and opened a beer. As he drank, he stared at her over the top of the bottle, a lecherous grin on his face.

Sheila curled into a fetal position as a warmth filled her body. Dizziness overpowered her. Out of the corner of her eye, she watched Toothless, but now he seemed to be surrounded by a dark fog. Unable to keep her eyes open, she gave up and sank into blackness.

Toothless glanced at his watch.

"Soon I will have my dessert," he whispered, all smiles.

She tried to get up, but her body felt weak.

"Where am I?"

Toothless stood up and walked over to Sheila. He turned her gently onto her back and untied her hands. She groaned at the sensation of her hands being moved.

What's happening?

Sheila tried to move, but her muscles wouldn't obey her. She passed out again.

Toothless began kissing her inert body as she lay unconscious and helpless. He then raped her. He kept his eyes closed, and he made humming sounds as he went up and down on top of her.

---

[35] Murder

When he finished, he put her panties back on her and covered her with the canvas, leaving her head uncovered.

The pirogue continued its journey, taking Sheila to an unknown destination.

The sound of a running engine reached Toothless' ears. He rose and peered into the darkness, then picked up his pistol, ready to shoot.

A Coast Guard patrol boat was approaching. Toothless turned off the pirogue's motor and stared intently as it came alongside.

The patrol boat came to a halt right in front of him. Toothless stared suspiciously at the two men as they hailed him.

"Hey Toothless, is that you?" asked one of them. He wore a black cap, jacket, and pants. In his hand he held a long rifle.

"Yes, Emiliano, it's me."

The other stranger, a tall, broad-shouldered man, blew smoke from a cheap cigarette. He spat into the sea and spoke in broken English.

"Did you bring what we've asked?"

"Yes, Alejandro, I did," Toothless answered.

"Where is the woman?" asked Emiliano.

"Under the canvas." Toothless pointed to the inert mound at his feet.

He uncovered Sheila and pulled her up, making her stand at the edge of the boat. Emiliano leaned over the edge of the boat and grasped Sheila under her arms. He pulled her up and, hugging her, dragged her to the cabin.

Inside, two ladies sat on a bench. They were two sisters who were going to a Caribbean Island in order to escape poverty and hunger.

"Hey, *senoras*, please go outside. The boat came for you," said Emiliano.

After a glance at Sheila and then at each other, they edged toward the door, frowned at Emiliano, and left the cabin.

As they stood at the edge of the boat patiently waiting to get off, Toothless picked up two huge garbage bags from his pirogue and passed them to Alejandro. Emiliano joined them.

"Check the contents," Emiliano said.

Alejandro searched the bags. They were filled with toilet paper, diapers, medicine, and soaps.

Then Toothless tried to lift a burlap bag.

"Hey, I need help with this one," he said.

Alejandro crossed over, and both lifted the bag by the ends. They dropped it onto the deck of the Coast Guard boat. Alejandro inspected this bag also; he found rice, pasta, potatoes, and flour in it.

"Did you bring gasoline?" Emiliano asked.

"Yes, I did."

Toothless lifted two canisters and walked to the edge of the boat. Emiliano took them from him, then turned toward the sisters.

"Okay, *senoras*. Time to cross to the next boat," he said.

Toothless gave the women a friendly smile.

"Good evening, ladies. My name is Zane, and I am going to take you to a Catholic center of hope. Come on board." He held out a hand to help them.

They took his hand and crossed over to his boat. Toothless pointed at the bench.

"Please have a seat," he said.

He turned and spoke to the coast guards.

"Listen to me. Make sure the package is delivered unharmed to the destination, or else..." Toothless gestured toward his new guests.

"Don't worry. It'll be delivered today."

Emiliano started the engine, and the Coast Guard boat sped away.

As the ladies sat down on the bench, they looked at each other.

"No me siento bien con este hombre. ¿Y a dónde se llevan a esta mujer[36]?"[a] said Mia.

Toothless, who understood Spanish, listened in on their conversation.

"Senoras, you look concerned. Is there anything wrong?"

The younger sister spoke. "Mister, who was that woman?"

Zane's eyes went to her breasts.

Looks delicious. Spanish women too hot.

"She's a dying cancer patient. She asked me to take her back home, so she can die on her own land," he said without blinking.

The sisters looked at each other.

"Oh, she is a poor thing," she said.

"Do you have any other questions?" he asked.

"Not really," she replied.

Toothless started the engine, and the boat moved off.

24th December

Miguel sat at his desk in the police station. His bandaged leg rested on the table as he spoke over the phone.

"Evans. Any good news from tattoo shops?"

"I've visited seven of them, and they have never tattooed anyone's hand with a snake," Evans answered.

Miguel stood up and walked to the window.

"Someone must know something. Keep searching," he said. His eyelid twitched.

"What about the blood and the fingerprints?" he asked.

---

[36] I do not feel good about this man. Where are they taking this woman?

"The fingerprints belong to your wife, and the blood is AB positive. We might have to dig deeply to find the answers."

"Thanks, Evans. Keep it up. You're doing a great job."

He hung up the phone and sank down into his chair. He sighed as he lit a cigarette.

Where are they keeping you, Sheila?

His cell phone rang. When he recognized the number on the phone's screen, he ignored it at first. But it kept ringing.

What does she want now? I told her I can't see her till I find Sheila!

He answered the phone.

"Yes, Candice? What's up?"

"Nothing much. Since your wife got snatched, you have been avoiding me. I got concerned and called to find out how you're coping."

"How do you think I feel? They kidnapped my children's mother, and I'm unable to find her!"

"I'm sorry. I wish I could help. What about your leg?"

"It's in pain but healing slowly. But how did you find out about it?"

Miguel leaned back in his chair and put his legs on the desk again.

"Boy, news around here spreads fast. I heard people talking about it. But honestly, I feel your pain and I wish I could ease it up. Come nah by me tonight. I will take away all your worries and the pain."

Miguel rose again and closed the blinds to his room.

"Gyul, don't you understand? We can't see each other until I find she. Why can't you leave me alone!"

"Okay! Don't get on like a bad john[37]. I only wanted to help you. Are there any leads that can help you find Sheila?"

Miguel sank back in his chair and unbuttoned the top

---

[37] A bully or a dangerous.man.

40

button of his shirt.

"Yes. One of the kidnappers, the one who shot me, was a woman, and she had a snake tattoo on her hand. We're checking all tattoo outlets. We might find her soon."

Miguel's words stabbed into Candice's mind, spreading shivers over her body. Her legs became so weak that she felt as if she was going to collapse.

"I have to go now," she mumbled.

A frown formed on his face.

"Did I say anything wrong?"

"No, I just remembered that I have to do something important. *Ciao.*"

She hung up the phone and stared blankly at her laptop. Only a week ago, she had gotten a tattoo on her hand, and had been eager to show it to Miguel, but now she had to hide it from him.

Why wasn't I careful? I should have worn long sleeves.

She turned on her laptop and surfed the Net, looking for ways to conceal tattoos. There were many results.

Not bad at all, she thought after reading a few tips. *Makeup will hide it.*

She got up and walked towards her sofa, an old brown item she'd found in a charity shop. She sat down on it and let her gaze pass over her small living room.

I don't deserve to live in this shitty place.

She lived in an old wooden house that had only two rooms. One was used as a bedroom and the other as a living room. The bedroom, painted pink, was anything but cheerful when it rained. At those times, she was forced to use buckets to stop leaks from dripping onto her carpet. Flooding had damaged her appliances more than once.

She gazed at her plywood ceiling. It was rotten and eaten by termites. Wood dust caused by termites kept falling on the floor. The floor itself was made of grey concrete. Her sofa and the table set looked old, as if they had served for ages.

I need to move out of this area, and away from poverty. Miguel is my key to a better life. I can't allow anything to mess it up.

Her cell phone buzzed. She lay down on the sofa to read messages on her cell, responding to some of them. Then she spent some time reading posts on her social sites.

After his conversation with Candice ended, Miguel kept thinking about her, along with the puzzle about Sheila's whereabouts. He had been going to tell Sheila about his decision to leave her for Candice after Christmas, but the latest events had put a halt to his plans. He still loved his wife, but the spark and attraction between them was gone.

With Candice he felt younger and alive. His feelings toward her had become deeper and more intense the more he was around her. Whenever she was with him, his heart raced and warmth filled his body.

In addition, Sheila's behavior had become odd lately. She had been going out wearing makeup and bright-colored clothes—something that she had never done before. At times she came home late, and he could sense cologne on her. This made him wonder if she was having an affair behind his back.

Oh, Sheila. I am so sorry for all of this. I was going to leave you, and now you've been kidnapped. It's as if God is punishing me. I'm not even sure if you're alive or dead.

His thoughts were interrupted by a knock on the door. It was his friend Sameer, the assistant superintendent.

"Hi, Miguel. I haven't seen you for half the day," said Sameer.

"I've been making calls, trying to find a clue. She's somewhere out there waiting for me to rescue her."

He hit the desk with his hand. "Damn it, I feel so helpless!"

Sameer sat down on a chair near Miguel's desk.

"Please take it easy, boy. You can't allow your emotions to overpower you."

Miguel got up and walked to the window. He glanced outside. A few police cars were parked by the building, and people were passing by. A normal day – for everyone else.

"I'm trying hard not to lose my self-control, but right now I am so mad, I swear if I meet my wife's kidnappers, I will beat the crap out of them."

He squeezed his hand into a fist.

"I understand. But being edgy won't help you solve this case."

Miguel sat down and lit another cigarette.

"What's the latest on the hospital and clinics?" he asked.

"Nothing. No one with wounds searching for medical care."

"This damn thing is getting under my skin. I need to find my wife before they kill her," said Miguel, in an irritated voice.

His friend stood up.

"Boy, take it easy. You must be strong for your children. By the way, how are they coping with all of this?"

Miguel exhaled smoke and leaned his head back.

"Not so good. They keep asking for Sheila. I don't know what to say. The boy has nightmares. He gets up at nights, wet and screaming. They refuse to go back home and are afraid to sleep alone."

"Oh, man this is tough for you. If you need any help, I'm here for you."

As Miguel looked at his watch, his office phone rang.

He answered, "Miguel Seeglobin here."

"Talk to you later," said Sameer.

Miguel nodded at him.

"What's the address?" asked Miguel, as Sameer headed to the door.

He took the receiver away from his ear.

"Sameer, wait!"

Then he continued listening and writing on a piece of paper.

"Good. I'll join you," said Miguel, and put down the phone. "Let's go."

"Where?" asked Sameer.

"We got a search warrant for Mickey's. We might find a lead there."

"He always knows what's happening in the inner circles of the gangsters," said Sameer.

They walked out of Miguel's office. On the way to the front of the building, they stopped at a small room. They took out MP5 pistols from a burglar-proof cabinet and put on bullet-proof vests. Then they walked into the lobby area.

Four police officers sat by a long receptionist desk, and there were three men in the waiting area. Miguel approached Daina, a pregnant officer.

"How is your day going, Daina?"

"Hectic, with all kinds of calls and complaints." Her smile added to the beauty of her face.

"Something different about you today."

 Miguel eyed her, and his eyes stopped on her belly.

"Your skin glows. By the way, how is the little one doing?"

She shyly looked away and blinked a lot.

"Oh, thanks. You always find good words to say. He's kicking. His dad says he might become a footballer."

Daina smiled again and turned towards Sameer.

"I heard you had a little incident playing cricket. How is your hand?"

"It's still hurting, but muscle rub does miracles."

"I do believe you have an envelope for us," interrupted Miguel.

Daina looked through the mail and picked out a sealed envelope. She handed it to him. He removed a warrant from the envelope and dropped it into his pocket.

"Oh, I almost forgot to tell you. There was an accident on Perdowani Junction. Edwin and Ian are headed there. They'll join you at Mickey's later. Please be careful."

"Thanks. See you later," Sameer said, and both men walked outside. They got into one of the police cars, Miguel in the driver's seat.

They hit heavy traffic when they got onto the highway.

"This isn't a good time for traffic congestion," said Miguel.

"Why don't you turn on the siren and drive on the shoulder?"

"Why didn't I think about that!?"

Miguel turned on the siren and moved onto the shoulder. The ride was smooth, with no interruptions. However, when the police car's tires hit the Perdowani junction, Miguel was forced to join the slow-moving traffic.

As usual, the drivers drove slowly just to get a glimpse of the two cars that had collided. A Nissan sat on the left shoulder of the road, and a pickup truck was on the left side of the highway. Two police cars and a tow truck were parked not far from them. Edwin and Ian stood outside their car, talking to the driver of the tow truck. Sameer could hear an ambulance a few cars away. It was leaving the accident area, forcing drivers into the right lane.

The Nissan's hood and fender were dented, and the front window broken. Splinters of glass were scattered on the road. The truck's bumper had fallen off, and its headlights were smashed. The hood was wide open.

Miguel reduced his speed and gazed with curiosity at the accident site. He lowered his window.

"Edwin, waz di scene?[38]" shouted Sameer.

Edwin turned around and saw Sameer.

---

[38] What's up

"Two people got injured in the accident. One didn't make it."

"Do you need help?"

"No. Go and get Mickey. We'll be there shortly."

Miguel raised the window as Sameer took out his cell phone and took a few shots.

"Whenever an accident happens, this highway gets clogged with traffic congestion. It's ridiculous," said Miguel.

"Most car accidents occur because of the stupidity of the drivers. They're either drunk driving or rushing somewhere, endangering not only themselves but others as well," added Sameer.

Cars continued moving slowly as they passed the accident area, but as they got further down the road, the traffic bottleneck cleared up. On both sides of the highway were sugar cane fields or houses and business places. They passed under a bridge and between the government houses that had looked so short from afar.

After driving for about an hour and half, they came to the hilly area of Longtail Village. Sameer could see houses crowded on the hill.

They turned in at a narrow street, passing two shirtless men. After a few turns, Miguel pulled over and parked his car two houses away from Mickey's house. With their guns in hand, they got out of the car. Both cast their eyes around the area, watching carefully. They knew that this was an area where one could get easily killed by a stray bullet.

A few young men stood nearby drinking beer. As soon as they saw the police officers, they walked away.

Miguel walked up to Mickey's old-looking wooden house and pressed on the bell. They heard someone walking up to the door.

A woman of African descent opened the door. She was wearing shorts and a tank top.

"What do you want?"

"Police. We have a warrant to search your house," said Miguel.

She tried to close the door, but Miguel pushed past her. The policemen entered the hall. Loud music filled the house, along with the sound of a woman's laughter. However, the inhabitants weren't within sight of the front door.

"Where's the warrant?"

Miguel took it out and showed it to her.

Mickey was dancing with his girlfriend in the living room. He wore a white vest and black shorts. Around his neck was a chain with a big crucifix. He wore small earrings in his earlobes.

He raised both of his hands, holding a plastic cup of rum in one hand and a cigarette in the other, while his girlfriend wine39 on him. His jet-black dreadlocks hung down to his waist.

"I'm a law-abiding citizen and pay all my taxes. Why would you want to search my house?" Mickey's mother said, as she scrutinized the warrant.

Sameer gestured toward Miguel.

"This man's wife was kidnapped. We suspect that your son knows something about it. So where is he?"

"Why? Is it because he's black?" the woman asked.

She glanced over to where the music was coming out. Immediately, Miguel elbowed past her and opened the door, his pistol in his hand.

As soon as Mickey's girlfriend saw him, she stopped her gyrations on Mickey's pelvic area and moved aside.

Mickey tried to dash away through the open window. Miguel ran towards him and caught his hand. He pulled him in and pressed his hand to his back, then caught his other hand. He handcuffed him and pushed him towards an armchair.

---

39 Rotating of the pelvic girdle and hips in a winding position.

Mickey dropped down into it. The woman snatched her blouse off the floor and put it on.

"Go away before we arrest you!" Sameer said to Mickey's girlfriend. She stared boldly into his eyes with a grin on her face, tipsy and swaying slightly.

"Ever since Mickey came out of jail, you police have threatened to kill he," she said, her words slurred. "Why can't you leave he alone?"

Mickey began to sweat profusely. His mother stood in the room, silently watching them.

At that moment, officers Edwin and Ian walked into the house.

"Inspector Miguel, what would you like us to do?" asked Ian.

"Take these women out and search the house."

"Tanty40, please come with me," Ian told the older woman.

She stared at Ian, her jaw clenched.

"Why are you harassing my son? He didn't do anything wrong. Every time he leaves the house, you police search him."

"Leave the room, aunty!" ordered Miguel.

She, Mickey's girlfriend, and the two policemen left.

Miguel pointed a handgun at Mickey's temple. "Where did they take her?"

Mickey's legs trembled, and he shrank down into his chair.

"I have no idea who you are talking about," he said. He tried to get up but was pushed back into his seat.

"Answer me! Where is she?"

Mickey's lip twitched.

"Who?"

"My wife Sheila, the mother of my two children, was

---

40 Aunty

48

kidnapped two days ago. You had better tell me her location or I'll bust your skull!"

He pushed the pistol into his temple.

"I swear I don't know where she is. My hands are clean!"

Mickey shook like a leaf, fearful for his life.

Miguel had had enough of the man sitting in the chair before him. He wanted to solve the case as quickly as possible, so that he could find Sheila.

He opened the gun's cylinder and emptied the cartridges, leaving one bullet. He flicked the cylinder back in with a flick of his wrist, then spun the chamber. With a grim smile, he leaned over and calmly pointed the pistol at Mickey's head. "Spit it out! My patience is getting short."

"I...I am!"

A grimace ran across Miguel's face. He put his hand by his ear.

"I didn't hear," he said, still pressing the pistol to Mickey's temple. "You were you going to tell me something, weren't you?"

He pulled the trigger, and the pistol made a clicking sound.

Mickey flinched. The smell of urine filled the air.

"Are you insane? You could have killed me!" he screeched.

"If I had shot you, I would have done a favor to society."

"Please put that thing away, and I'll tell you everything."

Miguel lowered his hand. "I'm listening."

"There was talk about revenge. Someone was very angry with you for busting a drug deal, which caused losses of millions. The order was given to kill your children and kidnap your wife."

Miguel pressed the pistol against Mickey's private parts and tensed his finger on the trigger.

"Who gave the order?"

Sameer rushed to Miguel's side.

"Miguel, take it easy. Don't do anything stupid," he said.

"Please stop this madness! I told you everything I know!" said Mickey, sweating profusely.

"Give me a name, or say goodbye to your testicles," Miguel warned him.

"I can't tell you. Dem will kill me!"

"If you don't, then you will meet your brother in Hell."

Mickey gulped. After a moment, he said, "His name is Kingpin. He's the owner of the glass factory."

As Miguel was interrogating Mickey, police officers in the Mickey's bedroom were opening drawers and emptying the contents onto the floor. Mickey's mother stood apart and watched their every move.

"Why are you throwing everything on the floor?" she asked, biting her nails.

No one paid her any attention.

Edwin opened a closet and began looking through the clothes. He stooped down and searched the shoe shelf that was located below them. He removed the shoes from the bottom of the shelf. After some poking and prodding, he pulled out a wooden plank and noticed a hole below it.

Something wrapped in fabric lay in the hole. He lifted it out and removed the covering. It was an Uzi submachine gun with a loaded magazine.

Mickey's mother had been watching silently, rubbing her neck and nodding at times. However, when she saw the weapon, she fainted and fell on the floor. Ian and Mickey's girlfriend hurried towards her.

"Aunty, get up!" said Mickey's girlfriend, slapping her cheeks lightly.

She awoke and slowly sat up. With their help, she stood up. She made turtle steps to the bed and then sat on it.

"Only a few months ago he got out of jail," she mumbled.

"You stay with her," ordered Ian. The policemen left Mickey's bedroom and entered the other bedroom.

Ian rejoined Miguel. "I found an Uzi submachine gun," he reported. "We can arrest him now."

Miguel pulled on Mickey's shirt, forcing him to get up.

"Hey, why are you roughing me up? I have my rights."

"Just shut up and go with them." He turned to Ian. "Take him, with his mother and girlfriend, to the police station. We'll follow you."

All of them walked outside and were met with an angry mob. A woman in red shorts and a strapless top shouted, "Where yuh carryin dem? Yuh should jail dem big boys. Not dis small fish."

"Let them go!" shouted a man with short reddish hair.

"Allyuh police tink allyuh is God. Allyuh could do what allyuh want. You kill we boys and then saying dem tried to kill you," said another one.

"Go back to your house, before you get arrested for disrupting police work," said Sameer, his hand tight on his firearm.

The two policemen took Mickey away, along with his mother and girlfriend. Miguel and Sameer silently continued walking towards their cruiser. They got into the car with no more trouble, and Miguel sped off.

As Miguel drove, Sameer looked out at the mob.

"I can't understand these people. Instead of making our work easy, they defend criminals and then complain that the country is full of crime. No wonder it's in this state."

"Maybe it's a wake-up call for us police. We've lost the trust of our nation. Some changes must be done!" said Miguel, as he continued heading back to the police station.

"I agree with you, but we alone can't change the situation in this country. Transformation must start from every household, and people must work together."

Miguel looked briefly at the trees they were passing. They were full of pink flowers.

Our island is so beautiful, but crime makes it hard to live here and forces people to move away.

Sheila opened her eyes and found herself lying on a bunk bed in a small room. Her whole body burned, as if she was in an oven.

She lay still for a few minutes with a blank look on her face. Then her focus shifted to some yellow spots on the ceiling. A frown formed on her face, and her eyebrows came together.

She slowly sat up and stared at the window, which was barred. Unable to see anything through the tinted glass, she decided to walk to the window.

Sheila passed her hand over her head, which was hurting. Her hand hit a bump on the top of her head.

"Ouch! How did I get that?"

Then her attention moved to her wrists. She winced at her red, sore wrists and then rubbed them. With some effort, she got off the bunk bed, then looked at the top layer of the bed. A dingy bear and a doll lay on the mattress.

With a frown on her face she walked to the window. She held onto an iron bar and pulled it, then she peeked through the window.

Half of the window was underground. She could see the legs of people passing by through the top half.

She hit the glass, shouting, "Help! Help!" But no one heard her.

Suddenly the door opened, and a tall, broad-shouldered muscular man came in, accompanied by a fat, short woman. The man ran to Sheila. He took hold of her hair and began pulling her away from the window.

Sheila's hands clutched his, trying to pull them away.

"Let go, you fool!" she screamed.

"Ella puede causar algunos problemas. Mantén tus ojos en ella41," warned Victor.

He dragged her to the bunk bed and pushed her. She landed on the bed in a sitting position, hitting her head on the top part of the bed. Her tears spread all over her face.

"Let me go, and my husband will spare your life," she pleaded.

"Puede que tengas que domarla42," said the woman, laughing.

Her laughter irritated Sheila's ears.

"What's so funny?" she asked.

"Your husband is in Trinidad and you aren't. He will never ever find you," she said in English.

"What do you want from me? If you need money, we will give it to you."

"Listen to me carefully. Money can't buy your freedom, and your husband can't help you either," said the woman.

"Ella se ve como una mujer de voluntad fuerte. Podríamos tener algún problema con ella43," said Victor.

Sheila listened carefully as they spoke to each other. She was glad that she had learned some Spanish in high school. But she knew she had to keep quiet about knowing the language.

At least she now knew the names of her captors: Victor and Bernadette.

These two idiots speak Spanish. I'm in Venezuela! How am I going to find my way back home?

"Tu ve y déjame encargarme de ella44," said the woman. Victor walked away, leaving the two women behind.

Bernadette turned toward Sheila.

"If you want your family to stay alive, especially Nadia and Ronnel, you must follow the rules of this house and not try

---

[41] She might cause some problems. Keep your eyes on her.
[42] You might have to tame her.
[43] She looks like a strong-willed woman. We might have some trouble with her.
[44] You go and let me handle her

to run away," threatened the woman, a grimace on her lips.

She walked away.

"Please wait!" Sheila lifted her hand towards her captor.

Bernadette turned around by the door, a fierce smile showing her yellow teeth.

"No one is going to save you. You hear me? No one!"

She left the room, and Sheila could hear her climbing up the stairs.

Uncontrollable trembling and weakness overtook Sheila. She stood up and walked around the room.

What to do? They know where my children are.

She paced the room, frustrated. After a few minutes, she stopped at the door and tried to turn the handle. It was locked.

She put her ear to the door and listened. Not too far off, she could hear a man humming.

"*Hazlo otra vez*45," said the man.

"*Estoy cansada, por favor, no más*46," pleaded a woman's voice.

Sheila moved away from the door and lay down on the bed. She curled into a fetal position, and put her hand on her chest, feeling for the chain. Then she recalled Toothless pulling it off.

He took my ring as well!

She scanned her brain, trying to recall earlier events. She recalled being on the boat and could clearly see Toothless injecting her with something. In her mind, Sheila saw him turn her over, and then she felt heaviness and pain between her legs.

Oh my God! He raped me!

With the realization of the truth, tears of pain welled up in her eyes. She sat up, gazing into space.

What am I going to do? These horrid people are not going to let me leave.

---

45 Do it again.
46 I'm tired, please no more.

She tried to stand up, but the whole room began spinning, forcing her to lie back.

I should play along, then run away at the first opportunity.

As her thoughts scattered all about, she fell asleep, exhausted.

Miguel's workday came to an end, and he drove to his mother's house, where he was staying with the children. After Sheila's abduction, he no longer felt safe in his own home.

As his mother, Elisa, kept busy cooking in her small yellow kitchen, Ronnel sat in front of the TV playing his "Catch the Criminal" game. Nadia had a toy set of teacups and two dollies in front of her.

The doorbell rang. Nadia dropped her toys and ran to her brother. She grabbed his hand.

"They came back!" she said, overcome with trembling.

"Don't be silly. That's not them," he answered.

Elisa rushed out to the door. She opened it slightly and looked outside, trying to see the person by the gate.

Seeing her son Kevin, she shouted, "I'm coming!"

She walked to the living room to get the remote control for the gate, which was on the coffee table.

"Granny, the doorbell frightened Nadia. She thinks that bad people will take she away like Mummy."

"Nadia, no one is going to come for you. It's Uncle Kevin," Elisa said soothingly. "Come, dear. Let's go see him."

Nadia took her granny's hand and together they went outside to the gate. She opened the gate wide enough for one person to squeeze through.

"Hi, Mummy. I brought some gifts for all of you," he said.

He patted Nadia's head. "Hey, little one. How are you?"

"I'm fine, thank you," said Nadia.

"Hey, smarty, you have grown so much. What has Granny been giving you to eat?"

Her lips quirked upwards in a joyous smile. "Too many vegetables."

"Oh, they're good for you," said Kevin.

"Yuck. I don't like them. They taste bad." She grimaced and wrinkled her nose.

"Nadia go inside now, please," said Elisa. There was something she wanted to discuss with Kevin, but she didn't want her to hear their conversation.

Nadia slowly walked away.

"I don't see you much these days," she told him. "I'm concerned for Miguel."

"Since Amelia's birth, I don't get a chance to do anything or go anywhere. Ria still suffers with Chikungunya virus.[47]"

"Give she coconut water to drink and spray your house. You don't want those mosquitoes give your children Chikungunya virus or Dengue Fever."

"I already took care of that," Kevin told her. "How is Miguel doing? Whenever I try to speak to him about all of this, he brushes me off."

"You know men never show their feelings. He comes home, spends some time with the children, and then goes into his bedroom."

Kevin's phone rang, and he took the call.

He listened for a moment. "I'm coming now," he said, as he ended his call.

"I must go. Ria needs me. But I'll come back in the morning."

He took out four gift bags from his pickup truck and handed them to his mom. "I tagged all of them."

"See you tomorrow then, and thank you," said Elisa.

---

[47] Chikungunya is a viral disease transmitted to humans by infected mosquitoes. It causes fever and severe joint pain.

Kevin drove away, and Elisa walked back inside the house, straight into the living room. She put the gifts under the Christmas tree and left the room.

Nadia stood for some time looking at the gifts. Then she moved them around to find those that had her name. Ronnel stopped playing his game and went over to her.

"You can't touch the gifts till tomorrow," he said, pulling her away from the tree.

"Leave me alone! They're not yours!"

Miguel pulled up to his mother's house. He parked the car and looked carefully at his surroundings. Not seeing anyone around, he opened the gate and drove into the yard. He got out of the car and entered the house.

Miguel headed to the living room, where Nadia was going through the gifts. Miguel tiptoed behind her and lifted her up in the air.

"Hey, nosy parker. I caught you red-handed. No touching the gifts until tomorrow!"

"Daddy, put me down! I was only looking."

Miguel let her down and tickled her belly. Her laughter spread across the room.

"Stop it!"

He paused and glanced at his son, who was still playing his game.

"What are you playing?"

Ronnel's eyes were fixed on the TV's screen. "'Catch the Criminal'," he said, with a serious look on his face.

Elisa came into the room. "Turn off the TV and the game box. Both of you go and wash your hands," she said firmly.

Ronnel turned off everything, and the siblings went into the bathroom. Miguel headed to the kitchen.

He gave his mother a kiss on her forehead and sniffed the air.

"Umm, smells so good. What are you cooking?"

"Callaloo, white rice, plantain, kidney beans, and chicken already made."

"Did the children give you any trouble today?"

"Not at all. However, I'm a little bit concerned about Nadia. She's still full of fears. Maybe you should take them for counselling," she suggested, as she stirred a big pot of green callaloo.

"I've already made arrangements for that. The psychologist will come here and talk to them."

"Anything about Sheila?"

"We found out who might be behind her kidnapping. But I can't discuss it with you."

She turned off the fire.

"I understand. If you need someone to talk to, I'm here for you."

"I know, Mummy."

Elisa picked up the bowl of callaloo, and Miguel took a pyrex dish heaped with rice. They walked out of the kitchen and went to the living room, where they placed the food on the table. The children were already there, sitting patiently.

"Wey you too quick! I didn't expect to see you at the table so soon," said Miguel.

"Ronnel made me hurry," said Nadia.

Elisa made a few more trips to the kitchen to get the rest of the food and some coconut water.

She poured it for the children, and then sat down at the table. They ate silently.

As they ate, Miguel looked thoughtfully at his children.

They look thinner, and they're so much quieter. Ronnel used to be talkative and friendly, but now he refuses to even go to his cousins'.

Miguel's cell phone vibrated a few times. He took it out of his pocket and gazed at the screen.

It was a message from Candice.

'I have something important to share with you. Please come as soon as possible."

I told her not to contact me. Why don't women ever listen?

'Why can't you just spill it out over the phone?' he typed to her.

'No. It concerns you. I have to tell you face to face.'

'So what? Just type it out!'

He looked at the phone as he waited for the answer, but she didn't bother to respond. He put his cell away and noticed that Elisa was staring at him.

"You seem worried, what is it? Was that news about Sheila?"

She glanced at the grandkids. "Never mind," she said.

"No, Mother. It was a text from my colleague. I have to go back to the station."

"But you only now got home."

Miguel rose and picked up his plate.

"They want me to be there. I'll be working late, so don't bother to wait up for me."

He smiled at his children. "You kids go to bed early! Santa won't come if he sees that you're awake."

Nadia's eyes sparkled. "Are you sure Santa exists? Vidash's parents said that Santa isn't real."

Miguel gave his child a smile.

"Sweetheart, Santa does exist, and he might visit us tomorrow."

"Really?" asked Nadia.

"Yes," said Miguel, getting up.

"I'm leaving now. Don't give your granny any trouble."

Miguel walked out with his plate and cutleries. After washing his plate, he drove away to Candice's.

Once his car came to a halt in front of her wooden house, he took a small box out of the glove compartment and pushed it into his pants pocket. Then he got of the car and buzzed the bell.

She greeted him at the door, wearing shorts and a red strapless top. Smiling invitingly, she let him in.

"What was so important that you had to tell me in person?" he asked.

She took out a pregnancy test strip from her pocket and gave it to him. He took it, a frown on his face.

"What is it?"

A short-lived smile flickered on her face.

"Please look at it. Do you see the two lines going across?"

"Yes."

"This shows that I'm pregnant."

She clutched his hand, a huge grin on her face. "We're going to have a baby!"

The pregnancy strip fell out of his hand, and he pulled away from her.

"Oh, no! Not good at all! You should get rid of dat[48]," he said.

She picked up a cigarette from the table. After lighting it, she glared silently at him.

"Put that down. You'll damage the child!" said Miguel in an irritated voice.

"What's the point? You don't want it!"

Miguel stepped closer and took away the cigarette, which he put in an ashtray. Then he faced Candice and held her hands.

"Candice, if it wasn't for my wife's disappearance, I would react differently. I honestly planned to leave her for you. But my hands are now tied up till she is found, either dead or alive. Right now, my children are vulnerable, and they need my attention. I had to leave them with their granny so I could rush over to you."

Candice put his hand on her belly.

---

[48] That

"But this is your baby. He's the creation of our love. Why should he suffer?"

"I don't know. It's so confusing. If you want to keep it, then go ahead. But we must stay apart for some time. As soon as Sheila comes back, we'll be together."

A spark of joy appeared in her eyes. They began kissing, and then walked to her bedroom.

Candice went to use the bathroom and Miguel, after taking off his clothes, spread himself out on the bed.

Candice washed her hands as Miguel lay waiting. She turned off the tap and dried them.

It was then that she noticed that her tattoo had become visible again.

"Oh, shit!" she said.

"What did you say?"

"Nothing," she replied.

I must be careful. Can't afford to lose him or go to jail.

She quickly opened a small cupboard above the sink and took out her makeup bag. She put down the toilet bowl cover and sat on it. Candice pulled out some makeup primer from the bag and evenly applied it on the snake.

Why did I get this tattoo?

Next, she took out a color correcting crayon and applied that over her tattoo. After that, she rubbed full-coverage foundation on it.

She's gone now from the scene. I can move in with him. But he will not marry me until she's found. I should speak to Toothless.

She frowned at the idea. *But he never does anything for free. I have to pay him.*

Miguel looked at his watch.

Why is she taking so long in the bathroom? It's Christmas Eve, and I should be at home with my children. Why on earth did I come here in the first place?

He got off the bed and took out his cigarettes and a lighter from his pocket. He lit it and sat on the edge of the bed.

Now she carries my child, which make things complicated.

Candice dabbed concealer on top of the foundation, and then she dipped her brush in face powder and brushed it on over the concealer.

She put away her makeup bag and went to the bedroom, where she found Miguel sitting on the bed and smoking.

She lay on the bed and stared at his back. It was covered with bruises and had a few scratches. She sat up and began kissing them.

"Boy, they really beat you up badly."

"I'm lucky to be alive."

Miguel's body flinched at the thought of that unfortunate night. He rose and picked up his shirt and pants.

She stared at his leg. It wasn't bandaged anymore but had a square dressing on it.

He put his clothes on.

"What are you doing?"

He zipped up his pants and then gazed around. Candice's lips twitched. Miguel stared at her silently for a while.

"I shouldn't be here today. My children are waiting for me."

He always put children and she before me. If he finds out that I was...He would kill me for sure.

Candice sat up. "What will happen to us if no one finds Sheila?"

Miguel walked to the window. He gazed outside and stared blankly at Candice's muddy pathway.

"I don't know. You, she, and the baby are puzzling me."

"Any clues as to who might take she?"

"We're getting there, and as soon as we find out who has the snake tattoo, we'll crack the case."

Candice's eyes glanced briefly at her tattooed hand.

I might have to have it removed permanently.

"Okay, I'm leaving," said Miguel.

He kissed her forehead and walked towards the door, keeping his hand in his pocket. After a moment, she followed him.

As he opened the door, he stopped and turned around.

"I almost forgot to give you this." He took his hand from the pocket, and held out a small gift box.

She stared at the box and then took it, a questioning look on her face.

"This is your Christmas gift," he said.

"Oh, thank you, babe!" she said, kissing him.

She unwrapped her gift and opened the box. To her amazement, there lay a gold bracelet with a few shiny stones set in it. She put it on her wrist.

"Are these diamonds?" she asked.

"Yes, they are. I bought them before Sheila was kidnapped."

She put her arms around his neck and kissed him all over his cheeks and lips.

"I'm so lucky to have a caring man like you."

He removed her arms from his neck.

"I must leave now. Remember, no smoking or drinking for you anymore," he said, gazing at her belly.

"Alright, boss," she said.

"If you be a good gyul, I might come and see you again."

With a smile, he turned and walked to his car.

25th December

At 7 a.m., Nadia rushed into her father's bedroom. He was sleeping at the edge of the bed. She climbed onto it and hopped in excitement.

"Daddy, Daddy, get up! It's Christmas!"

Miguel awoke with the shaking of the bed.

"Which naughty one is jumping on my bed, and so early!" he said jokingly, pulling his daughter in for a hug and a tickle.

"It's me. I want to open my gifts," she said, trying to get away from him. She laughed and said, "Stop it now!"

He moved away from her and took his camera out of the dressing table. Nadia ran out to her granny's bedroom.

Miguel sat up on the bed and turned on the camera. He pressed the "on" button and looked through the pictures--and stopped on one.

In that picture, he was sitting behind Sheila and hugging her. The picture captured their happiness and mutual love.

Oh, Sheila. Where did I go wrong?

His smile was replaced by sadness and guilt. With heaviness in his chest, he left the bedroom.

Elisa and Ronnel were soundly asleep in her bed. Near the bed stood a table with her Bible and spectacles on it. Elisa loved reading it before her bedtime.

Elisa's mother was Muslim and father a Hindu, but she got pulled into Christianity after attending a Christian-based secondary school. She had been recently baptized in the Roman Catholic church, to her Christian uncle's delight.

Nadia rushed to the bed and touched her granny's hand.

"Nana[49]. Wake up. I'm ready to open gifts."

Elisa sat up and reached for her spectacles. She put them on.

"Girl, why are you worrying me at this hour?"

"It's Christmas!"

Elisa stood up, yawning. Ronnel jumped out of the bed

---

[49] Granny

and rushed out of the room, trying to reach the living room first.

Elisa and her granddaughter walked to the living room. They found Miguel sitting on a chair not far from their tall Christmas tree, which was decorated with snowflakes, red ribbons, and red and yellow ornaments. The blue lights on the tree made it look more beautiful. Under the tree lay quite a few gifts.

Nadia dashed to the Christmas tree and sat on the floor. Ronnel stood in the middle of the room, wondering if he should open his gifts as well. He looked over at his father.

Miguel readied the camera.

"Sit next to your sister and open your gifts."

Ronnel went over to the Christmas tree as Nadia searched the gifts, trying to see her name. Ronnel picked up a box wrapped in red paper and gave it to her. She unwrapped it right away and found a Barbie doll. She lifted it and showed it to her granny.

"Look what Santa gave me."

"That's beautiful," said Granny, who was now sitting on the floor not far from them.

"Where are my other gifts?" asked Nadia.

Ronnel walked around the tree and gathered all her gifts into one pile.

"These are all your presents," he said.

As he picked up one of his gifts, his eyes caught sight of a present that he had wrapped for his mother just a few days before she was taken away from him. Slowly he began opening his gift, his face solemn. Once Miguel had taken their pictures, Ronnel pushed his gift away.

"Son, what's wrong?" asked Miguel.

Ronnel silently gazed at his present for his mother.

"Why aren't you opening your gifts, boy?"

Ronnel's eyes darted toward the present. He lifted it from the floor with a cry.

Miguel rushed toward him. "What's happened?"

"Mu...mu...Mummy! I made this for Mummy. But she's not coming back. They took her away from us, Daddy."

His cries were as loud as thunder. Nadia stopped opening her gifts. She stared at Ronnel, upset.

Miguel hugged him. Ronnel buried his face in his father's chest.

"Tish. Calm down, son. She'll be back in no time."

"No, Daddy. You lie. People outside tell she dead."

Suddenly Nadia burst into tears as well. "Where's my mummy? Santa didn't bring my mummy back."

Elisa embraced her granddaughter. "Come on, stop crying. She'll come home soon," she said.

Nadia raised her head and gazed at her granny with watery eyes.

"Are you sure?"

"Yes, I am. Your father will find her."

Elisa looked at Miguel, and a few tears shone in her own eyes.

"I forgot to tell you that Santa Claus is coming today," said Miguel.

"Really?" asked Nadia.

"Yes, but first you need to finish opening your gifts, have breakfast, and take your shower."

Ronnel got up.

"Daddy I don't feel like opening presents anymore. Can I do it later?"

"Sure," said Miguel.

Nadia gazed at her gifts.

"Granny, I'll open mine with you when Santa comes," she said.

"Okay, honey. You just sit on the sofa. I need to make your breakfast."

Elisa went to the kitchen and began making breakfast. Soon a song came on the radio.

It's Christmas day today,

Hip, Hip, Hooray.
My dear Madina, pour sorrel for me,
Lots of nice things to have, you will see.
On the table roasted pork and ham,
You must cook bodi and some yam.
Don't' forget the pastelle and Christmas rice,
I'm feeling hungry, it all looks nice.
Black forest cake, rum raisin ice cream,
Hurry up, my dear, before I scream!

She put an iron *tawa*[50] on the stove and prepared to make *dosti* roti. First, she kneaded dough into thin circles. She then rubbed each circle with butter and pressed two circles of dough together. Then Elisa rubbed the tawa with butter and put a dough circle on it. When one side was cooked, she turned it over with a spatula.

When she had made enough, she warmed up some curried potatoes and pastelle.

Ronnel came in. "Granny do you need help?"

"Yes. Take the plate with pastelles[51] out to the table, and I'll bring the rest."

Ronnel left with the pastelles. Elisa picked up the plate of dosti roti and took it to the living room.

Ronnel and Nadia sat at the table and Miguel sat on the sofa. His attention was on a gift wrapped in blue paper; it was one that his wife had left for him.

"Miguel, come and have your breakfast."

Miguel got up. As he approached the table, he noticed that there was nothing to drink, so he went to the kitchen and brought back a big bottle of sorrel[52]. Elisa brought out the rest of the food and sat down at the table.

---

[50] Tawa is a large flat, disc-shaped frying pan.
[51] Pastelles are a steamed cornmeal pie wrapped in banana leaves and filled with olives,raisins and stewed meat.
[52] A preferred drink during Christmas in Trinidad.

Miguel dished out breakfast for his children and then himself.

"Mummy, pass the pepper please," he asked.

Elisa gave him a bottle of hot pepper sauce. He sprinkled some on his curried potato.

As they ate, they could hear rain falling, *pitta patta*.

"Oh boy, rain for Christmas. Last time it rained, the river behind Natasha's house rose and flooded it," said Elisa.

"It's the rainy season. We can't avoid rain or flooding," Miguel replied.

He put some roti with potato into his mouth.

"Are you working on Boxing Day?"

"Nope. I decided to take the day off and spend it with you. Plus, I want to watch the cricket match," answered Miguel.

Ronnel and Nadia finished their breakfast and got up from the table with their plates.

"Father, I'm going to go take a shower," said Ronnel.

"Okay, just don't take too long."

"Granny, come and bathe me," said Nadia.

Elisa left the living room with her grandkids. She allowed Ronnel to take his shower first, and then bathed Nadia.

While they were gone, Miguel cleared up the table.

The doorbell rang, and he opened the door. Once he recognized who was there, he unlocked the gate.

His brother Kevin ran to the door, wearing a Santa disguise and carrying a sack on his back.

"With this rain, I thought you wouldn't dare to leave the house," said Miguel.

"I didn't want to disappoint your children."

Raindrops were landing on Kevin's red clothes.

"Come nah inside before rain wet you up," offered Miguel.

Kevin dashed into the living room. After shaking off the rain, he sat down on the sofa. He dropped the sack on the floor.

Miguel went to the kitchen and brought two glasses and a bottle of Ponche de Crème.[53] He poured some for himself and his brother.

"Boy, take a drink. This is homemade Ponche de Crème. Mummy made it," said Miguel.

Kevin took the proffered glass and had a sip as Miguel sank into an armchair.

"I haven't seen you since last month," said Miguel.

"You know how it is, boy. With the crime rate going up, my wife doesn't want to leave the house after 7 p.m. Amelia is so tiny and fragile; we don't want to expose her to germs. So many people are getting symptoms of vomiting and diarrhea. There's a flu virus going around too."

"Yes, I understand it very well. Congratulations on Shantel's SEA results. I saw her name on the list. She made the top 100," said Miguel.

Kevin smiled and eased into the back of the sofa.

"She was accepted into her first choice of high school. I'm glad that she's leaving primary school. That place always ends up in some kind of bacchanal. Last term, a teacher wrote a love letter to an eleven-year-old girl."

Kevin sipped his Ponche de Creme.

"Yes, it was in the news." Miguel scowled. "I hope they'll suspend him. Children can't be trusted with this type of person. Today he writes a letter. Tomorrow he might want to have sex with she."

Kevin nodded. He then grinned and looked at his glass. "Oh, gosh, this Ponche de Crème is de bess. Did Mummy put aside a bottle for me?"

"Yes, she did."

Miguel got up and left the living room. He came back with a bottle of Ponche de Crème and two bottles of sorrel, along

---

[53] Ponche de Creme is a Christmas drink that is often compared to eggnog.

with a grocery bag. He put everything in the bag and set it on the table.

Kevin stood up. He put his glass on the table, then hefted his sack.

"I have to go home soon to help Ria, so I guess we'd better make Santa's presence known."

He then shouted, "Ho, ho, ho! Santa's here! Is anyone at home?"

Miguel winked, trying not to smile.

"Boy, with that red suit and the sack you really do look like Santa."

"Ho, ho, ho! Where are the children?"

Nadia and Ronnel ran down the stairs and rushed into the living room. They screeched to a stop, eyes wide, when they saw Santa standing there in the middle of the room. Ronnel stared at him intently, trying to see if the face was familiar.

Nadia ran to Santa and hugged him.

"Santa, I knew you were real!" she said.

"I am real for those who believe in me."

Nadia pulled his hand. "Come, Santa. Sit on the sofa."

Santa followed Nadia, carrying his sack. Then he sat down next to her.

"You're not Santa. He doesn't exist," said Ronnel, looking serious.

Nadia stared at Santa's face, frowning. She put both hands on his cheeks and then touched his beard.

"He is Santa. He has a long beard and a big belly like Santa. But why is he dark?"

Miguel couldn't stop smiling.

"He probably got too much sun. Santa isn't accustomed to the Caribbean weather," he said with a grin.

"Come here, Ronnel. I brought a gift for you," Kevin/Santa said.

Ronnel walked over to him. Kevin dug in his sack and removed a gift wrapped in green wrapping paper. He gave it to

Ronnel, who quickly took it out of his hands. He gazed at it, wondering if he should open it.

"Open it, boy," said Miguel.

Nadia touched Kevin's hand. "Santa, what about me?"

Kevin stroked his chin, pretending to be thinking.

"Hmm. Have you been on your best behavior?"

"Yes, and I put away all my toys," answered Nadia.

Kevin dug in his sack.

"Well then, you have a gift to get."

He took out a huge gift wrapped in pink wrapping paper. Nadia held out her arms, ready to take it.

"And this is for a special girl," said Kevin, giving it to her. She took it from him and quickly began to open it.

Elisa came in.

"Santa, would you like to have some breakfast?" She gave him a wink.

"No, thank you. I've eaten many cookies and drunk a lot of milk."

Kevin rubbed his belly. "My belly is certainly full."

Nadia unwrapped her gift and found a talking baby doll. She removed a pacifier from the doll's mouth and pressed on the button.

"Mummy, mummy feed me," said the doll.

Nadia put the pacifier back in the doll's mouth.

"This is the best gift ever!" she said, and hugged Kevin. "Thank you, Santa."

Kevin embraced her. "You're welcome, dear."

He stood up. "Santa has to leave. There are other children waiting for their gifts."

He put his sack over his shoulder, and then picked up the grocery bag with his drinks from the table.

"Miguel, call me later," whispered Kevin as he passed him on the way to the door.

Miguel accompanied him.

"Thank you for bringing some joy into my children's

lives. Both cried earlier for Sheila, but your presence has cheered them up."

"Why don't you come over tomorrow? Let them play with Shantel."

"I'll see how it goes."

Nadia got up from the sofa. "Santa, wait!"

Kevin looked at her.

"Where's my mummy?"

Santa stared at Miguel, not knowing what to say. "Help me," he whispered.

"Nadia, you're keeping Santa back," said Miguel.

He opened the door. Kevin stepped out and glanced at the sky, and then at his mother's yard. The rain had stopped falling, but the hibiscus leaves and buttercup flowers were still wet.

"The child's question took me aback."

Miguel nodded his understanding. He looked over his shoulder. "Yes, it happens a lot these days."

Kevin put a sympathetic hand on his brother's shoulder. "See you later."

Kevin walked out of the yard and put his sack in the truck. Miguel went back inside.

***

Sheila discovered that she was being kept in a two-story house that belonged to Bernadette. The upstairs had one huge guest room with a toilet and shower, and three smaller bedrooms, one of which was occupied by Bernadette and Victor. Four bedrooms and a kitchen took up the downstairs. This was where customers were taken for paid sex services.

Each bedroom had burglar-proof windows with tinted glass. The building itself had only one iron door, with five locks. It was occupied mostly by local women who paid Bernadette a rental fee. However, a new teenage girl, Daniela, had been brought to the brothel from Romania and was being kept there against her will.

Bernadette had tried to make her place Christmassy by decorating it. A few red and golden ornaments shaped like icicles hung down from the ceiling of the guest room. There was a tall Christmas tree. Small yellow and green gift box ornaments and garlands were used as decorations. A few gifts stood under the tree.

Two women were in the room, entertaining clients. One couple sat on a brown fabric sofa, which was covered with oily stains.

The woman, a 29-year-old, olive-skinned young lady by the name of Camille, was a bit chubby, but liked by her clients for her big breasts and an unusually big, round bottom. Despite the disgust she felt when she was touched by her customers, she kept coming to the brothel.

She and her 45-year-old companion, who had black hair and a fair complexion, were wrapped up in kissing each other. His hands were under her blouse, caressing her breasts. They were too busy to care about what was going on around them in the room.

After unsuccessfully searching for employment, Camille had chosen a path of prostitution to provide for the loved ones who were dependent on her. Camille's mother was paralyzed, and her father had lost his job. She also had two children, ages eight and five, from a relationship with a married foreign man. The father of her children had moved back to the USA and had refused to help financially. He wasn't interested in the welfare of his kids and kept demanding a DNA test to confirm his fatherhood. In addition, her dad was a diabetic whose life depended on his medication. Therefore, for the sake of her family, she had swallowed her pride and dignity in order to sell her body.

On the other sofa a fat, baldheaded 60-year-old tourist

by the name of Jackson licked Daniela's toes. She was only 17 years old, a fair-skinned teenage girl from a wealthy family. She averted her gaze from what was going on, feeling scorched and dirty. The stench of alcohol mixed with his odor was making her nauseous. To make matters worse, he kept farting.

Anger stirred in her heart as she hatefully gazed at this stranger. It grew steadily, until she had finally had enough.

"Get your dirty self away from me! You're sickening!" she said. She tried to push Jackson away.

He slapped her. She quickly moved to the other end of the sofa and put her hand on her cheek.

"Shut up, you little whore. I didn't pay to hear your whining."

"But you stink, and you keep farting like a pig."

She tried to get up, but he pushed her back onto the sofa. Her black eyes filled with fear. She looked over at Camille, hoping that she would help her. However, Camille pretended that she had not heard anything, and tried not to look at Daniela.

Jackson started unbuttoning Daniela's blouse, but she pushed him off.

"Please go away," she pleaded.

However, he was aroused and ignored her pleas. He continued working on getting her blouse off. His eyes opened wide as she fought him.

"Stop being naughty," he said. Now his hands went down her body.

"Please come back later."

Hearing Daniela's pleas, Camille got up.

"Let's go to my bedroom. There's no privacy here at all," she said.

She walked away, pulling her partner with her.

Daniela pushed her tormentor away and got up. Right then, she caught a glimpse of Victor standing by the door. He glared at her and swiped a finger across his neck, giving her a sign. It was only too clear that, if she did not obey her customer's desires, her head would be cut off.

She shook as she turned back to her customer. With a feeble smile, she took his hand and said, "Please come with me. I feel uncomfortable doing this in here."

"I knew you were a good girl," he said. His face was red, and saliva dripped from his lips.

"Lead the way, puddin'," he said, hitting her bottom. Trembling like a leaf, she led him to the bedroom.

Late in the evening, Sheila lay on the bed. She stared at her latest client, Mateo.

His head was covered with grey hair, and wrinkles crisscrossed his unshaven face. He was unhealthily thin, in such a way that his ribs were bulging out through his skin. The smell of cigarettes on his breath bothered her nose. He kept passing his hands over her hair, and then massaging her legs and slapping her bottom.

Yesterday's incident had left a horrid feeling in her mind, and the memory haunted her.

She recalled her last client. He had smelled like a fish and his back had been covered in acne. As soon as he had taken off his clothes and tried to kiss her, she had pushed him away and had run out of the bedroom. She had puked in the garbage bin that was in the guest room, and then had sat on the sofa crying. The man had followed her into the guest room, stripped to the waist.

"Hey, you. I didn't pay good money for you to relax in here. Come back to your stupid bedroom."

She had looked up tearily at him, ignoring his words. He had snatched her hands and pulled her up.

"You little trash, I want to get what I paid for!"

Sheila had tried to pull her hand away. "Let go my hand, you nasty dog. I'm not your slave!"

Hearing loud voices, Victor had entered the guest room. "What is happening here?"

The man had released her hand and grinned.

"I paid 300 US to sleep with this slut, and she refuses to do her job. I want my money back."

"Mr. Price, please calm down. Go back into the bedroom. I give you my word you'll get value for your money."

Price had walked away. Victor had grabbed Sheila's hair and made her get up.

"Ouch! Please stop! I'm not a prostitute. Why are you making me to do these things?"

He had pulled her in front of him. "Walk to the toilet," he had ordered.

As soon as they had gone in, he had locked the door and pushed her to the toilet. He made her kneel.

"In this house, you are to please every desire of the clients without questioning," he said.

He had grasped her neck from behind and pushed her head into the toilet bowl. Then he had flushed the toilet with her head in the water. The water had gone all over Sheila's face and into her mouth.

She had put her hand out, searching for something to grab onto. At the same time, she tried to lift her head up out of the bowl.

Finally, he had taken her head out of the toilet bowl. She began coughing and puking.

"Now you know what will happen to you if you disobey. Clean yourself up and go back to your room," he had ordered.

He had unlocked the door and left. Sheila stood up, crying, and began rinsing her mouth and face. Right after that she sat on the floor and pulled her knees up to her chest, trembling.

"Please, please, God! Free me from this trap. I can't

handle it. I beg you, help me to escape."

She had leaned her head against the wall and stared at the celling.

"Father, it's too much for me. I want to go back to my children. Why has this happened to me? Why? This monster comes every night and rapes me. I try to be strong for my children. But I might not last. Please save me!"

For a while she sat in silence, letting her rage build up inside her. Finally, she made a fist, stood up, and left the toilet.

Now, as she lay there with Mateo, she started to feel weak, as if someone was draining the life out of her. She glanced at her unfinished drink on the bedside table.

Victor must have drugged me.

Mateo removed a small pack of white powder from his valet and a short straw. He sat on the bed and glanced at Sheila. Then he emptied some powder into his palm. With a straw in his nostril, he brought his palmful of cocaine closer to his nose. He began snorting cocaine with closed eyes. His eyes became teary.

"Hey, chick! You want some?" he offered, staring at her.

"No." She turned her head aside.

He grabbed her chin and made her face him. He brought his palm closer to her face.

She pushed it away, and the powder spilled on her.

"You little slut! You wasted it!" He raised his voice and made a fist.

"Please, no! I am very tired and unwell," she plead staring at his fist.

He put the powder and straw back into his valet.

Then he started undressing her. He suspected that she was under the influence of another drug, but he didn't care. Before him was a beautiful woman who couldn't say no, and would be used to satisfy his dirty dreams and desires.

He rubbed her breasts.

"You idiot. Leave me alone," she said, as she tried to raise her head. It was too much of an effort, so she dropped it back.

"Oh, you want to play." Mateo leered down at her.

"Listen, I don't belong here. I have children and a husband," she mumbled.

Mateo ignored her words. Instead, he pulled down his underpants and climbed on top of her. Sheila put her hands on his chest and tried to push him off but lacked the strength to do so.

As Sheila lay there helplessly watching him rape her, she felt as if part of her soul was dying, together with all her values and hopes. She had an urge to yell but swallowed it when she saw that the door was slightly open. The one who had almost drowned her in the toilet bowl stood there watching them.

She forced herself to look in another direction and closed her eyes, trying to get lost in her thoughts.

It's Christmas. I should be with my family, not in this whorehouse or with this jerk on top of me.

She swallowed her bile as she felt the pain between her legs. Finally, Mateo got off and put on his shorts. Then he sat on the bed and leered at Sheila. He caught hold of her hand and began caressing it.

"Where are you from?" he asked.

Sheila stared straight into his eyes, playing mute and deaf.

He squeezed her wrist. "When I ask questions, you had better have answers," he said.

"Please let go of my wrist."

He loosened his grasp.

"Are you a new girl? I've been here before and have never seen you."

As he caressed her cheek, she turned her head away. "I don't belong here."

"Every whore says they don't belong here, playing innocent and pure," he said.

Sheila rose slightly and slapped him on the cheek.

"Look nuh! I'm not a whore! I was forcedly brought here!"

Mateo got up, rubbing his cheek. He spat on her face and then squeezed her throat with both hands.

"You nasty bitch. I can smell a whore like you from afar. Don't play virgin with me."

Sheila clutched at his hands, trying to loosen his grasp. Her face got red and her eyes became teary.

The door opened, and Victor walked in. Sheila's tormentor let go of her neck.

"Is everything alright here, Mateo?" Victor asked.

Mateo picked his clothes up off the floor.

"Oh, yes. We're just getting to know each other. But I think I'm done for now."

As Victor gazed at Sheila, Mateo slipped into the rest of his clothes. Then he took out a few dollars from his wallet and threw them on her.

"Here, this is for you. You should buy some soap and take a shower. You stink like a shit."

Sheila raised her head slightly and stared at him and at Victor. She wanted to say, 'I don't need your dirty money,' but was too afraid of being punished.

Mateo walked away. However, he stopped at the door and turned around.

"You need to tame her a little bit. She's too wild for me."

Victor smirked at Sheila. "She's new here. But I guarantee that the next time you won't have any problems with her."

"And please do not come into the room when I'm naked."

A grin formed on Victor's face.

"Sorry, I didn't mean to interrupt you."

"Forget it. I'll be back in two weeks," Mateo said, with a smile on his face.

After he left, Victor clutched Sheila's hand, squeezing it firmly.

"Remember, the customer is always right. It's your job to make them happy. If they express dissatisfaction with you, I will make sure that you drown the next time we have to 'discuss' your behavior."

He let go of her hand, picked up the money from the floor, and left her alone.

Sheila got of the bed, trembling all over. She rubbed her aching wrist silently as an urge to cry filled her. The feeling of being filthy pushed her to the bathroom. She managed to get there just in time to puke in the toilet bowl.

She got into the shower and let the water run. As the cold water poured over her, she soaped herself over and over, trying to remove all the pain and disgust that she felt.

"Yuck. Get out of me."

"Sheila!" It was Bernadette. "When you're done, come into the guest room."

What does she want now?

Sheila's left eyelid twitched, and a stabbing pain developed behind her eye.

"Did you hear me?"

Can't even take a shower in peace! "Yes, *Senora*. I'll be there."

"Stubborn woman. I will break her spirit," whispered Bernadette as she left the bedroom.

Sheila turned off the water and wrapped herself in a towel. When she came out of the shower, she gazed at herself in the mirror. Her face looked thinner, and there were dark shadows under her eyes. With a frown on her face she whispered, "I will find a way to get out of this damned place."

She walked to the small closet and took out a top and skirt that had been given to her by Bernadette. She put them on and went to the guest room.

To her surprise, all the girls of the brothel were in the room. They had wine glasses in their hands and were chatting merrily.

Daniela, however, sat silently by herself. She was thinking about the last Christmas with her sister and parents. She recalled opening gifts with them and then going to church. Her face was sad as she sat there missing her family.

Sheila sat quietly on another sofa, watching the ladies in the room.

Bernadette picked up gifts from under the tree and handed them out. When Daniela got her gift, she hugged Bernadette and said, "Thank you."

With a smile on her face Bernadette said, "Don't thank me but Victor."

She glanced at her watch and then walked away.

Daniela began unwrapping the gift. Suddenly she heard Camille's loud laughter.

Camille took out the contents of her gift box and held them in the air for everyone to see. They were red panties, condoms, a pregnancy test kit, and a lubricator.

"Victor is a real idiot. Couldn't he get a better gift for us?"

Others also opened their gifts and found the same items.

"Is this some kind of joke? Just throw them away," said a woman by the name of Luciana. She stood up and left.

Sheila didn't even bother to unwrap hers. As soon as Daniela opened her gift, disappointment was clear on her face. Sheila walked towards her.

Without saying anything, Daniela took out a pack of condoms.

"What kind of gift is this? They are cruel animals."

Tears formed in her eyes. "They sell my body to make money and give me this rubbish." She stood up, dropping her gifts.

"I guess they want to make sure you don't catch a disease."

"They robbed me of my virginity, my soul, and my innocence. I'm unable to bear this anymore."

Trembling, Daniela dropped back onto the sofa. Sheila sat down next to Daniela and rubbed her back.

"Please don't make a scene, or Victor will come back. I promise we'll walk out of here free as birds," Sheila whispered, glancing at the others.

One by one, the brothel's dwellers left the guest room with their gifts.

"Wipe your tears and get up. You must not show your weakness to them."

Daniela lifted the edge of her blouse up and wiped her tears with it. Then she clutched Sheila's hand.

"Whatever you're doing, please free us soon. I can't handle this any longer."

I don't even know where to start, or how to free us.

Sheila rose. She felt as if something was stuck in her throat.

"I'll try. Now go to your room and get some rest."

26th December

It was Boxing Day, a public holiday. Candice, wearing shorts and a strapless green top, sat on the sofa in her living room with a tall dark-skinned man by the name of Terrel. She held a glass of Sprite and he was drinking beer.

He put his glass down and began kissing her shoulder. She laughed as she squirmed away.

"What happened to you, gyul?"

"I'm just ticklish," she said.

He took the glass from her hand and put it on the floor. Then he pulled her top up. His lips passed over her breasts.

She stiffened and moved away.

"You kind of seem uninterested and edgy today," he said.

"I have a headache, and it's killing me," she answered, trying to pull down her top.

He pulled it off and threw it across the room. He took off his pants and lay down on the sofa. "Jump on top," he said.

She undressed and slowly sat on top of him, and they started having sex.

"Ouch! It hurts!" She grimaced and got off him.

Terrel sat up. "What's wrong with you today, gyul?" he asked.

"My tummy is in pain. Maybe because of the pregnancy."

He grasped her hand and stared into her eyes.

"Ah always wondering if dis[54] child is really mine."

Her eyebrows knitted. "Wah yuh[55] talking about, boy? When did you started doubting me?"

"Weren't you sleeping with *him* as well?"

"No, we've only been dating."

"Yuh[56] lie. Men wouldn't see a woman for so long without having pussy."

She pulled her hand away from him and walked towards the table. She took a cigarette out of a pack and lit it, then sat down on a chair and smoked silently.

"Yuh pushed me to date him so I can spy on him. Now yuh[57] accusing me with dis shit?" she asked in a loud voice. She flicked her ashes into the ashtray.

Terrel put on his shirt and walked to the table. He poured another glass of beer for himself and stood in front of her.

"[58]Me eh hah no other choice. I borrowed money from de boss and couldn't return it. When I told him that I had no money, he put a Smith and Wesson revolver to my head and said, "Either pay back my money or find out what Miguel knows

---

[54] This
[55] What are you
[56] You
[57] You are
[58] I had no other choice

about my operations."

Candice put out her cigarette and dropped it in the ashtray.

"Both of you are dotish. Why would he tell me anything about police stuff?"

"Why yuh doh leave him?"

She wrapped her arms around his neck and kissed him. He kissed her back. She pulled her lips away from his.

"Your jealousy is suffocating. You know my heart belongs only to you."

"I don't want his hands all over you."

"Why yuh cah[59] understand? I'm doing this for you!"

He gently removed her arms from around his neck and walked over to the window. He gazed at a shop that was across from her house.

"You know, I can easily get money just by robbing shops or neighbors. Chen's shop can give me a good income. Isn't this shop run by a Chinese man?" he asked, pointing outside.

She came to the window and looked at where he was pointing.

"Yes, he runs it with his wife. Dem come here and doh even talk English," she said.

"I went there a few times and didn't see any security. It would be easy to rob them," Terrel said.

"Leave that Chinese man alone. He's already been robbed a few times this year."

"Who cares how many times he was robbed? Dem come to our country opening restaurants, little shops taking we money. Why can't I rob dem?"

"You might get another jail term if they catch you. The streets have cameras."

On the other hand, if he goes to jail, I'll be free of him.

---

[59] Why can't you

"You know what? Just go ahead with your plans. The baby will need a lot of things."

If dem lock him up, I can for sure marry Miguel.

His phone rang, and he answered. The smile on his face disappeared and his eyes narrowed.

"Yes, boss. I'll be there shortly."

He ended the call.

"What bossman wants?" asked Candice.

"I dunno[60]. He asked me to come by immediately."

"You're like a loyal puppy ready to run after a bone," she said with a grimace.

"Hush nah."[61]

He walked away. As he left, Candice took a cigarette from the pack and lit it. She sat on the sofa and sucked some smoke in. She held it in her mouth and then blew it out.

I need to have a better plan so I can leave him. Next thing I know, he may slice me with a cutlass or shoot me.

Candice gazed at her tattoo.

I have so much to worry about. This damned tattoo is causing so much trouble. I can get caught for this.

She picked up the cell phone from the table and dialed Miguel's number. It rang but no one answered.

They should kill she, and then I wouldn't have any problems. He's avoiding me because of she.

Candice turned on the radio and listened to the chutney music.

Then she closed her eyes and began visualizing her wedding day. She saw herself going to the altar with Miguel and exchanging rings. Daydreaming about her future, she fell asleep.

It was mid-morning, and at the primary school Ronnel

---

[60] I don't know
[61] Shut up

was playing outside with his friends. The schoolyard, as usual, was filled with noisy students during recess time. Some played a game of catch, while others sat on a bench munching on their lunch.

Suddenly shots echoed in the school yard. The children began running into their classrooms.

Ronnel dashed into his and ducked under his chair.

"Where's Miss Tyler?" he asked a girl next to him.

"I don't know," she said, trembling.

Miss Tyler came in and shut the door behind her. The students started coming out of their hiding places.

"Everyone, please stay in the classroom till your parents come for you," she said.

"Miss, I'm scared. Did someone die?" asked Kamla, a girl who sat behind Ronnel.

"No. There's nothing to be afraid of."

The room buzzed with the chatter of classmates talking about what had happened. However, Ronnel sat soundlessly and lay face down on his desk. He remembered the events of the night that bandits had entered his house. Tears fell on his desk.

"They took her. I'm not going to see her anymore," he whispered.

Within an hour, parents were rushing to the school to pick up their children. Everyone hurried to leave.

Miguel arrived and walked towards Ronnel's classroom. As soon as he came in, Ronnel rushed towards him.

"Hello, Miss Tyler," Miguel said to the teacher.

Ronnel clutched at his hand. "Father, take me home now, please!"

"Just give me a minute." He looked up at the teacher.

"Do you know what happened?" asked Miss Tyler, who knew that Miguel was a policeman.

"It was a shootout between police and two bandits. One of the gang members was killed and the other one injured."

"It's so scary to come to this area. When these things happen, no one dares to leave the school's compound to check on it," said Miss Tyler.

"Father, where's Nadia?"

"She's still at school."

Miguel addressed the teacher once again. "How is Ronnel doing with his schoolwork?"

"He's become less talkative, and his marks have dropped. He was one of my best students, but now he's lagging behind."

"Hmm. I'll talk to him about it," said Miguel.

He looked at his watch. "Sorry, Miss Tyler. I have to go to pick up my daughter. Stay safe this afternoon."

"You too," she answered.

Father and son then left for home.

GRUESOME END

26th January

Toothless earned extra cash by working as a taxi driver. On an unusual hot day, at 4 p.m., he was on the road driving his Nissan Almera and occasionally looking at his mirror. He drove at 60km/h in order not to attract the police to himself. In front, on the passenger's seat, he had a small ice box with a few drinks in it. Because the AC in his car refused to work, his shirt was soaking wet.

Images of the events earlier that day kept popping into his mind, as if he was watching movie. He saw himself in the car, laughing and talking to a neighbor's daughter, Layla.

Right before picking her up, he had taken an extra dose of antidepressants in order to deal with his anxiety and anger episodes. Consequently, he felt free of worries and at peace as he chatted with Layla.

She showed him a photo of her son, which she carried in her wallet, and spoke about his achievements in school. She was going to the Shopping Centre to buy gifts for his birthday.

At some point she began fanning herself with a booklet.

"Can you please let down the back window? I'm boiling here," she said.

With a smile on his face he opened the window. Then he took out a drink from his ice box.

"Gyul, why don't yuh drink dis. You'll feel better."

He removed the cap from the bottle.

Layla took it from him and drank it all.

"Thank you. This is just what I needed."

She leaned back and gazed outside. They were passing the governmental houses.

"Any news on your government house?" she asked.

Toothless glanced at Layla in the mirror.

"No news. I'm still waiting for approval."

"You'll get it. Don't worry."

Layla felt herself getting sleepy and relaxed. She yawned a few times and was soon asleep.

Toothless glanced at her in the mirror, a grin on his face. He closed the windows. Seeing her unconscious, he pulled off the highway and drove onto a road lined closely on both sides by sugar cane. Then he parked along a gravel road and dialed Candice's number.

She was riding in a taxi between two passengers. She glanced at the phone's screen and, seeing Toothless' name, answered the call.

"Yes, Toothless."

"I'm ready to proceed."

Candice's eyes looked from left to right at the people beside her.

"What are you talking about?" she whispered.

"You have a short memory. Didn't you ask me to kill a woman and pass her off as Sheila?"

Candice again looked at the travelers, making sure that they hadn't heard anything.

"Call me later. This isn't a good time."

"Listen, I'm going ahead with the plan. Put seven thousand in an envelope and drop it at the designated place tomorrow."

"Okay, you'll get it once the job is done. Don't call this number again."

"If you try to play games with me, I'll come for you."

He put away his phone and got out of the car, making sure to scan the area beforehand.

Not seeing anyone, he pulled Layla out of the back seat and carried her into a nearby, dilapidated wooden house. He put her on the dirty floor and began unbuttoning her blouse. When her breasts were exposed, he took some photos of her.

Layla opened her eyes and rose, blinking sleepily at her surroundings and then at Toothless. She then noticed that her blouse was unbuttoned.

"What are you doing?" she spluttered as she tried to get up.

He put a finger on her lips.

"Sh, sh. Everything is gonna be alright."

His memories were suddenly interrupted by a car horn. He had drifted into the oncoming lane.

He swerved back and continued with his reverie.

His memories focused on a moment where he was raping Layla, who was screaming and clawing at him. She had very long nails, and as she tried to push him away from herself, she scratched his face.

Why do these silly women grow long nails?

He tied her hands and taped her mouth. After injecting her with something, he put her in the trunk of the car and started the engine.

He felt sorry for her. After all, she was his neighbor, but she had seen his face, and he needed his seven thousand. In the end, he decided to go ahead with Candice's suggestion. The question was, what to do next?

Where can I take her? Oh--Grande Forest will do.

As he drove his maxi taxi on the unpopulated road, his thoughts were interrupted by the noises coming out of his trunk. Layla was kicking the trunk's lid, trying to open it.

She's making too much noise.

He pulled off the road and drove towards Grande Forest and parked his car not far from the trees. He took his gun out from underneath the seat and opened a can of beer. For some time, he sat there drinking it.

"Help me! Somebody please let me out!"

"Stop it. It won't help you!" he shouted.

He got a look at his face in the mirror and saw oozing scratches on his cheeks.

"Please free me! Let me go to my son!"

Scraped up all my face, stupid woman. I should have end she in that house.

He took out a roll of wide masking tape and a pair of pliers from the glove compartment and got out of the car. He put the pliers in his pants pocket. Looking around suspiciously, Toothless contemplated his surroundings. Then he put his gun in his pocket, walked to his trunk, and raised the lid.

Layla stared up at him, wide-eyed and trembling with fear.

"Are you going to kill me? We grew up together!"

He tore off a piece of masking tape. She tried to sit up, but he pushed her back, then pasted the tape across her mouth.

Toothless pulled her out and put her on his shoulder. Then he took out a canister of gasoline from the trunk. Carrying both, he walked to the forest. Layla kicked and writhed, trying to get off.

"Ow! Stop that or I'll finish your life right here!"

He kept moving into the forest, sweating and in pain. Once they were surrounded by the trees, he stopped and dropped her on the ground.

He stared at her silently. Her blouse was covered with blood and her lips were bruised.

Layla's entire body ached, especially between her legs and in her stomach. She felt so very weak.

Being around helpless and lonely women gave Toothless a feeling of gratification. They were easy prey for him. He merely had to give them a little attention or gentleness, and they fell for him like fools. As he raped them, their pleas were like a lullaby for his ears, and he felt powerful and in control.

Layla was his fourth victim. The last three he had released, but he had prepared something horrid for Layla.

Layla sat up, too scared to move. She stared around as her lips and chin trembled.

Toothless stooped down and pulled the tape off of her mouth. Next, he took the gun out of his pocket and directed it at her.

Slowly she moved backwards, her eyes focusing on the barrel.

"Please, Toothless, don't do it. You used to come to our house. You were like a brother to me."

"And what? I've been in many houses. [62]Yuh real dunce and naïve woman."

His eyes wandered around, doing a quick scan of the area. Then he put the gun to her temple.

She cried and kept pleading. "I beg you, don't kill me. I have a son. Don't leave my child motherless."

Her pleas made him recall an event from his childhood:

Once when he was only eight years old, he had woken up at night feeling someone's touch on his groin area. He opened his eyes, and right before him stood his Uncle Dylan, who was living with them after returning from the US.

Toothless had tried to get out of bed, but Dylan had pushed him back. He had wanted to scream, but his uncle had covered his mouth with his hand and whispered, "If you make a sound, I will kill your mummy."

Toothless' body had shuddered with fear. His face had paled, and his legs weak. Dylan had pulled down his underpants and said, "Lie down on the bed and do what I say, and everything will be fine."

---

[62] You are really stupid…

Layla managed to grab Toothless' hand and stared at him with teary eyes. "Caleb please, don't do this."

He made a fist and kicked her a few times.

"Oh, God, I'm going to die. Please stop it!" she pleaded, as her body moved jerkily.

"You will not hurt me anymore. You hear me, Uncle? This is your end!"

He knelt next to Layla, who was crying loudly, and held onto her chin. He stared into her face—but it wasn't Layla he was seeing. It was his uncle's face.

His hand slid down to her neck.

"I hate you, Uncle."

As he stared at her, his eyes flashing hatred, another past event popped into his mind.

He was in his dark bedroom, being choked by his uncle because he had refused to follow the monster's demands. How Toothless wished to be rescued by his parents, but they were never at home when he needed their protection.

After work, his father stayed out late messing around with his lady lovers. His mother was too busy with gossiping and partying with her own friends.

As his uncle let go of his neck, Toothless stared into his eyes and pleaded, "Uncle, please stop hurting me. I don't want do this anymore." The poor child's eyes ran with tears, which poured down his wet cheeks.

Toothless' memories were interrupted by Layla's voice.

"Caleb I beg you, take me to the hospital. I won't tell anyone anything about what happened."

He pulled her up to a standing position and pushed her towards a tree, all the while seeing his uncle's face. He turned her around and silently stared into her eyes. Toothless then moved aside and took out a pack of cigarettes from his pocket.

As he did so, some money rolled out of his pocket. He leaned over and picked it up.

Layla took the opportunity and ran, holding her tied hands in front of herself.

Toothless looked up. He grinned as he watched her flee.

"Oh, she wants to play hide and seek now. What a waste of time!"

He walked in the direction, slowly and purposely, giving her more time to run.

"People always run somewhere, but the end still comes," he mumbled. "Can't cheat death."

As he chased after his victim, his mind brought back new images of his past.

He recalled a time when he was thirteen, getting up at night and rushing to the toilet. As soon as he had finished urinating, Dylan came in. Toothless had tried to pull up his pants, but his uncle had stopped him and began touching his groin area. He had managed to push Dylan away, and had run out of the room. Trembling, he had dashed into his parents' bedroom and had hidden under their bed. As he lay there teary-eyed, his heartbeat increased, and his palms became clammy.

"Stop hiding. Come out or you'll regret it."

His uncle had walked through the house searching for him. Toothless could hear him coughing.

He had stopped in Toothless' bedroom, out of breath, and had looked under the bed. Then he had entered his brother's bedroom.

Dylan's coughing had worsened; he was having an asthma attack. He had knelt on the floor, breathing heavily. As Dylan looked in the bed's direction, he had noticed Toothless' legs under the bed.

"Son, please help me. I know you're under the bed."

Dylan felt a stabbing pain in his chest as he gasped for air.

Toothless had gotten out of his hiding spot and stared at

his uncle from afar.

"I am not your son."

Dylan' s face had become pale.

"Go and get my inhaler from the top of my chest of drawers."

Toothless hadn't moved a muscle. Dylan's eyes became watery as his chest wheezed loudly.

"No, you did bad things to me." Toothless' body trembled as tears appeared on his eyes.

"Please, go. I promise I will never touch you again."

Toothless looked over at the door and then at his uncle.

"You were putting your thing in my mouth. I begged you not to do it. But you didn't listen."

Dylan spread himself on the floor, lying on his left side.

"Go and get dat damned thing before I dead."

Feeling sorry for him, Toothless ran out of the bedroom and in a few minutes came back with the inhaler.

He approached his uncle who, upon seeing Toothless, had reached for the inhaler. Toothless stretched his arm out to pass the inhaler to his uncle. However, even then Dylan had touched him inappropriately.

Anger roared through his brain.

"No, Uncle. You get it yourself."

He had thrown the inhaler and it had rolled under the bed. Dylan had attempted to get up.

"Go and get it, stupid boy!" he had ordered.

"No, you get it yourself."

"You're an idiot. I'll get you!"

Dylan managed to sit up. The scared boy had run out of the room like a bullet.

Layla ran into the overgrown foliage, which scratched her face and hands. Her leg hit against a branch that had fallen from a tree, and she fell facedown.

Her sobs filled the air. "Ouch! Help me! Why is no one

helping me?" She tried frantically to get up a few times and failed.

Finally, she was able to get on her feet. She took off again, running for dear life. She paused once and looked around, trying to see where to run, but was surrounded by trees. There didn't seem to be a way out.

Then she heard the sound of gushing water and ran towards it.

It was a river. Afraid of being drowned by Caleb if he found her there, she ran back into the woods and hid behind a huge tree. She stood very still and peeked out from behind it. Feeling worn out, she slid down to a sitting position against the tree.

Toothless kept walking, patiently and relentlessly, holding the gun in his hand and ready to shoot.

"Where are you? Come out! There's nowhere to go."

He looked at the ground and saw the grass that had been crushed under her feet. After a few minutes of following the trail, he came to the river. He stopped and gazed toward the other side.

"No, she couldn't have crossed it," he said.

He stared at the ground, looking for footprints.

She must be here somewhere.

Hearing his voice, Layla tried not to move or to breathe loudly. She closed her eyes.

Please Lord, don't allow him to find me.

Toothless looked at the trees suspiciously. Then he walked slowly towards them.

A huge black centipede crawled up her leg and bit it. She jumped up, screaming.

Hearing her voice, Toothless ran towards the tree. As soon as he found Layla, he grabbed her blouse. Then he pushed her against the tree a few times, bashing her head.

Blood gushed down her scalp. Toothless let her go and moved aside. She took a few steps, then fell on her belly. Yellow lights flew before her eyes, and her head was spinning. Slowly she crawled forward, trying to get away from him.

Toothless let her crawl little bit further, and then he kicked her all over her body. She grabbed his leg and lifted her head to stare at him, unbearable pain in her eyes.

"Please shoot me and end this."

He stopped kicking her and sat on a rock. He lit a cigarette and put it in his mouth.

As blood oozed from her nose, ears, and mouth, Layla raised her head and gazed at Toothless.

"Why Caleb?"

"Don't take it personally. Your death will earn meh cash."

"You're a monster. You'll burn in hell," she whispered, and then coughed out a gob of blood.

Toothless glanced at his watch. He threw his cigarette on the ground and then stepped on it.

He walked towards her and gripped her neck with both hands. She held onto his hands, trying to free herself. As he squeezed her neck, her face became blueish pale and she let go of his hands.

Toothless let go as she became still. He put his finger on her wrist and checked her pulse.

She was dead.

Toothless lit another cigarette and, with trembling hands, put it into his mouth. He inhaled the smoke as he stared into her wide-open, dull eyes. He flinched and dropped the cigarette on the grass. Stepping on it, he walked to Layla's lifeless body and closed her eyes.

He picked up the canister and doused her with the gasoline. Then he lit her blouse with his lighter and stood aside, watching the fire slowly spreading over her body. Flames rose up, making Toothless move away further. He sat on a rock, smoking and watching the fire. When the flames got smaller, he began pulling out her teeth with the pliers. One by one, he removed them all and put them in his pocket.

No one will be able to identify her.

Then he doused her with gasoline again. As the flames rose, he looked at his watch.

Didn't expect this would take so long.

He dialed Candice's number.

She was at her friend's house in the bedroom, going through some clothes. Her friend was selling them, and Candice had come to buy some.

Her phone buzzed nonstop. She looked at the screen and then answered.

"What now?" she asked, with annoyance in her voice.

"It's done."

A frown formed on her face. "What are you talking about?"

"I killed a woman as you asked. I'll be waiting for my seven thousand tomorrow. Actually, since the work took more time than expected, make it nine thousand."

Candice looked over at the door, making sure that her friend wasn't nearby.

"Are you insane? I can't pay you that amount."

"I don't care. If I don't get my nine thousand, I'll call Miguel and tell him everything."

Candice closed the bedroom's door.

"I swear I have no cash right now. Give me a week."

Toothless spat on the ground. "Why don't you ask your pimp, Teller?"

"He's struggling himself."

"Fine. No more than a week!"

"What did you do with the body?" she asked in a low voice as she stared at the door.

"I burned it and dumped it in the forest."

"Did you leave Sheila's ring near her?"

"Oh no, I forgot. I'll do it now."

He pressed the end button and put his cell in his pocket, then took the ring, which he'd put in a fire the day before, out of his pocket and went over to the corpse. He pondered a moment, wondering where to leave the ring. Finally, he bent down and slid it onto Layla's burnt finger.

"I wish I hadn't had to spoil that ring. Oh well—maybe I can steal it off her before she's buried."

Then he picked up the canister and walked out of the forest.

As he sat in his car, Toothless heard a cell phone ringing somewhere. He looked at the back seat, but it was empty. Then he got out and searched in his trunk.

There he found Layla's cell phone. He picked it up and looked at the screen. The word "Mummy" appeared on the screen.

Damn it, her mother is calling.

He turned off the phone and slipped it into his pocket. Then he got back into the car and drove away.

The next day, at 8 a.m., two police officers sat at the desk in Monrel police station. One of them was talking on the phone and the other one was reading a report.

A plump 60-year-old lady walked into the police station. She went to the desk.

"Excuse me?" she said.

One of the officers looked up at her. "Good morning. How can I help you?"

"My daughter has been missing since yesterday. I came to make a report for a missing person."

The officer picked up a huge journal of entries and a pen.

"What is your name, Aunty?"

"Indriani."

"Your daughter's name and age, please."

"Her name is Layla, and she's 29 years old."

The officer kept taking notes.

"When was the last time you saw her?"

"Yesterday. She left the house at 7 a.m., for work."

"When was the last time you spoke to her?"

"She called at around 4.30 p.m., and said that she was waiting for a taxi."

"What was she wearing?"

"She wore a white blouse and a black skirt."

The officer closed her journal and put her pen down.

"Why don't you come back in a few days. She might be somewhere with she man or having a good time with friends."

"No, she never stays away from home. Can you please search for her?" Indriani pleaded, putting her hands on the desk.

"Please don't panic. I'm sure she's fine. Go home and come back in two days if she doesn't show up."

"But she..."

"Aunty, we will look for her."

Layla's mother slowly walked away.

"Are you going to do anything about it?" asked the other officer.

"No, we should wait for two days. She's probably somewhere having fun with she lover."

"What if you're wrong? I'll make some calls and see what we can do," said the officer, as she lifted the phone receiver.

Indriani drove home. She went straight into Layla's bedroom. It was a cream-colored room with a queen-sized bed, two bedside tables, and an oak dressing table.

She opened the drawers of the dressing table and searched for Layla's phone book.

In her search, Indriani found a huge photo album. She took it out and sat on the bed, where she spent some time looking at every picture in it. On one of the photos, Layla was standing with a bunch of children. Everyone was smiling except Caleb, who stood near her. He looked dejected.

Where are you, my child? You never stay away without telling me. Are you hurt?

Her attention shifted to a picture of Layla taken in a restaurant. She sat next to her boyfriend, radiating joy.

Stop it. Nothing wrong with she. She probably with her boyfriend.

A tall, thin boy with a short haircut came into the bedroom.

"Granny, when is Mummy coming home?"

Indriani glanced at him, not knowing what to say.

"Granny, why are you ignoring me?"

"Sorry, I got lost in thought. I don't know, okay?"

"Why don't you call her?"

"Go and do your homework, and I'll try to get her."

Indriani's grandchild left. She put away the album and searched the rest of the drawers.

She found a telephone book and looked at the names in the book. Then she picked up the phone and called Layla's friends.

The first call was made to her boyfriend, Jason.

"Hello."

"Hi, Jason. This is Layla's mother."

"Oh, hi, Aunty. What happened?"

"Layla didn't come home yesterday. Did you see her?"

Jason sat up on his bed.

"Yesterday she called me and said that she was boarding a taxi to go home. Something might have happened to her."

Fear filled Indriani, making her tremble. "No, not to my sweet daughter. She's my only child."

"Aunty, stay calm. Maybe there's a rational explanation. I'll come over in a while and help you to look for she."

Indriani hung up and, for some time, sat unresponsively. Then she dropped the phone on the floor.

Someone might have captured her and is holding her against her will.

She picked up the phone and made a few more calls.

"Hi, Karissa. Did you speak to Layla yesterday?"

"No, Aunty. Why?"

Brick by brick, her wall of hope was crumbling. She broke down, sobbing.

"She went to work yesterday and didn't turn up. I feel that something horrible has happened to her," she said through sobs.

"Aunty, take it easy. She probably went out with friends and stayed with one of them."

"But my child doesn't do that. She always calls me."

Indriani put down the phone as tears escaped her eyes.

MISTAKEN IDENTITY

29th January

A farmer walked into the forest, looking for his dog, which had run off.

"Brono! Come here!"

He could hear the dog barking from far off.

"You're a naughty dog. Come here now!"

He followed his dog's barking and was soon able to see him.

When he got to Brono, he spied something gruesome--a corpse burned beyond recognition. His dog walked around the corpse, sniffing it and yapping. As the farmer grabbed the dog's collar, the sickly-sweet aroma of cooked flesh hit his nose, making him throw up. He put his hand over his nose and pulled his dog away from the corpse.

The dog got away and jumped over the remains.

"Oh, shit," he said, and vomited again.

He got hold of his dog's collar and put on a leash on it.

"Let's go. I have to call the police."

He ran to his pickup truck. He put his dog in the back of the truck and dialed the police.

"Irva Police station."

"Yeah, listen. I was walking in the Grande Forest looking for my dog, and I've stumbled on some burnt human remains."

"What's your name?"

"Gary."

"Did you see anything else by the remains?"

"I didn't really look properly. As soon as I saw the corpse I ran out."

"Thank you for your call. I'll have this looked into immediately," said the dispatcher.

"Please keep my name anonymous," said the farmer.

"We never give out names. I assure you of that."

The farmer put away his cell phone and started his engine. He drove away, trying to forget what he had seen and smelled.

30th January

In the evening, after the church service, Father Piero sank down comfortably in his armchair in front of the TV, watching the local news. He was drinking tea.

'Another tragedy has struck our society. Yesterday, human remains were found by a farmer in Grande Forest. The body was burned beyond recognition. Police have yet to identify the gender and identity. The police are still searching for a kidnap victim by the name of Sheila Siglobeen. There's a possibility that the remains might belong to her.'

Another innocent life perished. Almost every day they announce more death. No wonder why some people don't read or watch the news. So many lives are ruined. Indeed, the Demon is not sleeping at all. Could it be Sheila?

Father Piero turned off the TV and dialed Miguel's number.

Miguel was sitting at his desk, going through some bills that had to be paid soon. He picked up the phone.

"Good evening, Miguel. This is Father Piero."

"Good evening, Father Piero."

"How is everything going? I have not seen you for quite a while. You've missed all my Masses since Sheila's been gone."

Miguel lit a cigarette.

"I can't force myself to come to church without my wife. It's not easy to live, not knowing where she might be. Is she hurt? Is she dying or hungry? My mind is like a boiling kettle that's ready to explode."

"You shouldn't be missing out on Mass for any reason. You'd feel much better in God's house, taking communion and surrounded by people. Why don't you attend tomorrow with your children? You need God in order to cope. He is our hope and our strength."

"Father, I'm not sure about that. I would rather stay away from everyone than hear questions about her or see their gazes directed at me."

"I understand perfectly. But If you attain God's grace, you'll be able to manage your pain in a better way. A seed of hope will grow in your heart, warming you with joy."

Miguel shook his head. "I'll think about it."

"Good."

There was a pause, then Father Piero said, "Did you see today's news?"

"Yes, I did."

"Do you think it could be Sheila?"

Miguel put his cigarette in an ashtray and then rubbed his neck.

"Father, honestly I don't know what to think any more."

Father Piero's doorbell rang. He looked at his door.

"I have to go, Miguel. We'll chat later, and please don't neglect God's house or lose your hope. As long as there a little spark of hope, everything is possible."

"I'll try, Father."

The priest put down the phone and rushed to open the door.

There on the doorstep was his childhood friend, Indriani. Her face was ashen, her eyelids swollen, and she was trembling like a leaf.

"Can I come in, Piero?"

Father Piero led her to the living room.

"What happened? You look like you saw a ghost."

She gazed around and then took her seat. Father sat on a chair.

"My daughter has been missing for four days. She's not answering my calls. As I was driving back home today, I heard horrible news. They have found her remains in Grande Forest."

Indriani felt a lump in her throat and a heaviness in her chest.

"Some heartless person killed and then burnt her. She never hurt a fly. Why would anyone want to end her life like an animal?"

Father Piero got up and came over to her. He patted her shoulder.

"You don't have to hurt anyone to gain an enemy. If you're beautiful, successful, or have something that others don't have, people will always be jealous of you. They will wish to have what you have."

Indriani let go of her sorrow and wailed as her whole body shook.

"Why did this happen to my child??"

"Calm down. They couldn't identify the victim. It could be someone else."

Indriani shook her head.

"No, Piero. It's her. I can feel it."

He took a tissue from his table and passed it to her. Her sobs echoed throughout his house.

"The victim could be anyone else. Don't make rash decisions."

Indriani shook her head, and then blew her nose.

"I know it's my Layla. I'm her mother and can feel it. Knowing that my child faced a gruesome death has torn my heart apart. It's as if a part of me died with her."

Father Piero again patted her shoulder.

"Please pardon me for being emotional."

"Sometimes crying is good. It helps to release the pain. However, you shouldn't lose hope. Wait until the police identify the body."

Indriani's cell phone rang. She looked at the screen. Her husband was calling.

"I must go before my husband gets worried. I don't know how to carry this news to him."

She got up, and Father Piero led her to the door.

"Maybe you should keep quiet till you know for sure."

"That would be so tough. Please forgive me for this late-night visit and all this drama."

"No need to apologize. That's what friends are for. To support and be there for each other. If you need to talk to someone, I'm a call away."

"Thank you, Piero. But you already have too much to deal with."

Father Piero opened the door and Indriani rushed outside.

31st January

Miguel sat at the desk in his office, speaking over the phone. His hands shook slightly, and his face was covered with sweat. After seeing the news the night before, he hadn't gotten any sleep at all. He had worried all night, wondering if the corpse belonged to Sheila.

"Where exactly was it found?"

"On the finger of the corpse," said his friend at another police station.

Miguel unbuttoned the first two buttons of his shirt and gasped for air.

"Please look at it and tell me what initials you see inside of it."

"R +S=L."

"The ring belongs to my wife. She was wearing it the night she was kidnapped."

His eyes teared up, and the room spun.

"I'm sorry. I wish I wasn't the bearer of bad news," said his friend.

"Was the autopsy completed?" Miguel strode towards the window and gazed outside, breathing heavily.

I'll deal with Kingpin and his bastards. I'll bring hell upon them.

"Yes. I got a report an hour ago, but it was inconclusive. It was confirmed that the corpse is female. There were no marks left by a knife or gunshot wounds. However, autopsy indicated hyoid fracture and possibility of strangulation. The killer removed all her teeth which makes it difficult to identify her."

Miguel returned to his seat.

They took her away from us and killed her. Kingpin will pay dearly if he was indeed behind this.

He lit a cigarette.

"Miguel, I'm truly sorry for all of this, but please don't do anything that you will regret later. You have to consider how your decision would impact your children and your job."

Miguel let go a circle of smoke.

"I won't, thank you. Where is her body being kept? I must claim it and give her a decent burial."

"It's at Judy M.D. Forensic Pathology Centre."

"Okay. Thanks."

He disconnected the call without saying goodbye. Miguel sank into his chair.

It's all my fault. They followed me all the way to my home. I should have noticed them. How am I going to break this news to the children?

He sighed deeply and picked up the phone.

I need to organize a funeral for her.

He pulled out the yellow pages from his drawer and looked for the pathologist's number. Then he dialed it.

"Judy M.D. Forensic Pathology Centre," he heard.

"Yes, I am Sergeant Miguel Siglobeen from Lystra Police Station. A few days ago, burnt remains were taken to your Centre. I've just learned that it is my wife, Sheila. I would like the body to be released for a proper burial."

"You must come with your and your wife's ID and sign the documentation. Then we can release her body."

"No problem. I'll be there shortly."

Miguel ended the call and dialed the number for the funeral home. He arranged for them to pick up the body and transfer her there. Then he called Father Piero.

"Father Piero, they've found her."

"I'm so happy for you."

Miguel took a deep, shaky breath. "Father, they found her corpse."

The priest was silent for a minute.

"Oh, my God. Where and how?"

"A farmer searching for his dog in the Grande Forest stumbled upon her."

"This is so horrible. May God be with your family. Is there anything I can do for you?"

"I would like to get a date for her funeral service."

"I have something going on almost every day. But I can fit you in on February 2nd. The service will start at 9 a.m. Does that work for you?"

"Yes, Father."

"I'm really sorry for your loss. So devastating."

"Thank you, Father. There's so much to do. I have to register her death and transfer her to the funeral home. Bye for now."

"Okay, bye."

Miguel left the office in a hurry without saying a word to anyone. He drove to the forensic pathology centre.

As soon as he parked his car, a black hearse stopped near him. A man got out of the driver's seat.

Miguel looked at him. "Are you from Angela's Funeral Home?"

"Yes, I am."

"My name is Miguel. I believe you came to pick up the body of a burnt woman."

"Yes, I did. By the way, I'm John Henkison. Are you related to her?"

"I'm her husband."

"Oh, I'm really sorry. I heard that she was burnt badly. You won't be able to display her body for viewers."

"I thought so. Let's go inside," offered Miguel.

They walked to the building and Miguel rang the doorbell. It opened automatically. They went inside and walked to the lobby area. At the desk was a woman of about age 30.

"Hello. I am Miguel Seeglobin. We spoke about an hour ago. And this is John Henkison. He will transfer my spouse's remains to the funeral home."

"Can I see your ID please, as well as hers?" she asked.

He removed his and Sheila's driver's licenses and gave them to her. She filled out an application form with the information provided and then handed the IDs and the documentation to Miguel.

"Please check it, and then sign it."

Miguel read the documents and then signed the forms.

"You'll need to talk to Jude," she told him.

She then directed him to a lab room, where his wife's remains lay on an examination trolley under a white sheet. A pathologist's assistant stood by a man's body on another trolley. He was busy stitching an incision in the man's abdomen.

"Jude? My name is Miguel Siglobeen. I'm here to collect my wife's corpse. She's being transferred to a funeral home."

"Oh, sorry. I'm not Jude. I'm Drake Willum, his assistant."

Miguel stared at the corpse that Drake was working on, and started feeling quite dizzy. Dead bodies always sickened him. Seeing the look on his face, Drake left the needle on top of the body and covered it with a white cloth.

"I hope you have a strong heart. The fire disfigured her body."

"I can take it."

Drake walked towards another examination table and lifted the covering from it.

Miguel's eyes caught the most horrible view of a human body. There was nothing familiar left of his wife's body. Her remains were now blackened, and pieces of clothing were melted into her skin. Her face was totally gone, leaving only scalp.

Miguel gasped for air, and his heart raced. Seeing his reaction, Drake covered her corpse.

"I'm sorry that you had to see this."

"How did she die?"

"There are no traces of gun shots or knife injuries. The findings on her neck area suggests she might have been choked to death and then burned. We found traces of blunt force trauma to her head. There is a small crack going across her scalp. This could be caused by the force of hitting her head on something. We were planning to perform DNA to confirm her identity. However, since you've identified her based on the ring, we have cancelled all of that."

The driver from the funeral home entered the lab room with a stretcher on a wheeled frame.

"I have to pick up another body. Is the corpse ready for my collection?"

"Yes, you can proceed," said Drake.

Unable to take the smell of death any longer, Miguel left the room. He allowed the driver to transport the body into the funeral van, then drove straight home.

Upon arriving home, he found his children in the living room, occupied with a jigsaw puzzle.

"Hey, I'm back," said Miguel.

Nadia got up and ran towards Miguel. She embraced him.

"Daddy, did you get ice cream?"

"Oh, no, your old man forgot it. I'll get it tomorrow."

"You're not an old man. You're still young," said Nadia.

"Oh, thank you. Where's Granny?"

"She's in the kitchen," answered Ronnel.

"Thanks, Ronnel. You go and complete your puzzle," said Miguel.

He walked into the kitchen. Elisa stood next to the stove, turning *bake* over with a spatula. On the counter, Miguel noticed cooked saltfish and avocado cut into thin pieces. On the next plate lay a peppery mango chutney, inviting Miguel to take a piece.

"Hi, Mummy. I need to talk to you."

"You're back early today," she said.

"Please move away from the frying pan and go sit down."

"My cooking is done," she said, and turned off the stove.

She left the spatula on a plate and sat down on a swivel chair. She looked straight into his eyes.

"Did they found her?" she asked.

"Yes, Mummy. She's the one whose corpse was found in the forest. She's so badly disfigured. It's sickening."

"They just killed her, like a pig without any disregard to a human life." Her mouth was set in a grim line.

Elisa noticed tears in her son's eyes.

"Mother, I can't handle it. It hurts so much."

Elisa got up and moved towards her son.

"That is horrible. I'm so sorry. I wish there was a magical wand that could bring her back."

She embraced him. His body trembled as he cried on his mother's shoulder. Tears sparkled in her own eyes.

She put her hands on his cheeks and looked into his eyes.

"Listen, son. Calm down. The children might hear you."

She walked to the counter to get a tissue. As she did so, a fly flew over the food that had been left on the counter. She covered her food with a paper towel and picked up a tissue. Miguel took it from her and dried his eyes.

"What are you going to tell the children?"

"Mummy, I don't know. I still have to digest all of this myself."

"Go and change your clothes, and after dinner we'll deal with it," said Elisa.

Miguel walked to the door, and then turned around and looked at his mother.

"Oh, I forgot to mention. I've spoken with Father Piero. The funeral will be held in his church on the 2nd February at 9 a.m. Please get a picture of Sheila for the service and put a notice in the newspaper about it. Can you please call our relatives? I'll get her death certificate and speak to her mother."

He wiped his eyes again. "Oh, dear Lord, that will not be an easy task."

"Let me call her. Khalisha will be in a state when she finds out. It's so painful to lose one's own child," said Elisa.

Out of nowhere, Ronnel appeared in front of Miguel.

"Daddy, who died?"

His eyes stared intently at Miguel.

"There's something I have to tell you." Miguel gazed at his mom.

"Am I in trouble?"

Granny walked to Ronnel and stroked his cheek.

"No, honey. You're not. Let's go to the living room."

They walked into the living room and sat down on the sofa. Miguel glanced at Nadia. She was trying to fit a piece of the jigsaw puzzle together with the rest. She left it on the floor and walked over to them.

"Daddy, I don't like jigsaw puzzles. They're hard."

"Leave it alone, and come sit on my lap."

She followed his instructions.

"Do you know what happens when people die?" Miguel asked his children.

"They go to heaven to be with the Lord," answered Ronnel.

"When will I go to heaven? I want to see Him," said Nadia.

"I don't know. Only God knows. Today I've found out that Mummy went to heaven."

A frown formed on Ronnel's face.

"Mummy couldn't have gone to heaven. She's alive!" said Ronnel, raising his voice.

Miguel glanced at his mother and took a deep breath.

"She died, and we are going to bury her," Miguel told him sorrowfully.

Ronnel got up. "No! You lie! Mummy can't be dead. She's going to come back soon!"

Ronnel ran out of the room. Elisa rushed after him.

Nadia gazed silently at her father, trying to digest what she had heard. She pulled his hand.

"Daddy, am I going to see my mom?" she asked.

"No, you won't. But she will be in your heart."

Miguel put Nadia's hand to her heart.

"As long as this heart beats, she will be there."

He then touched Nadia's head.

"And the memory of her will always live in your mind."

She moved closer to her father and hugged him.

"I want Mummy to come back home."

Miguel hugged her.

"I know, darling. I want that too, but that isn't possible."

Nadia's eyes became moist. She moved her lips, whispering something.

"Why did Mummy go to heaven? Doesn't she love us anymore?"

"She loves us. God decided to take her there."

She stared into his eyes. "But why?"

"Maybe He wanted her to become an angel in heaven."

"Will he take you as well? I don't want you leave me alone."

Miguel kissed her head.

"I won't, sugar. Go and play now. Daddy has to make some calls."

"I don't feel like playing," said Nadia. She rushed out as well.

Miguel got up from the sofa and went to his bedroom. From there he called some of his relatives and friends to notify them about Sheila's death.

As he went through his contact list over WhatsApp, he stopped on Candice's profile. He noticed that she had changed her profile picture. The current picture showed her in a strapless top, exposing her toned and muscled shoulders and arms. He hesitated for a moment and then texted her.

'Hi Candice. They've found her.'

At the time, Candice was doing pull-ups on a pull-up bar in her door's frame. As she worked out, it was easy to see her biceps and toned-up broad shoulders.

She dropped to the floor and walked towards her phone, where she typed in her password and checked her WhatsApp. She read Miguel's message and typed.

'Is she at home with you now?'

'No, she's at the funeral home.'

Toothless did a great job. Finally, some good luck coming my way. Hallelujah.

A smile crossed her face. She decided to play naive.

'What's she doing there?'

'Why are you asking so many questions? She's dead. Are you happy now?' typed Miguel irritably.

If you knew where she is now, you would wish her to be dead.

'I'm sorry. I didn't figure that out. How did she die?'

'They killed she and then burnt she. I'm organizing funeral for she.'

Candice opened a bottle of water and drank it all. Then she typed again.

'Where will the funeral be held?'

'At Father Piero's church.'

'I'm truly sorry that things ended up this way. If you need anything, I'm here for you.'

'Thank you', typed Miguel, then he put away his phone. He lit a cigarette and smoked, feeling edgy. He gazed at his cell phone.

In the evening Indriani sat on the sofa in front of the TV, watching the news, a cup of coffee in her hand. Her husband had fallen asleep in his armchair not far from her, a newspaper on his lap.

"A Chinese businessman was killed during a morning robbery at a Super Market shop. Two armed bandits stormed his shop, and during the struggle between them he was shot in the abdomen. By the time police arrived, he had succumbed to his wounds.

"Remains found in Grande Forest have been identified. It belongs to Sheila Seeglobin, the last for this year, and the victim of the kidnapping we reported a few days ago. Funeral arrangements are currently being arranged. Up to now no one has been arrested. Investigation is still going on."

Indriani dropped her cup on the floor and it shattered. Indriani's whole body shivered.

"Oh my God. My child is still alive!"

She got up and nudged her husband. "Afzal, wake up. They're going to find our child!"

Afzal opened his eyes.

"What happened, woman? I was in the middle of a funny

dream."

Indriani picked up the cup.

"The remains that were found in Grande Forest don't belong to our daughter. They are of a woman named Sheila."

The wrinkles became deeper on Afzal's forehead and his eyebrows met. He rose, dropping his newspaper.

"Why did you think they were hers in the first place?"

"Man, when you get up from your sleep, yuh act dotish."

"Sorry. My mind is still in sleepy mode."

"Our daughter is somewhere waiting to be rescued. The police must have some information by now."

"Why don't we visit the police station?" said Afzal.

"We'll go tomorrow."

"I'm going to bed now. You come as well. You've been on your feet all day," said Afzal.

"I can't sleep knowing that my child suffers who knows where. Why is life so cruel?" said Indriani.

They walked out of the living room.

"Life isn't cruel, but people are." Afzal caressed her back with his hand. "Try to get some sleep, honey."

They went into the bedroom and changed into pajamas. Indriani lay down on her left side with her husband behind her. He embraced her.

"Darling, get some rest. I'm sure they'll find she soon."

Indriani took hold of his hand and closed her eyes.

Jesus, please bring my only child home. Don't leave my grandchild motherless.

As the day for Sheila's funeral approached, Miguel felt more and more guilty, and blamed himself for his wife's death.

The day before the funeral, he called his childhood friend Aneesh and invited him to the pub.

They spent the day sitting outside the place, drinking beer. The pub was filled with women and men. Some sat at the tables and others stood around outside with drinks in their hands. Music wafted softly from overhead speakers.

"Are you still seeing that chick?" asked Aneesh.

"No, I told she to stay away from meh."

"I know this isn't the place and time to talk about it, but did Sheila know that you horn she with Candice? Where did you find she?"

Miguel put his glass down on the table and glanced over at some other men sitting not far from them.

"Man, your mouth is indeed big. Just hush a little bit nah. I met she on the highway. Her car shut down and seeing she on the road, I stopped to help she. I must say if it wasn't for she curves I might have passed she straight by. Later she invited me for a drink to thank me."

"And you run to meet she like a happy puppy?!"

Miguel signaled a passing waitress. "Hey, can I have some whisky with Sprite please?"

He turned back to Aneesh with a frown on his face. "Please stop it. I don't want to talk about she now. If I had known this was coming, I would have behaved differently and would never have taken late shifts. It's my fault."

The waitress brought a whiskey with Sprite, and as she was leaving Aneesh stared at her big, round bottom.

"Boy, she has a big bumsee[63]! It makes me horny."

"I can't stop blaming myself for her death. I should have been there more for her."

Miguel poured some Sprite into the glass of whisky. He took a few sips.

Aneesh looked over at his friend. "It's too late now to think about it. Life is such a thing that today you're alive and

---

[63] Bottom

tomorrow you might not get up. You should have thought about it when Sheila was alive. However, you were too busy running after another skirt."

A tall dark-skinned woman with curly hair approached them.

"Hey, boys. What's up?" she said.

She hugged both of them and then sat down next to Aneesh.

"Nothing much, Vanessa. We're just talking," said Aneesh.

The waitress walked to another table. Aneesh couldn't take his eyes off her bottom.

Vanessa looked back and forth between her boyfriend and the waitress.

"What the hell is dis? I sit here and you watch she with your hungry eyes as if you want to take she right here!"

She got up and started to leave. Aneesh caught her hand.

"Gyul, behave nah. Yuh always causing bacchanal. I looked at she chain on she neck. I only want you. Come and sit on my lap nah."

Vanessa grinned and sat on his lap, looking quite cozy. Aneesh ordered tequila for her.

The music changed to something livelier. Vanessa got up and pulled Aneesh's hand.

"Let's go dance."

They went a short distance from the table and moved to the music. She leaned forward and pressed her bottom against his private parts, moving in a such a way as to get him aroused. He grabbed onto her waist and closed his eyes.

Miguel sat gazing silently at them.

Then she faced Aneesh and put her arms around his neck. They kissed while some men leered at them.

"Waitress, bring my bill please," said Miguel. When it came, he gave some money to the waitress and got up.

"I'm leaving. You stay and have fun," he said to Aneesh.

"Okay, see you at the funeral then," said Aneesh.

Miguel walked away.

It was four in the morning. Miguel tossed from side to side, in the midst of a nightmare. He saw himself running in a huge and murky forest. As he ran, his wife's sobs echoed in the air, getting more and more distant.

"Miguel, please help me!" she cried out.

Miguel peered through the trees, hoping to see her, but the fog affected his ability to see.

"Miguel, why aren't you coming for me?"

Miguel turned around. "Sheila, where are you? I'm coming!"

The fog began to ease up. He found himself surrounded by tall, huge trees that resembled monsters in the darkness.

As the fog lifted, he saw a woman walking slowly towards him. Her long hair fell over her face and her red dress was torn. Drops of blood fell from her, creating a puddle of blood around her.

She stopped and pushed her hair from her face, then she raised her head and stared into his eyes. Her arms stretched towards him. He noticed that she was being held back by hands holding her tightly.

"Miguel, please help me!"

When Miguel stared into her face, he recognized his wife. The bloody puddle grew bigger until it reached him.

The hands pulled her away.

"No! No! Let me go!"

The puddle of blood surrounded him, and then it rose up to his waist. Miguel began drowning in Sheila's blood. He struggled to raise himself above it, but he sank

He awoke, sweating profusely. As he got out of bed, he could hear rain falling. He walked over to his window and gazed outside, where he could see water running down the road. He lit a cigarette and sat down on his bed. Guilt crawled like a spider, spreading webs into his heart.

He got her killed because of me. I must find a way to prove it. Kingpin must go to jail.

By 7 a.m., everyone in Elisa's house was up, preparing to attend Sheila's funeral service. Miguel put on a black suit, and his son got dressed in black pants with a white shirt. Nadia wore a grey dress with black shoes.

As Elisa combed her hair, Nadia entered her bedroom.

"Granny, Granny! Comb my hair please," she said, holding a white bow in her hand.

"Come closer then," said Granny.

She gently passed a brush over Nadia's hair.

"Granny, you're combing my hair softly, like Mummy did."

Elisa put her hair in a ponytail and gave her a smile.

"You go and sit on the sofa. I'll be there shortly."

Nadia hugged her and left the room.

At 8.30 a.m., they all left the house.

Miguel stopped the car right in front of the church's entrance. He opened the passenger's side and, holding an umbrella, hand walked his family one by one to the entrance. Leaving the umbrella by the door, he ran back to his car and drove it into the parking lot.

As Elisa entered the church with her grandchildren, she bumped into Father Piero, who stood not far from the door greeting the guests.

"Good morning, Father Piero," Elisa said.

"It is so nice to see you," Father Piero responded.

Nadia shyly hid behind her granny.

"How are you doing, Elisa?" Father asked.

"With Sheila gone, I'm taking it one day at a time. It helps to be looking after them."

The priest glanced at Miguel's children.

"I hope they don't give you trouble," he said jokingly.

"Not at all," said Elisa.

Father Piero glanced outside. A few guests rushed inside, soaking wet.

"Quite a rainy day we got today," he said.

"Yes, it is."

Elisa looked around and saw her son Kevin with his family.

"Where's Miguel?" Father asked.

"He went to park the car."

The hearse arrived, stopping not far from the church's entry.

"I'll talk to you later, Father," said Elisa.

She gestured to the children. "Let's go."

Elisa and her grandchildren walked towards her son Kevin. He was standing in the aisle with his wife and daughter. He was chatting with someone.

"Thanks be to God we made it on time," said Elisa.

Kevin's family turned around.

"We came not too long as well," answered Kevin.

"Hi, Granny," said Shantel. She hugged her granny.

"You did well in SEA. Congratulations."

Shantel smiled, showing the braces on her teeth. "Thank you, Granny."

"Hey, you got braces as well?!"

"Yep, and every month I'll have different colors."

Elisa gazed at Ria.

"Ria, you look so slim—as if you were never pregnant. I need to shed a few pounds as well. What's your secret?"

"Maybe it's genetics. Or maybe it's because looking after children is one big exercise."

Elisa glanced at Miguel's children. "I know what you mean."

Kevin tousled Ronnel's hair. "Both of you look so grown up." He addressed his mother. "By the way, where's Miguel?"

"He's parking the car," answered Elisa.

Ria glanced at the guests. "Can I borrow your grandchildren, please? We need to start giving out the program brochures."

"Sure."

Nadia gazed at Ria with a frown on her face. Ria gave Nadia, Shantel, and Ronnel brochures.

"Please walk through every row and distribute one to each person," she said.

Nadia took her brother's hand, ready to leave.

"Nadia, you come with me," said Ria.

Nadia let go of her brother's hand. He and Shantel walked away.

"Aunty, let's go," said Nadia, pulling Ria's hand. They walked towards the people coming in and handed out the programs.

Miguel walked up the stairs, soaking wet. As he came through the door, he bumped into Father Piero.

"Sorry, Father Piero, I was running away from the rain." said Miguel.

"Not a good day for rain at all. I remember it rained when your wife, er, disappeared," said the priest.

"I am unable to forget it myself," said Miguel. His lip twitched.

"Please accept my condolences. May God be with you at this heartbreaking moment."

"Thank you, Father," said Miguel, staring inside the church.

"Your jacket is soaking wet. You should take it off."

Miguel nodded. "Perhaps you're right." He took off his jacket.

Kevin walked up to them and hugged his brother.

"Man, I am so sorry for your loss," he said.

They were interrupted by the driver from the funeral home, who had run inside.

"I need help taking the casket out of the van," he said.

A friend of Kevin's was standing by the entrance. Kevin asked him for help, and the four men went outside.

The driver pulled out the casket. Two on each side, the men took hold of the handles on the casket and lifted it.

A taxi stopped not far from them. A woman got out, wearing a black dress that stopped five inches above her knees, and black high-heeled shoes. She held a rose in her hand.

"Thank you," she said to the taxi driver.

Hearing her voice, Miguel raised his head and glared at her.

What the hell is she doing here?

She looked at him with a grin on her face. "Hi Miguel," she said.

The other men greeted her, tongue-tied.

She slowly climbed the steps and entered the church as the men stared at her bottom and legs.

"Who was dat? She couldn't find a better dress?"

"First time I see she."

Miguel watched as she left and noticed changes in her figure. Her body had become more toned and her bottom seemed to be firmer and larger.

She doesn't look like a pregnant woman.

Slowly the men headed into the church. Everyone's eyes were on them as they carried the casket to the altar.

Miguel, however, didn't even notice. His mind was on other things.

Why did she come here?

The casket was set down on a wheeled stand by the altar. The priest walked towards it but stopped by the microphone.

"Please take your seats, and we will start celebrating Sheila's life."

Everyone sat down in the pews. Miguel, with his children and mother, took the first row on the right side. His brother and his family sat behind him. Sheila's relatives, including her mother, sat down in the first row on the left side.

Indriani and her husband took their seats a few rows behind Sheila's family.

Indriani stared at the coffin, feeling heaviness in her chest. For some unknown reason, she was unable to take her eyes away from it. A few drops of sweat formed on her temple and rolled down her cheek. Her brain felt as if something was squeezing it.

Feeling hot, she fanned herself with the brochure. She then clutched her husband's hand. He glanced at her, feeling her tension.

"Are you okay?"

"I don't know. I'm feeling weird."

"If you want, we can leave."

"No, it'll look bad."

Her attention fixed again on the coffin. Her heartbeat increased alarmingly.

Why am I feeling this way? It's as if my own child lies in the coffin. Oh, Lord I do feel their pain. Please strengthen this family in this hard time. And thank you for my child's life. It could have been her lying in this coffin.

Her eyes became moist, and sadness overwhelmed her heart. She looked at Jesus over the altar.

Jesus, please bring my child home. Without her our lives are empty.

A few rows up, Candice approached Khalisha.

"I am so sorry for your loss," she said, trying to look sad. It was hard to hide the spark in her eyes.

Sheila's mother lifted her head and looked at Candice.

"I'm one of Sheila's friends. She was a good soul."

"May I ask your name, please?"

A man stopped next to Candice, waiting for her to move.

"I am Candice."

She stared at the man. "Sorry," she said, and moved out

of his way.

Miguel turned around and stared at Candice. His eyebrows furrowed.

Did she come here to intentionally cause trouble? Or does she really care?

He turned back around, blowing out a frustrated breath. *I never could understand women.*

Candice sat down behind Sheila's mother, and then gazed intently at Miguel.

Their eyes met. She smiled, then her attention fell on the coffin.

You're kept in a brothel, suffering like an animal, but everyone thinks that they're burying you. Ha! What a life!

Two women sitting in the back whispered to each other as they stared at Candice's back.

"I saw Miguel entering a hotel with this jagabat64. He's been sleeping with this slut," said one of them, Sarah, whose nose was always in everyone's business.

"You could be mistaking her for someone else," said her friend Jahni.

"Gyul, my eyes are not blind. I know what I see."

"She's bold-faced. How could she show up at poor Sheila's funeral?" said Jahni.

Their conversation was interrupted by the priest as he began his speech.

"Our beloved Sheila was a mother, wife, and daughter, as well as a good friend to many. She lived her life peacefully, hoping to see her children going to university and getting married, but unfortunately her dreams were cut short by a death brought on by a heartless killer.

"She isn't the first or last victim. This country has buried many sons and daughters. And today the Caribbean pours its

---

64 Prostitute

tears for every life taken away.

"Let Sheila's death be a wake-up call for all of us. Something must be done to change the crime situation on this island. Changes should start from us, and in our houses, first.

"Look into your lives and behavior. See what must be altered. Are you negligent as a parent or partner? Have you been abusive, or have you indulged in alcohol or an unhealthy lifestyle? Are you a bad influence on your family? What example do you set for your children?

"In many cases, crime is committed by those who have been neglected as a child, grew up without a father figure, were victims of abuse, or have witnessed a parent being abused.

"Ladies, make sure that your children are safe. Don't rush to bring a man into your life and under the same roof with your children. Know him well first.

"The next problem in our society is the fact that some men appease their sorrow and pain with a bottle of rum instead of finding a solution. They leave their wives and children alone at night while having fun in cheap rum shops. Rely on God instead, and find a solution to your problems. Is being around friends and consuming alcohol better than having quality time with family? Be there for your wives and children. If you can't, you'll be replaced by someone else. Alcohol will never solve your problem.

"Women, spend time with your children instead of planning your[65] liming, your carnival time, or spending so much time on social sites. Families, spend quality time together.

"Do you try to solve arguments in a civilized manner? Parents, do you monitor your child's online activities? So much lives are ruined because of dysfunctional relationships.

"I must say, death is not far. It is right behind you. Death is a painful experience for everyone. It can't be cheated, and it's

---

[65] Partying

a separation where you're no longer able to see or hear the ones that you love. It finds us unexpectedly, and it brings pain and sorrow. But what can we do? We must continue to carry on with our lives, hoping that one day we will meet our loved ones again. We should also keep praying for departed souls and give charity in their names.

"After death our bodies will rot and be eaten by worms, but the soul never dies. It will either enter the eternal fire of Hell or Paradise. The destination of our souls will be determined by the way we lived our lives. The soul of a man who built a good relationship with God, led a righteous life, and showed kindness to others will dwell in Paradise. However, a sinful life and unrepentance pushes one to Hell.

"Death is a rebirth, where the soul can finally go back home to the Lord. As you know, at the beginning of the existence of humanity there was no death, but only endless life. Unfortunately, due to Satan's work, humans invited sin into this world. And the cycle of life has changed. Humans were introduced to illnesses, suffering, pain, and death.

"By our own fault we allowed Satan to bring destruction to this world. That's why we're now saying goodbye to Sheila."

As the priest talked, Miguel kept wiping his face with a handkerchief. He cast his eyes on the casket, his heart feeling empty. He felt as if the whole world had collapsed over him.

If I had stopped them, she would be alive. But what can one man do against two?

Nadia was holding onto his hand tightly. He glanced at her.

Poor children. At this young age, they have to grow up motherless. How will I manage on my own? Maybe Candace will help me.

Nadia stared at the casket. She knew her mother lay in there but couldn't understand how she had gotten there.

Ronnel cried silently on the other side of his father. He couldn't take his gaze away from the casket. Understandably, he wanted to see his mother one more time.

Out of the blue, a loud wailing echoed throughout the church, making people turn their heads towards the sound. Miguel did the same, and realized that it was Sheila's mother, Khalisha.

Her crying became louder. Dark mascara spread on her face.

"My only child has gone! My joy of life was taken away from me. Why did they kill her?"

Tears rolled from her chin, landing on her dress. When Ronnel heard her sobs, the walls that had kept him strong collapsed. His cries became as ferocious and loud as hers.

"Daddy, Mummy died! I won't see her anymore!" he said through sobs.

Hearing their cries, the congregation poured forth a silent sympathy for the bereaved family.

Nadia also began crying.

"Why is Mummy in that box? Who put her there?"

The priest stopped talking and looked over at them in sadness.

Ria rushed towards Nadia and picked her up. "Don't cry, sweetie. Everything is going to be fine."

Nadia lifted her head and gazed at Ria. Her eyes were filled with tears.

"Aunty, Mummy went to Heaven."

Ria walked outside, carrying Nadia with her. The church quieted down a little.

"I understand that today is a difficult time for all of you, but you must be strong and keep going on," said Father Piero.

Sheila's mother got up and rushed towards the casket. She embraced it, resting her head on it.

"Why did they take my child away from me? She never did anything to anyone."

Her son Dan rushed to her side.

"Mummy, please calm down."

He gently removed her from the casket. "Let's go, mummy."

"I didn't give her life only to have someone cruelly end it."

"Come, Mummy."

"Please leave me alone. She was my angel and the joy of my eye. What am I going to do without her?"

Dan embraced his mother. "Mummy, let's go back to our seats. It's hard for all of us."

She finally let go, and they walked to their seats.

"I can't even see her. They hid she in the casket."

Father Piero's eyes followed them. He took a deep breath and spoke.

"It is a sad day for all of us. Today many of you pour out tears of pain and sorrow. And your hearts are filled with anger. No matter how painful it is, you must find forgiveness and peace in your minds and hearts. You should continue living and keep moving forward. One day, when the time comes, you'll meet your loved ones.

"I do hope that this negativity will serve as a catalyst for change, where you not only look after yourself but after your neighbor as well. So many times, people have witnessed someone being abused, but they have never bothered to interfere or report it to the police. Consequently, abuse has continued and, in some cases, resulted in death. So please do not let Sheila's death go in vain. Change and change."

After talking for a while, Father Piero invited other people to say a couple of words about Sheila.

Her friend Anisa walked to the microphone. She was a tall, dark-skinned woman.

"Sheila was my childhood friend. We went to the same high school and university. She was a very caring and ambitious young woman."

Tears formed in Anisa's eyes. Her voice became shaky.

"She was always there for me and for others. I've always admired her personality--especially her stubbornness, fearlessness, and the strength of her spirit. She's gone, but she will always be in my memory and everyone else's too. Thank you."

She walked back to her bench, wiping her tears.

Then the priest said a few prayers and blessed the guests. The funeral service ended.

People got up. Some began talking to each other while others left.

Ria came back with Nadia. Kevin, with Shantel and Elisa, stood not far from Miguel.

Elisa came up to her son, and they hugged for a brief moment.

"I'm here for you, son," she whispered.

"Thank you, Mummy," he said.

As soon as Nadia saw her father, she took his hand.

"Daddy, the rain stopped. I saw puddles outside."

He stroked her head. "They'll dry as soon as it becomes hotter."

Ronnel slowly walked to his mother's casket. He put his hand on it.

"Mummy, I wish you weren't dead. I miss you really a lot."

Miguel gazed at his son and made a step to go to him. Kevin took hold of his hand.

"Leave him. He needs to say good-bye to her."

"Daddy said that you're in a better place now. But how am I going to live without you? I need you. Why did criminals take you away from us?"

Ronnel's eyes became teary again. He gazed at his father and then at the casket.

"Ronnel, come son," said Miguel.

"It's unfair, Mummy. I won't be hearing your voice or seeing your face anymore."

Elisa went over to him. "Let's go, child."

"Bye, Mummy. I have to go now," he whispered.

He hugged his granny and they walked away.

When Miguel turned around, he almost collided with Candice, who had approached them unnoticed.

"Please accept my condolences," she said.

She embraced him and then let him go.

Miguel glanced at his family and then at her. "Thank you."

She made a few steps towards the casket with a rose in her hand. Miguel followed her.

Candice set the rose on the casket.

Miguel whispered, "What are you doing here?"

"I came to show my support, and I missed you a lot."

"You shouldn't be here at all. What if they suspect something?"

Miguel turned and gazed at his family. Then he wiped his forehead with a handkerchief.

Ronnel stared at Candice's back. He tried to recall where he had heard her voice. And her perfume smelled familiar to him.

"Granny, who is that lady?" he asked.

She shrugged her shoulders. "She must be one of your mother's friends."

"Oh. Okay."

"Please leave now. I'll call you later," Miguel said.

"See you later then," she whispered.

She turned around and glanced at his family. Then she walked away and left the church, unable to hide her joy. With a triumphant smile on her face, she stood outside waiting for a taxi. A few men stared at her figure, but she paid them no mind.

My plan worked well. I can step in and marry him.

A private taxi stopped.

"Hi beautiful. Do you need a ride?" asked the driver, a leer on his face.

Candice stared at his car and then at him.

"No, thank you," she lied.

A couple of months ago a woman had been raped by a taxi driver, and this made Candice cautious. She refused to get driven by unknown drivers.

Another cab stopped.

"Hi, Candice. Are you waiting for a ride?"

She smiled, "Yes I am."

"Hop in then," he said.

Candice sat in the back next to two women passengers, and the taxi drove away.

After his lover had gone, Miguel rested his hand on the casket.

I never imagined that we would be separated this way. I loved you. You were the mother of my children. I'm so sorry that I couldn't protect you or do anything to stop your kidnapping. I promise that I'll find whoever did this to you and make sure he spends the rest of his life in jail, along with Kingpin.

The hearse driver came up to Miguel.

"Sir, it's time to take her to the cemetery. Can you please help me carry the casket back to the van?"

Miguel looked over at his assembled family. "Ria, please take the children with you. I'll see you later. Mummy, are you coming with me?"

"Yes, I am."

"Daddy, can I come with you too?" asked Ronnel.

"No, son."

Miguel, Kevin, and the driver walked to the casket. Father Piero joined them, and together they took hold of the handles and carried the coffin to the van.

From there Miguel, Kevin, Elisa, and Sheila's relatives, as well as Father Piero, headed to the cemetery.

7th February.

Sheila woke up in the early morning hours to the sound of loud voices and sobs. Curious, she got out of bed and moved to the door.

"Please take me back home!" shouted a girl's voice.

Sheila opened the door and tiptoed upstairs. She crept up to the guest room's door and opened it a little.

A child of about thirteen years of age was struggling with Victor, trying to pull her hand away from his fist.

Sheila gasped as she saw the girl bite his hand.

"You stupid dog!" he shouted as he pushed her away from him. She fell, and stayed on the floor, trembling.

"I'll chain you and keep you like a dog."

"No! I don't want to be here," she mumbled.

Bernadette, who was also in the room, marched up to the girl and raised her hand, ready to strike.

"If you don't shut up, I'll beat you like an animal."

The girl became quiet and silently regarded the woman. Her eyes were red and wet.

"Fat meanie," she whispered.

"What did you say?" demanded Bernadette.

The poor child moved backwards.

"Listen carefully. You're going to stay here for some time. If you listen to us and do what you are told, we'll allow you go home. Do you understand?"

"Yes, I do," answered the girl.

Rage filled Sheila as she watched them. She wanted to rush in and choke Victor; she squeezed her hand into a fist as she worked to stop herself.

I'm not going to let them ruin this child's life!

"Take her to Camille," Bernadette instructed her henchman. "She'll look after her."

Victor grabbed the girl's hand. "Let's go, doggy," he said.

She refused to move. He pulled her ear to make her get up.

"Ouch! That hurts!"

He let go of her ear and took hold of her hand.

"Come with me!"

She began pushing him away.

"No, please!" She turned a pleading look toward Bernadette. "I don't want to go with him!"

He pushed her away, making her fall again.

Sheila opened the door and rushed towards the two of them. She stood in front of the girl.

"Victor, please don't hurt the child. Allow me to take care of her."

Victor stared into Sheila's eyes.

"Okay. Make sure she knows what she's expected to do," he said.

The poor girl's lips trembled, and sweat ran down her face. She stood up and hid behind Sheila, afraid to move.

Sheila turned towards her.

"Let's go, child," she said gently, taking her hand.

They hurried to Sheila's bedroom. On the way, Sheila saw Daniela standing by the door.

"What's going on?" she whispered.

"Go back to your room. We'll talk tomorrow," said Sheila.

As soon as Sheila entered the bedroom, she led the girl to the bed.

"Sit here and don't move."

Sheila left the bedroom to get a glass of water. On her return, she found the little one sitting on the bunk bed, staring at the door.

"Please drink some water."

The girl took the glass from Sheila and drank it slowly.

Suddenly there were footsteps in the corridor. The little guest, upon hearing the steps, clutched Sheila's hand and burst into tears. Sheila embraced her, and the girl buried her face into Sheila's chest, crying.

"They're coming for me!"

"Sh! No one is there."

"Please take me home."

"They lock the doors. I myself can't leave this place."

Sheila wiped the girl's tears.

They're going to take her innocence and childhood, and destroy her soul. I can't even prevent it.

"My name is Sheila. What's your name?"

The girl calmed down a little bit.

"I am Violeta."

"How old are you?"

"I'm thirteen." Violeta looked at the door.

"How did you get here?" asked Sheila.

"That monster came and spoke to my mom, and then took me with him."

Violeta told Sheila how Victor had come with Bernadette to her house very late at night. She had been in a deep sleep, dreaming about a sinking boat. The loud voices coming out of the living room had woken her up. She had gotten out of bed and, burning with curiosity, had tiptoed to the living room and had stood by the doorway.

She had seen her mother on her knees. Bernadette had been standing before her, looking down at her.

The mother had grabbed Bernadette's hand.

"I beg you, have heart! Please give me four more months."

Bernadette had pulled out her hand.

"No. I waited long enough. Either pay back the money or vacate this house."

Violeta's mother had stood up slowly and walked to Victor.

"I have children, and I've lost my husband. Where will I go with them? Only four months, please."

Victor had pushed her away and she had fallen.

Violeta had run towards her. "Leave my mummy alone!" She hugged her sobbing mother.

"Mummy, why are these strangers in our house?"

Her brother, upon hearing the voices, had hidden under the bed. As far as Violeta knew, he was still safe.

Bernadette had come up to Violeta and her mother and had pulled the girl away. She turned her around, and had scrutinized her, nodding approvingly at the girl's fair complexion and long hair.

"I'll take her instead of money," she had declared.

Violeta's mother had shaken her head and pulled her daughter to herself.

"Not my child!"

"Then give me my money. I'll call the police and accuse you of stealing. My patience is ticking away."

Violeta's mother had heaved a huge sob and pushed her daughter towards them.

"Take her and don't come here anymore," she had said through her tears.

Violeta had run towards her mother and grabbed onto her, but she pushed her away.

"You have to go. I have no choice."

"Mummy, please don't give me away!"

Victor had dragged her away, then had lifted her from the floor. She had begun kicking and screaming. Victor had pulled a gun from his pocket and pointed it at her forehead.

"Stop it or I'll shoot you."

Instantly, Violeta became quieter. She had twisted around and stared at her mother, teary-eyed.

She hadn't even raised her eyes.

"I hate you, Mother," Violeta had whispered.

Victor and Bernadette had then taken Violeta away from her home and family.

Back from her memories, Violeta raised her head and stared into Sheila's eyes. Her own eyes narrowed.

"My mother didn't do anything to stop them. She's a betrayer, and I hate her!"

Sheila stood up and pulled back the blanket on the top bed.

"Don't speak that way about your mother." Sheila couldn't help but feel the same rage Violeta was feeling, but she had to help keep some goodness in the child. "It's time for you to sleep. Climb up and go to sleep, and we'll talk tomorrow."

Violeta got up and climbed onto the top bunk. She lay down and covered herself with the blanket.

"Aunty Sheila, why are you here?"

"No more talking, please," said Sheila. She turned off the light.

Violeta leaned over the side of the bed and looked at Sheila.

"Aunty, where are we?"

Sheila looked into the child's eyes and smiled.

"Child, sleep nah."

Violeta lay back down on the pillow and turned onto her right side.

Sheila lay in bed, feeling very anxious. She tried to keep her eyes wide open, even though sleep was taking over. All of her attention was on the door.

She knew that, once Bernadette was in a deep sleep, he would come.

Eventually she was unable to fight off the sleepiness any longer. She had just begun to doze off when her ear caught the squeaking sound of the door and then cautious steps.

Sheila opened her eyes and sat up to see Victor carefully walking towards her.

"It's time for you to give me what's due," he said, taking off his vest.

Sheila got up and looked over at Violeta. She slept soundly.

Victor came up closer and put his hand on Sheila's hair. She pushed him away.

"Don't you see there's a child here?"

"So what? She's sleeping."

He caressed her cheek. She pushed him away again.

"Leave me alone, you freak!"

Victor grabbed her hair and pulled hard.

"Listen, bitch. I have to put up with your bullshit every night. Why can't you just obey me?"

Violeta turned on her left side, talking in her sleep. "Mummy! Mummy! Come back for me!"

Victor glanced at Violeta.

"I can get whatever I need from her. She's young and juicier."

He took hold of Violeta's blanket, ready to pull it off. Sheila grabbed hold of his hand and pulled him away from the bed.

"Don't touch her," she whispered. "I'll do whatever you want."

"Go into the bathroom," he ordered.

Dragging her feet slowly, Sheila went into the bathroom. Victor followed her. He closed the door and pushed Sheila into the shower stall.

Sheila shook violently, feeling disgusted. Her head felt dizzy.

"What the hell are you doing just standing there? Take off your clothes!"

"No! If you touch me again, I'm going to tell Bernadette that you're raping the girls at night."

Victor removed his belt from his pants.

"I said, take off your clothes. Face the wall!" he ordered.

She merely stood there and glared at him.

He swung his fist at her. Sheila put her arms up to defend herself. Tears of frustration and anger cascaded down her cheeks.

Sheila grabbed the belt and tried to take it away from him. "Why do you torment me?"

Violeta was awakened by the sounds coming out of the bathroom. Shaking, she put her blanket over her head and cried silently.

Victor pulled the belt away from Sheila and kicked her in the belly. The kick pushed her back against the wall. He lashed her with the belt. Then he put his hands around Sheila's neck and squeezed.

"Please stop it!" she begged, staring into his eyes.

He let go of her neck. She began coughing, holding onto the wall for support.

"You're a fighter. I kind of admire your inner strength," Victor told her.

Then he leered at her. "This only arouses me," he said, pulling down his pants.

Everything began spinning before her eyes. A weakness came over her. Then her vision became foggy.

Sheila passed out and slipped to the floor.

Victor pulled up his pants and checked the pulse on her neck. He then put his belt back on his pants and left the bathroom. Wasting no time, he ran out of her bedroom.

Once Victor left, Violeta got down out of the bed. She watched the door for a moment, shaking with fear. Then she tiptoed to the bathroom.

Seeing Sheila motionless on the floor, she hurried towards her. She stooped down and touched her shoulder.

"Please get up. Don't leave me here alone," she said, tears running down her face. She picked up a small hand towel and wet it. Then she wiped Sheila's face.

"Please wake up. Please! I need you."

Sheila groaned and moved. She opened her eyes and gazed at Violeta.

"Where is he?"

"He left."

Feeling weak and still trembling, she got up. Pain ran through her body.

"Ouch!"

She stumbled back to her bed, holding onto Violeta's hand.

"What did he do to you, Aunty?"

"He beat me with his belt. Stay away from him. He's an evil man."

Violeta helped her to lie down.

"Can I please lie down next to you? He might come back," she said.

"Sure."

Violeta lay down next to Sheila.

"Aunty Sheila, what place is this?"

"This is a very horrible place."

Sheila felt heaviness in her heart. She wanted to scream out so loudly that the whole world would hear her. But this helpless and innocent child in her arms caused her to refrain from showing her weakness and pain. She just lay staring at the celling.

"Aunty Sheila, are we going to get out of here?"

"Child, leave talking for tomorrow. Please try to sleep."

Violeta raised her head.

"But Aunty...."

Sheila put a finger on Violeta's mouth and said, "Tish. I'll answer your questions tomorrow."

Sheila turned on her right side.

How am I going to protect this child? I can't even protect myself. I need to find a way for us to get out.

Her tears ran down onto the pillow.

"Life can be so cruel." She sighed deeply.

HIDEN TRACES

After the funeral, most people returned to their usual activities.

All except Anil.

He had a heavy burden on his shoulders. His stepdaughter's belly was getting bigger, and eventually everyone was going to find out that she was pregnant.

He himself had found out one evening not too long ago. He had come home and found Gail sitting on the sofa in her shorts. She had been on the phone, and hadn't seen him.

"I don't know what to do with this pregnancy. If my mom finds out, I'm in big trouble," Anil heard her say.

"What did you say?" he asked loudly.

Her head had shot up, and she had stared at him wide eyes. Her hands trembled.

"Nothing," she had said.

"I heard everything. How could you do this to us?"

She hadn't dared to look him in the eyes.

"They're going to mock you in school. What will your mother say when she finds out?"

"Please don't tell she anything. She gonna kill me."

Anil came up closer and took hold of her hand.

"Who is the father?"

She burst into tears.

"I don't know. I don't recall sleeping with anyone. I'm sorry."

"Okay, calm down. I'll help you."

He hugged her. Her breast, against his chest, gave him an electrical shock.

He caressed her back. She frowned as she felt his touch.

"I'll take you for an abortion, and no one will know about it."

She moved away from him. "Will that hurt?"

"Not at all. But we must keep it a secret. You can't tell anyone or you'll be in trouble. You know how your madder is."

She embraced him, and their cheeks touched. Anil was barely able to keep himself from kissing her on her lips.

He pushed her away gently.

"Oh, thank you!" Gail smiled up at him.

"Okay, sure. No more hugging for today."

Later in the day he called a friend, who was a gynecologist, and told him about his stepdaughter's pregnancy. However, he had to formulate a lie to make him agree to abort the child.

On Saturday Anil, his wife, and Gail sat at the table having breakfast. They were having *sada*, which is roti filled with aloo[66], and ocro.[67]

Anil started coughing.

"Gyul, you put too much pepper in the potato. Your food either doesn't have enough salt and pepper, or too much of it."

"Boy, you never happy with anything. Why yuh doh cook for yuhself, if my food nuh good enough for you?"

"Meh to cook? Are you crazy! This is a woman's job.'

"Appointed by who?"

Gail watched them quietly, and then said, "Mummy, I'm going over to Lisa's today. I'll be there all day."

Her mother gazed at her suspiciously.

---

[66] Potato
[67] A flowering plant in the mallow family.

"To do what?"

"We have to work on a school project."

Gail looked over at Anil. "Can you drive me over there, please?"

Anil smiled upon seeing how well Gail played her role as he had instructed.

He looked at his watch.

"If you want me to drop you off, you had better hurry up. I have other things to do."

He got up, picked up his plate and glass, and headed to the kitchen. Gail followed him, carrying her plate.

"Gyul, you played off your mother well. I've always admired you."

Gail's eyebrows came together. She could sense that something more was behind his words, but she couldn't figure out what it was.

She had noticed that whenever she wore something a little bit revealing, his eyes were always on her.

"Let's go, Gail," he said.

They walked back to the living room. His wife was clearing the table.

Anil came up by her. "Babe, I'm going," he said, and they kissed.

Gail stared at them. *Why should they kiss in front of me?*

As they kissed, Anil's eyes slid to Gail.

Why is he always watching me?

"Mummy, I'm going to go get in the car," said Gail, and she left. Anil rushed out as well.

When he got into the car, Gail was already sitting in front. He started the engine and drove off.

Gail leaned her head on the seat's backrest, overwhelmed by her thoughts.

Why did I get pregnant? And how? I don't recall having sex with anyone. Now I have to get rid of it. And the pastor condemns abortion. What should I do?

She sat up straight and opened her eyes.

"Anil, I'm not sure if I should go ahead with the abortion. After all, it's the killing of a child."

Anil glanced at her with a serious face.

"What are you talking about? If you don't abort this child soon, how will you go to school with a big belly? You might get expelled."

"I don't feel good about this whole situation, and the lies. I should tell Mother."

Anil started sweating.

"Are you insane? How could you think that? If you tell your mummy, she might send you to your aunty in the country."

She sighed in resignation. "Why did this happen to me?"

Anil gently held her hand.

"I'm here for you and will support you."

He began caressing her hand. She stared at him suspiciously. Feeling uncomfortable, she removed her hand from his. Silently they headed toward their appointment.

8th February

Loud music played in Kingpin's big mansion. It was the afternoon of his birthday, and he was throwing a party.

Tables and chairs had been set up under umbrellas beside the pool, and bikini-clad women played in the water with a few men.

Some chatted and laughed while others stood in the pool with glasses of liquor-- rum, whiskey, vodka, or tequila.

Kingpin, Cyclops, Toothless, Wendel, Terrel, and Austin sat next to each other in the guest room, which was spacious enough to hold a pool table, bar, a sofa with matching armchairs, and a coffee table. A painting of a naked woman leaning against a tiger decorated one of the walls.

Kingpin held a cigarette in one hand and a glass of scotch in the other. He wore a thick gold chain around his neck, from which dangled a pendant carved in the shape of an "M". It was encrusted with diamonds, which matched the ones in the earrings he wore.

Cyclops stayed close by, a bottle of beer in his hand. Occasionally he stole a jealous look at Kingpin's jewelry.

He always likes to show off with his damned gold and diamonds.

Toothless laughed at something Kingpin said. Then his attention switched to his surroundings.

Kingpin's living room shouted money. A huge crystal chandelier hung from the ceiling. Its brushed-nickel finish frame and canopy had little diamond-like stones in it. Clear crystal strands and ball accents shone like diamonds. The corners of the ceiling held moldings of angels.

Then Toothless' eyes paused on the ladies in the pool, which he could see from the huge window. However, because the glass on the windows only offered one-way vision, the guests outside couldn't get a glimpse of the inside.

Although he admired beautiful things, Toothless didn't care about riches. All he wanted was sex and women, and for that he needed money. If he was as wealthy as Kingpin, he reasoned, he would organize huge pool parties, surrounding himself with pretty women.

"The shipment has arrived, and tomorrow it'll be cleared, God willing," said Kingpin.

He turned to his henchman. "Cyclops, I want you in the port tomorrow. If we're busted, you must take all the blame for it."

Cyclops looked at his boss with a grimace.

"What if they lock me up for a long time?"

Kingpin got up and walked to his bar. He poured more drink into his glass and added some ice.

"If that happens, your mother will get a house."

"We're talking about my freedom. Last time it caused me an eye. Only a house? My freedom costs more than that!"

Kingpin scowled. He pulled a gun from his pocket as he moved towards Cyclops. Before he could move, Kingpin threw his arm around his neck from behind and put the pistol to his head.

"Listen to me! When you became a member of my group, you swore that you would obey my orders. What the hell are you complaining about?"

Cyclops's eyes went wide, and he wet his pants. Toothless laughed when he saw the urine dripping on the floor.

"I got it, Boss. I'll do as you wish."

Kingpin let go of his neck and removed the gun from his temple.

"Get the hell out of here. Go and change," said Kingpin with a sneer.

Two women stood outside at the window. They cupped their hands around their eyes, trying to see inside.

Toothless and Terrel couldn't stop laughing.

"Why are you laughing, idiots?" Cyclops demanded angrily.

Toothless' face became serious. "Get rid of those pants. Your piss makes me ill."

Cyclops left, walking gingerly, a wet spot over his crotch.

Only two years before, Cyclops had gotten out of jail barely alive.

He would never forget the morning when he was left without an eye. As Cyclops was taking a shower in the jail's washroom, a huge inmate by the name of Naren came into the room. He stood behind Cyclops, eying him. As he watched him, Naren became aroused. He slowly came up to Cyclops, who had been paying no attention to his surroundings, and pinned him to the wall. Cyclops's soap fell on the tile.

"Hey gyul, you and me are alone in here. Why don't we have ourselves a little fun? I promise I'll be easy on you."

"Move away from me, you piece of shit," Cyclops growled, as he tried to push himself off the wall.

Somehow, he managed to turn around and push Naren away from him. Cyclops lifted his leg and tried to kick him. Unfortunately, he stepped on the soap, slid, and fell on his back, his head bouncing against the floor.

Naren sat on top him. He began punching Cyclops's face. Cyclops could feel the blood gushing from his eye. He screamed and cussed, writhing to get Naren off of him.

Hearing his shouts, other prisoners and officers rushed in. They pulled Naren from him, and Cyclops was taken to the hospital, where his damaged eye was removed.

He was very angry with his loss, but glad that he did not get raped by Naren. That would have been a black stain on his manhood.

"Didn't you pay the customs to make sure that those containers weren't searched?" asked Toothless.

"We tried to bribe a few, but it didn't work."

Kingpin walked to the window and opened it. The two women stepped back.

"What are you trying to see?" he asked.

"We were looking for a friend of ours. She wanted to pee. We thought she went inside," one of them answered. Kingpin could tell that she was a terrible liar.

"Oh, she's probably somewhere outside," said Kingpin, fixing a false smile on his face. He hated curious people.

"Okay then." The ladies walked away.

A few women waved at him. He smiled and waved back. Then he shut the window and sat down in an armchair. He sighed and leaned back.

"Listen. Mickey was arrested by Miguel himself. He poses a threat to our organization. We have to exterminate him before he gives out any information to the police."

"Boss, it will be hard to kill him."

Kingpin exhaled a plume of smoke.

"I've already organized everything. Tomorrow he'll meet his end."

"But how?" asked Terrel, sitting up straight.

"A prison officer was convinced to help us," said Kingpin. He rubbed his fingers together, signifying money.

"Your money always open doors and make things happen," said Toothless.

Kingpin got up. "Money is the solution to every problem."

He turned his back to them. "This meeting is over. Go and join the party outside." He turned around to face them.

"Except you, Terrel."

The men stood up. Cyclops returned, wearing a dry pair of shorts.

Kingpin walked to the door leading to the pool. He opened it, and the men walked outside. When Toothless got to the door, Kingpin grabbed his hand.

"The police are looking for the killer of a woman found in the forest. Did you kill she?"

Kingpin gazed into his eyes.

"No, Boss. That's wasn't me."

"I hope so. If it proves to be the other way, I'll deal with you myself."

He freed his hand, and Toothless left the room.

Terrel stayed sitting in the armchair. Kingpin poured a drink and passed it to him. Then he sat down opposite him.

"Your chick is taking too long to give us information. What's going on?"

Terrel's lip twitched. "Since Miguel's wife is gone, he's been avoiding she. Therefore, she has no way of getting any information from him."

Kingpin lit a cigarette. "She had better give me something soon. I'm losing my patience with her slackness and screw head."

Terrel's eyelid jumped.

"I will talk to she."

Kingpin walked to the window and looked outside. Toothless was in the pool, flanked by two women.

"Come here."

Terrel walked to the window.

"There is one more thing I want you to do."

Terrel glanced outside, feeling a sudden stiffness in his neck.

"Toothless is only trouble for our organization. I feel he killed that woman. Organize with the boys to exterminate him."

An elderly lady came in and whispered something into Kingpin's ear. He looked at his watch and then at the old woman.

"Tell him I'll be there shortly."

He opened the door for Terrel. "Go and join the party."

Terrel walked outside, and Kingpin accompanied the elderly woman to another area of the house.

9th February

At 12 p.m., a dark-skinned woman of age thirty or so, wearing dark sunglasses, sat in the waiting room of Picedale Jail.

The woman, whose name was Elizabeth, put her bag on the table and nervously tapped her fingers on the metal surface as she waited for Charles, one of the inmates. Her eyes wandered between the camera and the door. She dug in her bag and took out a vial filled with liquid.

Charles entered the waiting room, followed by a stout police officer, who removed Charles's handcuffs. Charles, who was tall and broad-shouldered, looked like a giant next to him.

"Hi, babe," he said.

"Hello, cookie," she answered.

He hurried over to his wife, and they hugged. As she

embraced him, she passed the vial to his hand. He sniffed her hair and made cooing noises.

The police officer kept staring at them, so Charles sat down at the table.

"We miss having you at home," she said.

"I miss all of you too. How are the children doing?" Charles asked, holding her hands.

"They keep asking for you. If you hadn't been mixed up with the wrong company, you would be with us."

"I did this for you and the children. I searched for decent employment, but only wasted my time."

He sneaked a look at the guard, and whispered, "However, the boss gave me a job."

She pulled her hands away.

"On what cause? He asks you to do a dirty job, and now to take a life. You know what they told me? If Mickey lives, they'll kidnap my kids and sell them away."

She put her hands on his cheeks. "I beg you, get out of it before it's too late," she whispered.

He put his hands on hers and gently removed her hands from his cheeks.

"I can't. Once you become a member of a gang group, there's no turning back. If I leave, they will come after you and the children," he whispered.

The guard approached them. "It's time to go."

He handcuffed Charles.

Charles stood up and regarded his wife. "Don't overthink. I'll figure out something," he promised.

Then he was led away.

Later in the evening, Charles lined up to get his food in the jail's canteen. The eating area was filled with prisoners.

Charles put his hand in his pocket and touched the vial.

Now or never.

He gazed around in search of Mickey and found him in the back of the line.

A fat man put green beans, potatoes, and beef on Charles' plate. He was also given a glass of orange juice.

He walked to a long table where other male prisoners sat. There were two empty seats. He sat in one, then took the vial out of his pocket and emptied its contents into his juice. Then he patiently waited for Mickey.

Mickey got his food and wandered over, looking for a seat.

"Hey, Mickey! Come and sit here," said Charles.

Mickey walked over to Charles's table. His hair was uncombed, and his hands trembled little bit.

"What's up, man? You're looking restless today."

"I haven't slept for a few nights," said Mickey, putting his tray on the table. He sat down.

"I heard you spoke to Miguel."

A muscle in Mickey's face spasmed.

"Where did you hear that?" His heart began pumping faster.

"Doesn't matter," said Charles.

Charles looked over at a fellow inmate, Zane, who sat at the opposite table, and signaled him with a wink.

Zane stood up and threw a spoon at Mickey. The spoon landed on his back and then fell on the floor. Zane sat back down quickly in his seat.

Mickey rose, a frown on his face. He picked up the spoon and looked around. Then he raised it.

"Which of you imbeciles threw this?" he demanded loudly.

The nearest guard pulled his gun halfway out of its holster as he stared guardedly at Mickey.

Charles quickly exchanged his cup with Mickey's. Then he got up and put his hand on his shoulder.

"Take your seat, boy. You don't want to have a problem with these watchdogs. They just look for a reason to beat you."

Mickey stared at the prison officers for a long moment, and then he slowly took his seat.

"Someone wants me dead. Yesterday I was attacked while sleeping. Someone put a pillow over my face and tried to smother me. I was barely able to push him away from me. He then took out a knife and tried to stab me. We fought, and the knife rolled under the bed. I kicked him and jumped on his back. Then the officers came and took him away."

"Who would want you dead?" asked Charles.

Mickey began eating his food.

"Kingpin. Someone told him that I spoke to Miguel."

"You've made so many enemies. Any of them would want you dead."

As Mickey swallowed the beans, he began coughing. His face grew red. Charles patted his back.

"Are you okay?"

Mickey grabbed his cup and drank the juice. The coughing stopped.

"Thanks, man. Guess the beans went down the wrong tube."

He went back to eating. "I heard you're getting out in a few days. Tell bossman I haven't given out any information to Miguel or anyone else, and I don't plan to do so. My loyalty belongs to our organization."

As Mickey spoke, his stomach started feeling heavy. His vision became foggy, and the voices of the other prisoners sounded distant, like the buzzing of a fly.

Suddenly he couldn't breathe. Wide-eyed, he gasped and brought his hand to his neck, gasping for air. He scrambled up, and then collapsed on the floor. As he lay there, his body moved jerkily, and white foam came out of his mouth.

"What did you put in my drink?" he whispered, and then blacked out.

The two prison officers rushed towards him. One of them leaned over and put his ear on his chest, trying to hear his heartbeat. Then he held his hand and checked for a pulse. But there was no heartbeat.

"He's dead."

"He seemed good all the time. How could he fall dead!?" said Charles.

The other inmates surrounded Mickey. One of the prison officers made a call, all the while keeping a hand on his gun.

"Go back to eating, or to your cells!" he shouted.

Prisoners began leaving the canteen.

Two other prison officers came in with a stretcher. They laid Mickey's body on it and took him out.

Charles picked up Mickey's mug in order to destroy traces of his involvement. Then he dropped it in a huge sink that held other dirty mugs.

The prison officer put Charles's mug on the tray with Mickey's unfinished food.

"Send this to the lab for inspection," he told his partner. "We need to find out if he was poisoned."

The other guard took the tray and left. Soon the canteen was empty. Only a few people stayed to clean it up.

11th February

The situation in Trinidad's neighboring country was getting worse day by day, as poverty hit the country. Food, water, medications, toilet paper, and even soap were scarce, and prices soared. Women in search of jobs were forced to come to Trinidad in order to provide for their families.

Their desperate situation allowed a man named Samuel to lure a few of them into prostitution. Therefore, along with his hotel business, he ran a successful sex trade business.

Recently he had gotten a group of young Spanish women. As soon as they had stepped onto the island, they had been taken to Samuel's Exotic Land Hotel. Scared, alone, and threatened with the loss of their lives, they had had no choice.

Samuel forced them into prostitution.

Without having documents or a place to go, and not knowing the language, the girls became the tools of a thriving money-making business for Samuel.

A red Ferrari was parked by the white two-story Exotic Land Hotel. The building itself was burglar-proofed and had mirrored one-way windows.

Samuel sat in the Ferrari, counting a wad of money. Next to him was his broad-shouldered bodyguard, Wayne. While Samuel checked the money, Wayne's eyes focused on the street.

Samuel put twenty thousand dollars in a black satchel.

"Give this to Andre. Tell him that he'll get the rest in a few days. Also, go over to Donald's and get more pills from him. It makes the girls wild and the clients generous."

Wayne took the satchel. "Anything else?"

"Don't go into any rum shops before delivering my money!"

Wayne had planned to take a drink the first chance he got. He grimaced, and then got out of the car. Without another look at Samuel, he walked towards his white Nissan and got into it.

Samuel stared at his hotel, and then made a call.

In a living room of the hotel, a bald-headed man by the name of Zachary answered the phone

"Yes, bossman."

"What are the clients doing?"

"Usual thing. Dem locked up in de room. But de gyuls are getting too noisy."

Samuel shook his head.

"You must be giving them too many pills. I told you don't overdose my girls."

"Sorry. I got distracted."

Samuel ended the call and drove away.

In the hotel, Zachary squeezed his head.

Man, I gotta be more careful.

While Zachary's mind filled with worries, one of the hotel's male customers lay on the bed in one of the bedrooms. He was accompanied by Olivia, who was only seventeen years old, nineteen-year-old Fernanda, and twenty-two-year-old Romina.

Two of the women, Olivia and Fernanda, chuckled and spoke together in Spanish. They held plastic cups filled with whiskey. The man, Kingston, was on top of Romina, having sex.

When he was done, he got out of the bed and took out a camera from the pocket of his discarded pants. He directed the camera at them.

"Aye chicas, get close to each other and howl while rubbing your breasts."

They just stared at him, confused. He picked up his cup of tequila from the bedside table and took a few sips, then licked his lips.

"Arh-wooooooooooooooooooooooo!" he said with a grin.

Romina, who knew English, glared at his camera.

"Él nos pide aullar como un animal y frotar las roturas. Él nos va a grabar en video y podría compartirlo con todos,"[68] she told the others.

"¿Está loco? No voy a hacer eso,"[69] Olivia said.

"Why are you taking so long?"

"Sir, we don't feel comfortable with your request. You can't videotape us either," Romina told him.

---

[68] He asks us to howl like an animal and rub breasts. He is going to video tape us and might share it with everyone.

[69] Is he crazy? I'm not going do it.

She got off the bed, and he grabbed hold of her hand.

"Where are you going, you friggin idiot?"

She looked into his eyes. "Sir, we're not your toys. Free my hand."

He hit her in the face and then pushed her onto the bed. She fell on the two other girls.

"You nasty Jagabat.[70] I spent de friggin' ten thousand to have some fun. Now I have to deal with dis shit?"

He then spat on Romina. Her face burned and her eyes watered as she wiped the saliva off her face. She got up soundlessly and stood facing him. As she glared into his eyes, she slapped him back.

Blood rushed into his brain. He punched her in the nose. She screeched and held her nose as blood dripped down her face. She wiped it with her hand and ran to the toilet.

Fernanda tried to get off the bed, but Olivia embraced her.

"*No te defiendas. Harás las cosas peor para todos nosotros,*"[71] she told her.

Fernanda burst into tears.

"*No vine aquí a vender mi cuerpo. Me prometieron un trabajo como sirvienta. Mi hijo es asmático. Él necesita sus medicamentos y comidas adecuadas. Vine a esta isla por su culpa,*"[72] she said.

Romina returned and glared at Kingston. He scowled back.

"Okay, gyuls, I didn't come to see a crying circus. So go ahead and make some noise. Do you want me to speak to your boss?"

---

[70] Prostitute

[71] Do not fight back. You will make things worse for all of us.

[72] I did not come here to sell my body. They promised me a job as a maid. My son is asthmatic. He needs his medications and proper meals. I came to this island because of him."

"Haz lo que te pide para evitar problema," [73] said Romina.

All three howled and rubbed their breasts. Kingston put his hand on his own chest and imitated them.

"Oh, yes! Rub it! Rub!"

They followed his instructions.

"Now lick each other's breasts."

After he got his pictures, he sat down on the bed and started kissing Olivia.

In the next room, Mia lay naked on the bed as Gary smeared chocolate on her. He himself was covered in the chocolate as well. When he was done, he began licking it off her body.

"Gih mih de friggin ting nah. [74]."

She handed the tin of chocolate to him. Gary dipped his finger in the sauce, then he put it in her mouth, moving it in a circular motion.

Nausea overcame her. She stood up and put on a robe.

"I need to run to the toilet. I'll be back," she said.

"Why don't you use the one in the room?"

"I don't feel comfortable when people are around."

"Don't take too long."

She nodded, then started out. Something caught her eye, and she paused.

By the bed stood a chair over which Gary had draped his pants. His cell phone had fallen out of his pocket and onto the floor. When Gary turned around, she quickly picked it up and ran to the guest room.

As Mia ran in, she almost collided with Zachary. She quickly hid the phone behind her back.

He grasped her other hand. "Why aren't you with a customer?"

---

[73] Do what he asks to avoid problems.
[74] Give me the damn thing.

"I...I...I need to use the toilet. I have an upset stomach," she said, as her hands trembled.

He stared into her eyes, and then let go of her hand.

"Go quickly. Leave the toilet clean."

Mia went into the bathroom and locked the door, then stood just inside, listening for footsteps. After Zachary walked away, she sat on the toilet, staring at the cell phone. Her heart raced.

Which number to call?

The man's phone was connected to the internet. She browsed a site in search of local police numbers. Then she dialed the number for Lystra police station.

At that moment, Sameer was sitting in the lobby area of the police station chatting with a female police officer. When the phone rang, he answered, "Lystra police station."

"Please help me," whispered Mia.

"Speak louder. I can't hear you."

Mia glanced at the door.

"They brought me here from Venezuela and took my documents. They also exploit other girls. They drug them every day and make them to do nasty things. Please hurry up and send someone here!"

Sameer picked up a pen and paper from the desk.

"Where are you calling from?"

"From Exotic Land Hotel."

"Do you know where it's located?"

"Netrotin Street. The building is white and has mirrored windows."

Zachary knocked on the bathroom door.

"What's taking so long in there?"

"I have the runs. Please give me a minute," she said.

Her whole body began shaking.

"I have to go," she whispered to Sameer, then she hung up the phone.

The other police officer stared at Sameer.

"Another complaint of abuse? We've been getting a lot lately."

Sameer put the piece of paper into his pocket.

"No, this is something serious, and involves a foreigner. Could be a case of human trafficking. We have to check it out. Send out two police cars to Netrotin Street. Have them look for the Exotic Land Hotel. It's a two-story white building with mirrored windows."

Sameer left the lobby area and rushed into Miguel's office. Miguel had been reading a report when Sameer interrupted him.

"We got a call from a Spanish woman," Sameer told him.

"She, together with other women, are being forced into prostitution. Let's go and catch whoever is behind this."

Miguel put his cigarette in the ashtray. He opened his drawer and took out a few handcuffs.

"We'll need these," he said.

Sameer walked out to the parking lot, his friend behind him. They got in quickly, Miguel in the driver's seat.

Miguel put a cigarette in his mouth and lit it with a lighter while keeping his left hand on the steering wheel.

"You with your smoking! You know, you could get cancer. How much can you smoke?" Sameer lowered his window.

"I'll stop someday, but not now."

Sameer picked up the newspaper and got busy reading it. He stopped on the advertisement section.

"Escort Services and exotic massage, by women between the ages of 20 and 35," he read aloud. "I bet these kinds of services offer sex. Look at how low we've stooped; even the newspapers allow prostitution to be promoted on their pages."

Miguel blew out a circle of smoke.

"You shouldn't be surprised. Money buys everything. You pay big money, and anything you want to advertise is allowed on their pages."

Sameer read aloud again: "A psychic with 20 years of experience will predict your future by reading your palm. Can also unite loved ones. Bring good luck and finances."

A grimace formed on Sameer's face.

"What fool would go to this so-called psychic? The only gift he has is to lie and spend hopeless people's money."

Miguel stuffed his cigarette butt into an empty soda can.

"Sameer, you always have to go into some kind of philosophy, wondering and asking questions. I really don't know what idiot would go to a man instead of God. Maybe desperate, depressed, and gullible ones will look for them. Just to get deceived or swayed away—at any rate, they pay good money for things they want to hear, rather than the truth."

"Yes, people look for answers or solutions in the wrong places. They think drugs, alcohol, or psychics have the answers. The solution lies with faith in God, a positive mind, and hard work. One must just turn to God and ask Him for guidance and help."

"Boy, why don't you become a priest?" said Miguel with a grin.

A smile danced on Sameer's face. At one time in his life he had been considering choosing the path of priesthood. However, he couldn't see his life without a wife or kids, which one day he hoped to gain.

After a short drive, they arrived at their destination. Miguel parked two streets away from the hotel, and they strolled leisurely toward it.

As they got to the door, Zachary opened it. He had been going out to buy a roti from the store on the opposite side of the street. He stood motionless for a second when he saw the policemen.

"I am Sergeant Miguel Siglobeen. We have reason to investigate this property."

"Do you have a warrant?" asked Zachary, not moving

from the door.

Sameer showed him a piece of paper.

"Now please step aside and allow us to do our work."

Zachary moved away from the door, and Miguel and Sameer went inside.

Another police car stopped in front of the hotel, and two officers, Constables Benjamin and Anora, got out.

Two residents of the brothel had been on the way to the guest room, but as soon as they saw the policemen, they ran outside through another door.

Anora ran after them.

Mia came out of the toilet and rushed to the policemen.

"Are you from Lystra police station?"

"Yes, we are," said Miguel.

"My name is Mia. I was the one who called you."

Benjamin came in and walked towards them.

"Both of you go and search the rooms. I'll talk to her," said Miguel.

Sameer and Benjamin, guns in their hands, began knocking on the doors of the hotel's rooms.

It wasn't long before they hit pay dirt. Two rooms down, a shirtless man of about forty years of age opened the door. As soon as Sameer saw him, he forced himself inside.

On the bed was a tall, slim teenage girl with curly hair. She was naked. When she saw Sameer, she pulled a sheet over herself.

Sameer's attention moved to the man. "Let me see your ID."

The man removed an ID card from his wallet and gave it to Sameer.

"Avinash Ramsak," Sameer read. He handed the ID back. "What are you doing here?"

"I just wanted to have some relaxation time with my babe."

"Put on your shirt," said Sameer.

Avinash picked up his shirt, as well as his watch, from the chest of drawers. After he put on his shirt, Sameer handcuffed him.

"I didn't do anything wrong. You have no right to arrest me."

Sameer's attention was caught by the sight of the girl's school uniform, which was hanging over a chair.

He handed it to her. "Get dressed."

He turned away, and she began putting on her clothes.

When she was done, he asked her, "What's your name?"

"Nisha." She shyly looked away.

"How old are you?"

"Fourteen."

"Why aren't you in school?"

"I was on my way, but he brought me here."

"You should be in school, not in this place with an adult man."

"But he gives me money to spend."

Sameer glared at Avinash. He turned a much gentler face to Nisha.

"You must not sell your body for money. It shouldn't be touched by anyone unless you're married. Your body is like a temple that needs to be kept pure."

"But he promised to marry me."

Sameer tightened his grip on Avinash's handcuffs.

"How did you meet?"

"I'm her driver," Avinash told him with a leer.

Sameer pushed him towards the door. "Move it! You're being arrested for raping a minor."

Avinash walked out of the room, followed by Sameer and the teenager.

"But I didn't rape her. She willingly gave in."

Sameer kicked Avinash's butt, and he fell. The girl rushed towards him and helped him to get up.

"Let's go," ordered Sameer.

"Can I go home? If my parents find out, they'll punish me!"

"You should have thought about that before coming here," said Sameer.

They walked into the lobby. Sameer glanced at Miguel, who was sitting in an armchair, talking to Mia.

"I'm taking these people to the car," said Sameer.

Miguel looked at Avinash and the teenage girl. "I'll be there shortly."

Sameer left the hotel.

Constable Anora went into the hotel and headed to the hotel's suites. At the same time, Benjamin kicked open a door and moved swiftly toward the bedroom. He barged in, his pistol in his hand.

Kingston lay between Fernanda and Romina and was kissing Olivia. His head whipped around at the noise.

He took one look at Benjamin and jumped off the bed.

"What de hell!" he shouted. He scrambled for his underpants and hastily pulled them on.

The women covered themselves with the sheet.

Benjamin picked up their clothes from the floor and threw them on the bed. "Put on your clothes," he said.

He looked at Romina. "You too."

Romina got up and walked to the other side of the room to get her clothes. Then she dressed.

While she did so, Benjamin turned to Kingston. "Let me see your ID."

Kingston glared at him. "I left it in the car."

"Move now. I'm taking you to the police station."

Kingston suddenly turned and picked up the lamp. He threw it at Benjamin, but it missed him. It fell and broke on the floor, sending splinters everywhere.

Benjamin pointed a pistol at him.

"Don't move." He moved swiftly toward him and handcuffed him.

"You blasted shit!" Kingston snarled. "I'm a lawyer. I'll take you all to court."

Benjamin pointed at the door. "Do as you wish. Ladies, let's go now."

They headed to the police car. As they were getting in, another one stopped in front of the hotel. Three policemen jumped out, wearing bulletproof vests and holding guns in their hands. They arrested Gary and Zachary and hauled them off to the police station as well.

All of Miguel's attention was now on Mia.

"We were promised to get help from the Catholic Center of Hope. When we got to shore, they put us in a van. They left Laura somewhere else and put me in here. They took my passport and kept me here against my will," she said.

"Can you describe the one who brought you onto the boat?"

"He was broad-shouldered and dark-skinned. One of his front teeth was missing. He drove away with my sister."

Mia clutched his hand.

"Please help me to find her and get my passport. I left two children behind, hoping to make enough money to buy food and medication for them. I never thought my job search would mean I would end up in prostitution. Please help me."

"Okay, Mia. I'll see what I can do. But for now, you have to go with me to the police station. After that, immigration will deal with the rest. Let's go."

He escorted Mia to his car and then went back into the hotel, where he walked through the corridors and opened the doors. In one bedroom, he noticed an open window. He put his head outside and saw three women running away.

He went back to his car and opened the driver's door. Sameer was in the front seat. Mia, Nisha, and Avinash were squeezed into the back seat.

"Let's go."

He started the engine and they headed to the police station.

15th February

Going through with the abortion caused Gail to fall into a deep depression and brought illness upon her, so bad that she missed four days of school. Every inch of her body hurt. She lay in bed, restless, turning from side to side, burning with fever.

Her mother, Chelsea, stood next to her bed. She dipped a rag in a basin of water and wiped Gail's forehead.

Gail pushed her mother's hand away.

"Baby is dead. They killed it."

Her mother picked up a thermometer from the chair and put it under Gail's arm.

"They took it away."

Gail turned on her other side, and the thermometer slipped out.

"Stay on one place, gyul. Let me check your temperature."

Gail raised her head a little bit and cried, "My baby is gone!"

Her mother shook her head.

I must bring down her fever. She is talking nonsense.

Anil came in and glanced at Gail. "How is she?"

"Not so good. Go and get nah medicine for she," she said.

"You go. I'm waiting for someone," said Anil.

"Ok, just watch she," said Chelsea.

They left Gail's bedroom.

Chelsea picked her bag up, and left the house in a rush, forgetting to change out of her sandals.

Anil sat on the sofa and turned on the TV. He browsed through the channels and stopped on a cricket game.

"Mummy, it's hurting! Where are you?"

Anil turned up the volume of the TV to drown out Gail's shouting.

Gail slowly sat up and, out of the blue, cried out loudly, "Mummy! Anil murdered my child!"

Anil jumped up and rushed to the bedroom. He hurried to Gail and held her hand tightly.

"Lie down and stop talking bullshit!"

She pulled her hand away from him.

"Don't touch me. You insisted that I go for an abortion. You're a killer!"

She slowly stood up and took a few steps.

"Where are you going?"

She paused and looked at him, as if trying to figure out what she planned to do.

"I'm going to tell Mother about the abortion."

The whole room spun before her eyes, and she suddenly felt dizzy and weak.

Anil grabbed her hand. "Are you insane? You can't!"

"You're hurting my hand. Let it go!"

He freed her hand and walked to the door, where he stood in the doorway. When she got there, Gail put her hand on his chest and tried to move him out of the way.

"Go away. I hate you!"

"Go back to your bed now! You're not making things easy for me."

She pushed him harder.

"No, I need to tell the truth!"

He crossed his arms and didn't move. Her sobs became louder.

"Please get out of my way!"

She became hysterical and hit him a few times. He caught her wrists and held them.

"This is my bedroom! Get out of here!"

He grasped her hands.

"Don't you understand? If you tell she, they'll know that I had sex with you."

It suddenly got very quiet, and Anil shook from head to toe.

Why did I say that? Now she knows!

She paused and stared into his eyes.

"Why are you telling me this nasty thing? I don't remember having sex with you."

His grip on her wrists became painful.

"It's because I drugged you!" he blurted out.

Damn it. Why did I tell her?

As soon as he let go of her hands, she hit him again.

"You're my stepfather! How could you do this to me?"

"Stop it, girl. I couldn't help it. Ever since you blossomed into a young beautiful woman, I haven't been able to take my eyes off you. I love you!"

He tried to hug her, but she pulled away from him.

"You're crazy. I'm going to tell Mummy."

She managed get through the doorway, but Anil grabbed her hair and pulled her back.

"Leh go my hair, monster! You get me pregnant and then make me throw it away!"

He loosened his grasp, and she rushed to the living room.

"Mummy, where are you?"

She walked to the front door. Anil rushed after her.

"Please, Gail. Don't do it. Let's talk about it."

She put her hand on the door handle.

When she turned away, Anil seized a trophy from a nearby stand and hit her on the head.

She turned around and stared at him silently, her eyes full of pain. Then she collapsed.

Anil rushed to her. He checked her pulse, then carried her to the bedroom, where he lay her on the bed.

Then he went to the kitchen and picked up a bottle of beer. He returned to her bedroom and sat on the chair. As he took a few sips, he pondered his next step.

What to do? If she speaks out, I'm dead.

He heard a car park in front of their house. He quickly left Gail's bedroom and sank onto the sofa.

His wife walked into the living room.

"How is Gail?"

"She's been restless and cried for some time. Then she fell asleep."

Chelsea took out some medicine from the bag she was carrying. "I got for she fever reducer."

She left him and walked into Gail's bedroom.

Gail moved her legs. "Ouch! It hurts!" she wailed.

Chelsea put her hand on her forehead. Her skin seemed hotter than before.

"Mummy! Mummy! Where are you? I have something to tell you."

"I'm here, honey. Sit up and take some medicine."

Chelsea poured the liquid into a measuring spoon as Gail opened her eyes and looked dazedly at her mother. She rose halfway, but dropped back down.

"Mummy, he raped me and then forced me to get an abortion."

A frown formed on Chelsea's face.

"What are you talking about?"

Anil came up to the door unnoticed and stared at Gail. His heart raced and goosebumps pricked his skin.

Gail looked over at the doorway. She lifted her hand and pointed at Anil.

"He said he raped me because he loves me."

Her mother looked in the direction she pointed. Anil gazed silently at his wife.

"Is it true?" she asked, with a heavy heart. She sat down on the edge of the bed.

Anil came inside and stared at Gail.

"Me to rape she? Are you crazy? She's delirious," he said. Weakness overcame his body, and he felt as if his end was coming.

"Give she medicine, woman, before she gets cuckoo!"

Chelsea put the medicine and the spoon on the chair.

"She needs to see a doctor. Get up, child. I'm taking you to the hospital."

She held onto Gail's shoulders and helped her to sit up. Shaking, Gail raised her head and glared at Anil.

"Get out of my eyes, you sicko."

A doubt crawled into Chelsea's heart.

Why does she keep insisting? Did he really rape she?

She gave him a stern look.

He seems to be calm and collected.

"Go and start the engine," Chelsea said.

Anil left, and Gail followed slowly with the help of her mother. Chelsea helped her to get into the car, and then she got in as well.

"Ouch! My head is hurting. He hit me!"

Anil glanced at her in the mirror.

"Her delirious accusations are getting to me. She better stay in the hospital till she fever goes away," he said.

I might have to pack my clothes and leave.

"Just be patient. Don't you see she's burning with fever?"

Gail closed her eyes and fell asleep.

A GLIMPSE OF THE HOPE

In the late afternoon Sheila, Violeta, and Daniela sat at a table in the small kitchen. The paint on the walls was wearing off and had dark stains caused by dirt. There was a stove, and a small cupboard, its door falling off. They were having an early dinner.

"Aunty Sheila, how old is Ronnel?" asked Violeta.

A smile ran across Sheila's face, but sadness could be seen in her eyes.

"He's only ten."

Violeta's facial expression became serious.

"I have a brother, but I will never see him, or my mother, again." Tears formed in her eyes.

"What did I tell you yesterday?" asked Sheila.

Violeta stared into her eyes.

"One must never lose hope and faith but keep fighting till the end."

Sheila caressed Violeta's head.

"That's right. Just be a little patient, and one day we'll be free as birds."

Daniela sipped at her glass of juice.

"I've been here for two years with no way to get out. Why are you giving her false hope?"

Sheila gazed intently at Daniela's face, and saw a dark spot under her eye.

"Life is such a thing that, sometimes when we think there's no more hope, something good happens. Because God never leaves us."

Sheila peered closer at Daniela's eye.

"What's that on your face?"

"Nothing."

"Don't lie to me. I can see it."

Daniela got up. "Victor hit me for not following his instructions."

Sheila stood up. She clenched her fists.

"I have had enough of him! I'm going to talk to him right now."

Violeta shuddered. She clutched Sheila's hand.

"No, aunty. He'll kill you! Then who will protect me?"

Bernadette appeared at the door. She looked surprisingly clean in a tight green mini-dress, although it looked like it could burst at any time. Her long hair was neatly combed, and she had left it hanging loose. She had a makeup bag in her hand. The kitchen filled with the scent of roses.

"Why are you taking so long? Clients are going to come shortly, and they're paying US dollars. So, make sure you keep them satisfied at all costs."

Her stare stopped on Sheila. She held out the makeup bag.

"Take this and put some makeup on you and her."

She pointed with her chin at Violeta.

"Make sure Violeta wears the dress that I left on your bed. There's also a dress on the chair in your room, Daniela."

Bernadette stared at Daniela's face.

"Hide those bruises."

Sheila took the bag, and Bernadette left.

"I just hate her," Daniela said, irritated.

"She's a wicked woman. Camille said she sold her soul to a demon for money," said Violeta.

"I dislike her myself, but for our own good we can't express our feelings openly," Sheila advised them.

She took the dishes to the sink and rinsed them.

"Let's go now, before she sends that clown for us."

Daniela burst out laughing.

"A good name for Victor, although he's not funny at all. Just a jerk!"

The trio headed to their bedrooms.

Daniela found a blue silk dress on her bed. She picked it up and smelt it with closed eyes. It smelled so clean and fresh. It reminded her of her mother, whose favorite color was blue. She always smelled like a flower to her. Daniela hugged the dress as memories of the past entered her mind.

She saw herself having breakfast with her seven-year-old sister Andrea and her parents. They and their dad sat at the table while her mother stood beside it, rushing to finish her coffee. In her new dress, her mother looked more beautiful than ever. Even her daddy noticed her beauty and stared at her in astonishment.

"That dress looks as if it was made for you. You look so gorgeous. Doesn't she, girls?"

Andrea touched her mother's dress.

"She looks like a queen," she said.

"If I am a queen, then you are my princesses," she said, hugging both girls.

Their dad looked at his watch and then at his wife. It was evident, from his smile and kind eyes, that he truly loved his wife and children.

"My Queen, you must rush. The time is ticking," he said.

"Okay, my King, I'm leaving now. Girls, hurry up before the school bell rings," she said.

She kissed her husband and left. Her husband gazed after her.

"I don't know what I would do without her and you," he told his daughters.

When breakfast was over, the three of them hurriedly got into the car. Constantin left the front windows of the car open, and the wind blew their hair around. Daniela breathed deeply of the fresh air that she loved. As they got to the school, she saw other students she knew walking into the building.

He stopped not far from the gate and looked back.

"Have a nice day, little duckling," he said loudly.

Two teenage boys passing by their car stopped and stared at them. Daniela's ears burnt with embarrassment.

"Father, please don't call me duckling in public. Those boys heard it. It's so embarrassing."

"Sorry."

She got out of the car.

"I gone, bye," she said, and walked away.

Her school day passed as usual between schoolwork and short breaks. When lessons were over, Daniela rushed down the steps.

Out of nowhere, she was pushed by a boy who was running away from a classmate. She tumbled down a few steps and landed with her behind on her foot. The boy who pushed her came up to her.

"Sorry! I didn't mean to push you. I was running away from my friend."

She frowned at him. "Next time, open your eyes and look where you're going!"

She got up, grimacing with pain.

He picked her bag up from the ground. "If you don't mind, I'll carry it to the gate for you."

She limped slowly to the exit as he followed her. The pain on her foot was so unbearable that she stopped by the gate, sweating, her face screwed up in pain.

The boy handed her bag to her. "I must go. See you tomorrow."

"Bye."

He ran off.

Daniela's high school was twenty minutes away from Andrea's. After school, Daniela always walked to her sister's school, and their mother picked them up from there. But with the fall she wasn't sure if she could bear the walk. She took her phone out of her school bag and dialed her mother's phone number.

Why isn't she answering?

Other students passed by, busily chatting, paying no attention to her.

Daniela put away the cell phone. She took a deep breath and made slow steps. As she walked down the sidewalk, a car with tinted windows slowed down beside her. The driver, a man wearing a police uniform, called out to her.

"I see you're limping. Do you need a ride?"

Daniela stopped and gazed around. She hesitated for a minute, but then decided to take the offer. He stopped the car and let her in.

He continued driving, but soon slowed down and then stopped. Another man jumped into the car.

Gail's eyebrows met.

Where did he come from? I didn't see him.

He stared at Daniela with a wicked grin. Her heart pounded fast as uneasiness crept over her. She heard a click as the driver locked all the doors.

She looked outside and could see her sister's school.

"Excuse me, can you let me out right here, please?" she said.

As she turned around, she felt something sting her hand. When she looked over at the passenger, she noticed that he was holding a needle.

She put her hand on the door's lock button and tried to open the door, but the passenger pulled her away.

"Help me! Help!" she shouted.

She pulled herself away from him and pressed on the button that should have opened the window.

"Please, help me!"

Then she began feeling weak and blacked out.

Daniela took off her clothes and slipped into the dress. Her memories still haunted her. She recalled opening her eyes only to find herself in a moving lorry.

As she looked around, she noticed two men, three women, and a boy in with her. Their hands were tied, and their mouths were taped.

The boy, thin and lightly clothed, caught her attention. His eyes were wide, and he shivered. He gazed at her sadly with tears in his eyes.

The other hostages seemed to be in a daze, as if they weren't aware of what was happening. They stared ahead at one spot.

Daniela moved her hands, trying to free herself from the rope. Her efforts paid off; she pulled out one hand from the rope and freed herself. She got up and scrambled to the lorry's door and tried to open it, but it was locked.

The speed of the lorry made Daniela stumble from one side of the enclosure to the other. At one point, she lost her balance and fell. She regained her footing and began kicking the door with all her might. Helpless, she sat on the floor and burst into tears.

Where are they taking us? Is this my end?

She raised her head and looked at her fellow prisoners. She got up and gently pulled the tapes from the mouths of the adults.

"Please untie me," said the woman. Her eyes had cleared; only now did she realize that she had been kidnapped.

Daniela freed her hands. Then she went over to the boy and gently took the tape off his mouth.

"That hurts!" he said. His teeth were chattering from fear and the cold. Daniela quickly freed his limbs.

He scanned the other hostages. "Where's my mummy?"

"I don't know. How did you end up in here?"

"I was playing not far from our house. Then I heard an ice cream truck. It stopped right next to me. A woman was driving, and a man was selling the ice cream. They offered me a free cone. But then a man grabbed my waist and pulled me into their truck."

The men, now fully awake, rammed their bodies into the door, trying to open it.

"Where are they taking us?" asked the boy. He moved closer to Daniela and hugged her.

"I have no idea."

"I'm afraid," he said.

She embraced him. "It's going to be okay," she said.

The woman joined the men and began banging on the door.

"Somebody let us out!" she shouted.

The lorry slowed down and then came to a halt. The woman moved away from the door as someone slowly opened it from the outside.

Two armed men wearing respirator masks stood outside. They threw something inside the lorry. It rolled, and smoke poured out of it. One by one, coughing, the hostages fell to the floor.

The masked men had jumped inside, joined by two others. They had dragged the hostages out and put them into three separate vans.

The little boy and Daniela had been carried into a white van. A tall man tied Daniela's and the boy's hands with rope. Then he taped their mouths. He got out, shut the door, and the van started moving.

After a while, Daniela regained consciousness. She slowly sat up and looked around her. Again, she was able to free herself from the rope.

Noticing the little boy, she crawled towards him. She gently shook him, and he awoke. He stared at her, hopelessness in his eyes. She put a finger to her mouth, signaling to him to stay quiet. He got up, shaking.

She heard a phone ring. The driver answered and put the phone on the speaker.

"Where are you?"

"I'm on the main highway."

"Speed it up. The girl's condition is getting worse. He must be delivered soon. They can't operate without his kidney."

"What about Romanian girl?" asked the driver.

"She's been sold out to a brothel overseas. You need to drop her by C... Port."

The driver opened his mouth to ask another question, but the call had ended.

Daniela put on her blue silky gown and looked at herself in the mirror. The long dress hung on her beautifully, exposing Daniela's neck, shoulders, and back. She turned from side to side, inspecting the dress.

My whole life is ruined. From a student to a whore.

She sighed deeply. Her memory went back to the day when her cousin was getting married.

She stood with her mother before a mirror. At that time, she had been wearing a long cream-colored dress. Her mother was putting pearls around her neck.

"You have grown so fast, and have become a beautiful young lady. I'm proud of you."

"Thank you, Mother," said Daniela, putting her mother's hand on her cheek.

Andrea, wearing a pink dress with small blue flowers,

rushed in pulling her father's hand. He walked behind her, an amused look on his face.

"I'm ready! Let's go!" she exclaimed.

Her father stopped, speechless, as he looked at his wife. In her white dress, she looked like a bride.

His attention turned to Daniela.

"You're looking gorgeous. Just like your mom."

Andrea ran towards the mirror and gazed at herself.

"What about me?"

Andrea's mother caressed her head.

"You are the most beautiful girl in the world."

As Daniela returned to her current situation, tears sparkled in her eyes. She missed her home and her family and wasn't sure if she would ever see them again.

Beautiful young whore. They took everything away from me. It's my fault. I shouldn't have gotten in a car with a stranger. I should have just kept walking.

She wiped her tears off with her hand.

It's too late for regrets. I must be strong.

She stared at herself and forced a smile. Then she imagined herself running in the field with her sister. Her hair swayed in the air and her feet swished the green grass. They laughed nonstop.

Freedom! Sweet Freedom!

Coming back to reality, she looked at herself again. On her neck she could see a reddish hick left by her last customer.

She pulled up her dress and checked her legs. They were still covered with bruises. A customer, Silvester, had pushed her and then kicked her legs because she refused to perform oral sex.

As she kept looking at herself, the forced smile on her face died away.

Hope shouldn't die. But there's no way out of this.

She sat down on the floor, overcome with hopelessness. Her sobs echoed in the room.

When Sheila and Violeta returned to their bedroom, Violeta ran towards the bed, where she found a pink dress. She picked it up.

"Aunty Sheila, look at this pretty dress!"

"Put it on, please."

Violeta took off her clothes. She was so thin that her ribs all showed plainly. Sheila noticed a huge dark bruise on her back.

"Child, what is that on your back?"

Violeta faced her in order to hide it.

"I don't know."

Sheila went over to her and checked her back.

"How did you get it?"

"Bernadette asked me to take coffee to him. When I went to the room, he was smoking."

"Who?"

"Brian, a man from another country. When I gave him the cup, it spilled on him. He got very angry. He kicked me in the back. He said if I told anyone he would choke me."

Sheila suddenly felt weak, as anger and disappointment filled her. She gazed at the ceiling as if trying to see someone there.

I need to find a way to free us. She will not survive in here.

Violeta put on her dress.

"Aunty, please don't tell Bernadette or Victor. He's a monster."

"I'm not going to tell them."

Violeta ran towards the mirror.

"Wow, aunty! I look like a princess."

Just for a moment her face shone, spreading rays of joy. She spun around.

"You are indeed a beautiful princess."

Violeta sat on the bed and stared quietly out the small window.

"Why are you quiet?"

"Princesses live in castles and are free, but I live in this nasty house with bad people, and I feel ugly inside."

Sheila fingered the makeup bag, which was lying on the bed. She lifted it and sighed deeply.

"One day you'll be free as a bird."

She opened the makeup bag and took out silver eye shadow, red lipstick, and mascara. She picked up a small mirror and put it before Violeta's face.

"Look at your pretty face. It can never look ugly. Always remember, you are beautiful from the inside, which makes you beautiful on the outside. It's just that the world has become populated with ugly-hearted and evil people."

"Why does Bernadette want makeup on my face?"

"New customers are coming today from another country. Bernadette wants everyone to look special, and a little bit different."

Violeta walked to the small window. She peered outside, but could only see the feet of people going by. She shook the steel bars of their prison.

"I don't want to look special for bad people. I want to go home," she said, her eyes getting wet.

Sheila walked towards her and gazed outside.

"I want the same thing as well. My children are waiting for me. But for now, we have to follow Bernadette's instructions."

Violeta buried her face in Sheila's chest.

"Those people took me because Mummy didn't have money. Why did Mummy give me away? Didn't she love me?"

Sheila patted her back.

"Honestly, I don't know. Sometimes adults do stupid things when they're frustrated."

As they spoke, they could hear loud laughter and the voices of men as they came into the house.

"Bernadette, I hope your girls will show extraordinary service to us."

"My girls know how to please customers. They're here to satisfy all your needs and desires."

Daniela opened Sheila bedroom's door.

"Are you ready? Bernadette sent for you."

Sheila turned around and her eyes widened.

Daniela's eyelids were covered with green eye shadow. Her eyelashes had mascara on them, and her lips were colored with bright pink lipstick. Her dress showed off her figure, and just about revealed her breasts.

Poor girl. They turned her into a prostitute, and now she looks like one.

"Hey, I'm talking to you!"

"Oh, sorry. My mind was somewhere else."

Daniela's eyes were still red from crying. Seeing her sad hurt Sheila to the core. She wished that she could help this kid in some way, but she was powerless. The only thing she could do was to pray and hope.

They left the bedroom and walked to the sitting room, which was now crowded.

A blond-headed man was being entertained by Camille. Both sat on the sofa with drinks in their hands. The man was whispering something in her ear as she giggled.

"Oh, Christopher, you're too funny," said Camille.

Bernadette stood on the other side of the room, conversing with two men. She noticed Sheila and waved.

"Sheila, come here," she said.

"Stay here," Sheila told Violeta and Daniela.

As she started away, Victor entered the room. His eyes met Sheila's.

Upon seeing him, Violeta clutched Sheila's hand. "I'm coming with you."

They walked over to Bernadette. As they approached her, one of the men, John, eyed Sheila.

"You didn't tell me you had a gem in your place," he said.

"I keep a gem hidden for the generous customer," said Bernadette.

"What's your name?" asked John.

"My name isn't important."

John exposed his teeth and then looked at Violeta. "Who is this girl?"

Violeta began shaking nervously.

"She's a cousin of one of the girls," said Bernadette.

As Violeta's heart raced, she saw yellow lights flying before her eyes.

"Isn't she too young to be in here, exposed to all of this?"

Bernadette's face became serious.

"Her parents died, and her cousin brings her here in order not to leave her alone at home."

"Aww. I got it now. Is it okay if I spend some time with her? We'll just talk."

Violeta's face became pale.

"Are you okay?" asked Sheila, peering at her face.

Violeta suddenly passed out.

Victor ran towards her and lifted her up. Everyone paused to see what was happening.

He took her to the bedroom. Not trusting him, Sheila walked behind him. Once they were in the bedroom, he put Violeta on the bed.

"You can leave now. I'll look after her," said Sheila.

Her heart raced so fast, it seemed as if it was going to jump out of her chest.

"You can't stay with her all the time. There are customers waiting for you."

"As soon as she gets up, I'll come back," Sheila told him.

Without saying a word, he left.

Sheila gently shook Violeta's shoulder.

"Get up, child."

Violeta opened her eyes and stared at Sheila. At first her vision was blurry. She couldn't see Sheila's face clearly.

She slowly sat up.

"Where am I?"

"In our bedroom."

They heard a knock on the door. Violeta quickly lay down and closed her eyes.

Daniela entered and walked to the bed. She stared at Violeta.

"What happened to her?"

"Honestly, I don't know. Violeta, stop pretending."

Violeta sat up.

"Don't tell anyone that I'm awake, please."

"You foxy one. I won't," said Daniela.

A smile ran across Daniela's face. Violeta reminded her of her sister Andrea.

"But what happened to you?"

"He looked at me strangely and wanted to stay alone with me. I got frightened."

Violeta grasped Sheila's hand, sweating profusely.

"I want out of here, Aunty Sheila."

She embraced Sheila and began to cry.

"If I was alone with that man, he might do bad things to me."

Sheila patted her back.

"Stop crying. Everything will be fine."

"I forgot to tell you. Bernadette asked me to send you to Camille's bedroom," Daniela said.

"Why?"

"I don't know."

Sheila got up and looked at Daniela.

"You stay with Violeta, and I'll be back."

Violeta stood up.

"Please don't leave me."

"If I don't go, Victor will be back here again. So please get into your bed."

Violeta scrambled up into her bed and snuggled under the cover, turning onto her left side.

Sheila left the room and went to Camille's bedroom, which looked empty. On the chair, she found a black bag belonging to a man. Curious, she picked it up and went through its contents.

Between some papers she found a few cutouts from newspapers. She began reading them.

"A teenager of 14 years has been kidnapped after leaving school. The girl was seen getting into a black Mazda."

The picture of the girl caught her attention.

Oh my God! This is Daniela!

Suddenly she heard a cough behind her. She spun around, dropping the newspaper on the floor.

Right before her stood a tall man. He had a long beard, long brown hair, and green eyes.

"Oh, sorry. I didn't mean to interfere with your belongings. I'm not here for that." Sheila couldn't control her shaking.

"What are you here for?"

"To make you happy."

He looks quite handsome.

The man crossed his arms. His eyes looked cold.

"Do I look unhappy to you?"

"Not really, but I see a coldness in your eyes, and you sound too angry."

He picked up the newspaper from the floor and sat on the bed.

"How should I react? I caught you digging in my bag!"

"I was only checking who it belonged to."

His gaze softened.

"Come and sit next to me."

She stood motionless, looking at him uncertainly.

"Please come here. I don't bite."

She took a few steps and then sat at the edge of the bed. For some unknown reason, her cheeks burned and she felt uncomfortable.

He unbuttoned the two top buttons of his shirt. A sweet aroma of hibiscus mixed with jasmine wafted into her nose.

The scent of his cologne reminded her of home. In her own yard, she had a few hibiscuses growing that bore pinkish-reddish flowers. She inhaled deeply, enjoying the scent. Most men who she was forced to sleep with were too sweaty and smelled like a sewer or a dirty sock.

They sat for a moment looking at each other awkwardly. She gazed at him, studying his face. Dark circles and puffiness under his eyes were indications of sleepless nights. His blue shirt was ironed neatly and had a scent of corn starch.

She smiled.

"It looks like you haven't been getting enough sleep. Were you occupied with the Spanish ladies?"

He grinned, showing his white teeth, and got up laughing.

"No way. I have no time for that luxury."

"Then what are you doing in the brothel?"

He turned his back toward her and dug in his bag. As he did so, she took off her top and lay on the bed.

He faced Sheila and scanned her body with a frown on his face.

"You look appealing and quite cute," she said.

He picked up her top and threw it to her.

"Please hide your assets. They don't entice me. Not today."

A piece of newspaper was in his hand.

"I've met quite a few weird men here, but you're the strangest one," she said, putting on her top. She felt hurt. For the first time, she actually liked her customer, but he had rejected her.

"I can feel your disappointment, but I'm not here for sex."

"What was your purpose of coming into this horrid place?"

He looked at the door.

"I traveled all the way here from Romania looking for a teenage girl. Two years ago, a 14-year-old girl got snatched after leaving school. Her father came to my agency and hired me to find her."

Sheila's eyes widened. "Are you a detective?"

"Yes, I am."

He gave her the newspaper.

"Please take a look at this. Do you recognize her?"

Sheila gazed at it with a big smile.

"This is our Daniela. She was outside with the others. Didn't you see her?"

He got up and put away the newspaper.

"Are you sure that's her?"

"Hundred percent."

They heard steps approaching the door. Sheila grasped his hand.

"We must pretend to be having sex. Victor is coming to check on us."

She took off her top and he his shirt. Then she lay on the bed. He lay next to her.

"Hug me," she said.

He cuddled her. Her heart raced, and blood hit her brain. She felt so good next to this man.

The steps stopped.

"He's by the door. Kiss me."

Victor crept to the door and opened it slightly. He peeked inside and, seeing the couple kissing, he closed the door again.

"I think he left," whispered Sheila.

He sat up. Sheila got a good look at his six-pack abs and muscular body.

She got up also. The man put on his shirt and then buttoned it. He gazed silently at Sheila. The coldness that had been in his eyes before had melted. Now his eyes were kind as he smiled.

"I must say, for a woman in a brothel you have really soft lips and a clean body."

Sheila's eyebrows came together.

"Women in a brothel are no different from others. I don't see a need for comparison."

"Pardon me. I didn't mean anything bad."

He gestured toward the door.

"Who is that guy? Why are you afraid of him?"

"He's Bernadette's lover or puppet, and a cruel man. He forces the women to have sex with him."

"Doesn't she know about this?"

Sheila shrugged her shoulders.

"I'm not sure. But with her love and greed for money, she probably looks the other way."

He picked up his bag.

"By the way, I'm Adrian. And you?"

Once again, a smile lit up her face.

"I'm Sheila."

"I have to leave now. But after some thought and planning, I will be back to rescue Daniela."

He began walking away.

"Wait! Please!"

He turned around to see Sheila's eyes tearing up.

"I was forcibly brought here a few months ago. There's also a 12-year-old girl. Can you please help us to get out as well? My husband will reward you."

He paused and eyed her.

"Three instead of one is kind of a tough task. I'll think about it. However, be ready."

"Thank you."

"No need to thank me. I'm not promising anything."

He hung the strap of the bag over his shoulder and left.

Sheila walked out of Camille's bedroom. She felt so light and joyful that she forgot about Bernadette and Victor. With a spring in her step, she walked to her bedroom, overwhelmed with happy thoughts.

When I was ready to give up, the Lord gave me hope.

Oh, yes, I'm going to see my children soon. I can't believe it!

As soon as Gail was admitted to the hospital, she was hooked up to IV fluids and given antibiotics. She was put in a huge grey-colored room that had about twenty more beds, most of them occupied by other patients. Her doctor, Darion Ramkissoon, ordered a few tests, including a CBC blood test, as well as an ultrasound to properly diagnose her condition.

The next morning Dr. Ramkissoon stood by Gail's bed, the results in his hands. Gail was sound asleep. As he read them to Chelsea, she stood listening silently.

"Mrs. Singh, your daughter was admitted to the hospital with dehydration and a high fever. We've managed to lower her fever. However, her body is still fighting an infection. I went ahead and ordered a complete blood test, as well as an ultrasound. I'm not happy with the results."

Chelsea looked down at Gail, feeling dizzy.

"Is she in danger?"

"Not at this moment. Has your daughter been sexually active?"

A frown formed on Chelsea's face.

"No. I brought up my child with values and morals."

"Your daughter's hymen is broken. To be precise, it's stretched, and there is also a smelly vaginal discharge. Usually the hymen is stretched if there's sexual activity. Usage of tampons can break it as well. Did she use any?"

Chelsea began feeling as if someone was squeezing her brain.

"I don't understand what's going on."

"Further tests, as well as bloodwork, showed that your daughter has an endometritis and septicemia."

Chelsea sat on Gail's bed, feeling hot.

"Mrs. Singh, are you alright?"

Chelsea's lips became pale.

"This is too much for me to digest. What is endometritis and septicemia?"

"Endometritis is an infection of the lining of the uterus, as well as the genital tract. And septicemia is a serious bloodstream infection."

"How did she get that?"

"I don't have any idea. One of the reasons for endometritis is usually abortion. It can also be transmitted by a partner. It looks like bacteria got into the bloodstream, causing septicemia.

Chelsea's eyes narrowed as she gazed at her daughter. She slowly got up.

Why did this happen to my child? Did he really rape her and then force her to get an abortion?

A tall nurse approached them. She had a tray in her hands that had a syringe on it.

"How is the patient doing today?" she asked.

"She's out of danger but fighting a serious infection."

"I'm sure that with your good care she will be on the mend soon."

The nurse went over to the IV pole and injected the antibiotic into the bag through the centre of the injection port. She put the syringe back onto the tray and looked at the doctor.

"Dr. Ramkissoon, the patients in Ward B are waiting for you."

"Thanks. I'll be there shortly."

The nurse walked away.

"When can she go home?" Chelsea asked him.

"We'll keep her for four days. Once her condition improves, she'll be able to go home."

The doctor's cell rang.

"Darion here. Okay, I'll be there in five minutes."

He put away his cell phone and looked at Chelsea.

"I have to attend patients in other wards."

"Thank you, Doctor," said Chelsea.

The doctor walked away, and Chelsea was left alone. She regarded her daughter in silence. Her eyes filled with tears.

Someone suddenly cried out, "Oh, Jesus, take away my pain! It is unbearable!"

Chelsea moved away from the bed and looked in the direction of the voice.

"The judgment day is coming! The wicked will be punished. The good ones rewarded!"

A moment later: "Worship and praise the Lord. Turn away from your evil ways before it's too late!"

Other patients sat up in their beds. One of them shook her head in annoyance.

Two nurses ran to the end of the room, passing Chelsea. She followed them.

The nurses stopped at a bed where a dark-skinned woman lay. Her left leg was bandaged, and there were spots of blood on it. Her uncombed hair was curly and long. She was trembling, rubbing her arms as if feeling cold.

One of the nurses covered her and said, "Calm down. You're disturbing the other patients."

Instead, the patient sat up and looked at Chelsea.

"The wicked one will burn in Hell. Turn your hearts to the Lord. Repent and change before it's too late. Get rid of the evil in you."

She lay back down, and a grimace appeared on her face.

"Oh Lord I beg you, end my suffering."

"Who is she?" asked Chelsea.

"She's a vagrant who lives on the streets," said the nurse.

"What happened to she?"

"No one knows. A good Samaritan found her walking down the street and bleeding. He called the police and they brought her here."

The patient writhed, then sat up again.

"Lord Jesus Christ, son of God, have mercy on me, a sinner!"

The nurse injected her with a relaxer.

"Okay. Behave. Be a good girl."

The woman in the bed raised her head and again stared intently at Chelsea.

"Don't believe in lies. Evil is working against you. Pray and fast a lot. The snake is around you."

Chelsea shook her head.

They bring everyone into hospitals. She should be in the mad house, not here.

The woman closed her eyes and became quiet. Chelsea walked back to her daughter's bed.

Gail was awake. She gazed at her mom.

"Mummy, where am I?"

"You're in the hospital."

"What am I doing in here?"

She raised her body up slightly, but lay back down, feeling weak.

"Don't you remember anything?"

"No."

"You were burning with fever. I tried to reduce it with medication, but it didn't work. So, we brought you here."

At Gail's bewildered look, Chelsea asked, "Don't you remember anything at all? You were saying strange things."

Gail again tried to sit up, a frown on her face.

"What I have been saying?"

Chelsea looked at her watch.

"Why don't you rest now. We'll talk about it tomorrow."

She approached her daughter and kissed her forehead.
"Don't worry about anything. Okay? I'll be back later."
Gail closed her eyes. "Okay, Mother."
Chelsea walked away.

When she reached home, Anil was lying on the sofa, a cell phone in one hand and a bottle of beer in the other. He was watching a movie on his phone. As soon as she came in, Anil sat up.

"Where have you been? I got up this morning and didn't see you."

Chelsea shook her head.

"Stop liming at nights, getting drunk, and you'll be able to wake up early and see what happens. Why aren't you at work?"

"Me eh feeling so good nah. I getting ah headache."

Chelsea sat on a chair.

"Did anyone push alcohol into your mouth?"

"Shut up, woman. Always talking too much."

He took a sip of beer.

For a moment she stared at him, her eyes narrowed.

Did he touch her? I'll chop him up if he did.

"Why are you watching me so?"

"I went to the hospital, and they told me that Gail got an infection that was caused either by an abortion or intercourse. Did you interfere with my child?"

"What the hell are you talking about? Do I look like a child molester?"

His left eyelid twitched, and his heart raced. He tried to stay calm and collected.

"She kept saying that you raped her, and she had an abortion. Why would she say that?"

Anil got up and walked to the table. He set the bottle of beer on it.

"Woman, you really dotish. The gyul had a fever and spoke rubbish. You should know better."

She got up from her seat and walked towards him. Before he could move, she grabbed his groin.

"If I find out that you touched her, I'll cut the things between your legs off!"

She walked away, leaving Anil alone. He rubbed his forehead.

She's going to find out sooner or later. What should I do?

He lit a cigarette and sat at the table. His hands trembled as he smoked.

22nd February

Carnival was coming soon, and women were crowding into the gyms, aiming to flatten their bellies and shed some weight for the two-day Carnival parade. Some even tried to firm up and enlarge their bottoms by doing squats, in order to look sexy in their Carnival costumes.

They bought expensive outfits and attended carnival parties called FETE. Even though costumes were costly, women didn't care about the price. They couldn't miss out on taking part in a fun activity where they could be themselves- free in spirit and body, and feeling beautiful as well as sexy and wild!

Although Candice wasn't fat, long before Carnival she became serious about fitness. At least three times a week, she was seen in the gym lifting weights and running on a treadmill.

So, one mid-morning she was in the gym walking on the treadmill in shorts and a light top. She was chatting with her friend Nia.

"Did you get your Carnival costume yet?" Candice asked.

"Yep." Nia paused her treadmill and took out a cell phone from her pocket. She searched through the pictures and chose the one in which she posed, wearing her Carnival costume.

"Here it is."

Candice stopped her treadmill and stared at the picture.

Nia was wearing a red costume, which consisted of a bra and panties, with a lot of sequins on them. On her face she had a nice silver mask, covered with red and silver sequins. Her headpiece was made of red feathers.

"Wow! It's so beautiful! How much did you pay for it?"

Nia put away her cell.

"Don't even ask, gyul. Ten thousand."

Candice's eyes widened.

"Wow! You must be insane!"

"Carnival makes me feel alive, wild, sexy, and sometimes horny. Just for this, I don't mind spending the money. Didn't you get yours?"

"Not as yet."

"Gyul carnival is next week. Why are you taking so long?"

"I've been very busy. Didn't get a chance to look for any," Candice lied. She put on a headset and started her treadmill up again; hopefully, listening to music would keep Nia from digging further into her business.

While Candice was talking to Nia, Terrel was parking his Nissan Almira four buildings away from the Lucky Man rum shop. He slid it between two cars, then sat there a while, smoking. Then he watched a video on his phone.

On the video Zane, the owner of the Lucky Man Rum Shop, as well as a member of the governmental party, was lying on a bed naked. His lover sat on top of him. He rubbed her bottom as she moved rhythmically.

Terrel paused the video, and then sent it via text to Zane's cell number. He blew out smoke as he fixed his attention on his cell's screen, expecting a call at any time.

Two blue ticks appeared by his video. Zane had seen the

message. In a few minutes Terrel's cell phone rang.

"Who are you and how did you get that video?"

"I'm someone who knows everything about you and your lover, Luciana. I also have many pictures of you with she."

A few drops of sweat rolled down Zane's face. "What do you want?"

"I need some cash."

Zane took out his handkerchief from a pocket and wiped his face. His hands were trembling.

"How much?"

Terrel looked over at the rum shop. "Fifteen thousand. I need it now!"

Zane stood up. He picked up a bottle of rum from his chest of drawers and poured some in a glass.

"That's a lot. I can't get it right away."

Terrel threw his cigarette butt outside.

"Listen, I'm giving you ten minutes. Put the cash in a grocery bag and then drop it in the garbage bin outside the bar. If you call the police, the video will be sent to your wife and your party's chairman right away."

Terrel ended the call without allowing Zane to say a word.

Shuddering and pale as a ghost, Zane walked to a safe that was built in the wall. He moved the knob to certain figures and then opened its door. There lay documents, and on top of them, money.

Zane took out the money and counted it. When he reached fifteen thousand, he put the rest of the cash back. He found a grocery bag in a drawer and put the cash in it. Then he walked over to a window. He moved the curtain slightly to look outside.

Next he walked outside. He looked around but didn't notice anyone suspicious. As soon as he put the money in the garbage bin, his phone rang.

"How much did you put in the bin?"

"Fifteen thousand," Zane said irritably. He glanced at the street again.

"Go inside and stay there."

Zane returned to his office. He sat at his desk and looked at the video again.

Damn it! I should be more careful. If anyone finds out, my political career and my marriage will go down the drain.

Terrel put a hoodie over his head and donned dark sunglasses. He quickly got out of his car and walked towards the rum shop. As he got closer, he glanced around the area and then walked to the garbage bin. He took the bag out of it and returned to his car. There, he put the bag into his trunk and drove to meet Candice.

"He's so dumb. That's was so easy," he chuckled to himself. He turned on his music player and listened to rap, nodding his head slightly to a tune.

Terrel parked by the gym and walked in. Seeing his girlfriend and Nia, he headed towards the treadmills.

"Hey Nia, long time no see, gyul," he said.

She got off the treadmill and hugged him.

"I was thinking about you only yesterday," she said.

She eyed him.

"Are you coming out on Carnival Monday and Tuesday?"

Terrel turned to Candice and embraced, then kissed her.

"Yes, we are. My hot girl doesn't want to miss out on anything."

"Then you should come with me to Fete75 at Marcelo Hill. I have two extra tickets."

"What's the cost for one?" asked Candice.

"Six hundred."

Terrel whistled.

"So expensive," he said.

---

[75] Carnival Party

Nia grimaced. "It's all inclusive, and Andrea Parlo is going to perform."

Terrel took some money out of his pocket. He counted out and gave her twelve hundred.

Wrinkles ran across Candice's forehead as Nia took the money from him.

Where did he get cash from?

"Wait here. I'll be back," said Nia. She walked outside to her car and then came back with the tickets.

"Here they are."

Terrel took the tickets from her. "Thanks."

He looked at his watch.

"We must go. See you later, Nia," he said.

"I'll call you later, chick," Nia told Candice with a smile.

Candice and Terrel left the gym. Candice got into the car on the passenger side.

Terrel took the bag out of the trunk and then got in behind the wheel. As he started the Nissan's engine, he dropped the bag onto Candice's lap.

"What is this?"

"Cash, gyul."

"Where did you get it from?"

His face lit up as he smiled. "I won the lottery."

"You lie. Did you rob the Chinese man?"

"No. Just take the money and stop with the questions."

Her eyebrows knitted, and her eyes ran from the money to him.

"Open the bag nah, before I change my mind."

She quickly did what he told her and took out the money. With a gasp, she started to count it.

"Wow. It's a huge amount. How did you get it?"

"Oh, gyul. You wouldn't leave meh alone. Do you remember that fat man, Zane? At some point he was flirting with you."

Wrinkles became visible on her forehead. "Not really."

"The one who runs the Lucky Man Rum Shop."

"Oh yes."

"He's been horning his wife, and I got some pictures and videos of him with his chick. I blackmailed him, and he paid me to keep my mouth shut."

"Hmm. I heard he's a crazy fellow. If you push him a lot, you might pay dearly."

Terrel grimaced.

"He couldn't even hurt a fly."

Candice put the money back in the bag.

"You don't know what people are capable of when they're pushed into a corner or threatened."

"Just forget him. We're going to go get our carnival costumes."

"Boy, sometimes you surprise me."

After driving for about thirty minutes, they arrived at a building that housed a costume shop. Terrel parked in front of the two-story brick house.

Christian, a costume designer, lived at the top of the house with his wife, but he used the ground floor as a workstation to make costumes, as well as to display them. He was not only a costume designer but also the leader of the Extreme Masquerade band. Every year he and his wife, Sarika, made carnival suits for his band. Those who wanted to be part of the band paid handsomely for his costumes.

Every year, his band performed before the judges. Year by year, his band kept growing. From four hundred original members, it grew to three thousand. For two consecutive years, Extreme Masquerade had come in first for the best costumes.

Terrel and Candice got out of the car and stood before the iron door. Candice rang the bell, and it was opened by an employee. They went inside.

Candice noticed a TV screen on the wall. Not surprisingly, it was a security monitor; she saw herself and

Terrel in it.

Carnival suits were displayed near the walls. She walked towards the costumes and admired them. All of the costumes had the same style and colors. The women's costumes consisted of feathered headpieces, feathered backpieces, embellished bras and panties, and feathered leg bands.

Sarika, a tall woman with purple hair, bustled into the display room.

"Good day. How can I help you?"

"We would like to get costumes for both of us," said Terrel.

"What size are you looking for?"

"I wear 34 C in bra and medium size in panties," said Candice.

Sarika glanced at Terrel.

"What about you?"

"I wear medium size."

Sarika walked to the display, which consisted of a rod on which costumes hung, and shelves where headpieces as well as feather leg bands were displayed.

She pulled out a hanger with a bra and panties.

"Would you like to try it on?"

"Sure."

Sarika passed the items to her, along with a headpiece and leg bands, then led her to the changing room and opened the door.

Candice walked in.

While Candice was busy, Sarika handed a pair of purple shorts with a belt, legwear, and a feathered headpiece to Terrel.

"The changing room is next to hers," she said.

Terrel went to try on his costume also.

Candice came out of the changing room wearing the full outfit. She walked towards the mirror and admired her costume.

Her bra and panties were blue and covered with silver sequins. The bra exposed the top half of her breasts. Purple beads hung at the edge of the bra. She wore a headpiece that consisted of long purple and blue feathers. On her hands were purple bands covered with silver and purple sequins.

"Is it fitting you good?" asked Sarika.

"Yes, it is. Can I try on the backpiece?"

"Sure."

Sarika gave her the item. Candice put on the backpiece, which looked like angel's wings covered with purple and blue feathers.

"You look like a model from a magazine," said Sarika.

Candice smiled at her reflection. *Miguel should see me in this. He wouldn't be able to resist my charms.*

Terrel came out of the changing room. He wore tight purple shorts that outlined his manhood. On his waist he had a wide belt that glittered with sequins. On his hand he wore a handpiece similar to Candice's. His headpiece had short feathers.

He paused and gaped at Candice. His eyes ran from her face to her firm round breasts, then to her toned-up abs. They stopped on the panties.

He whistled loudly.

"Babe you look sooo sexy. I could eat you up."

He looked over at Sarika.

"We're taking them," he said.

"You both look so gorgeous. I'm sure the eyes of the entire crowd will be on you."

"How much for all of this?"

"Five thousand five hundred for the women's costume, and four thousand five hundred for the men's. That'll be ten thousand."

"The price is too high. Last time I paid three thousand," said Candice.

"We import our materials from overseas. They're costly. That's why the prices are high."

"We'll take them," Terrel told Sarika. To Candice he said,

rather reluctantly, "Go and change, babe."

With a huge grin on her face, Candice rushed into the changing room.

Terrel changed into his old clothes and went back to his car to get the money. By the time he came back, Sarika had put everything in big bags. She also gave Candice a piece of paper.

"This is a map of the road that we will be marching on. We'll start from Harvey Street and end in Nape's Stadium. So please be on time and follow all instructions."

Terrel gave her money. Sarika counted the cash and put it away.

"Thank you for your purchase, and for being part of our band."

"You're welcome," said Candice, and they left the shop.

While Candice and Terrel were busy with purchasing Carnival costumes Miguel, wearing a black pullover hoodie sweatshirt, parked not far from Kingpin's house, which was at a dead end. From there, he could see an empty, bushy plot. He put on dark shades and gloves. Then he put his gun in his pocket and picked up a plastic bag from another seat.

He got out of his car and pulled the hood over his head.

The houses on Kingpin's street had been constructed in such a way that the ones on the right had a street running behind them. However, the area beyond the houses on the left-hand side was full of wild trees and overgrown grass. Beyond the trees was a highway, hidden by the foliage.

Miguel checked the area out with a sweeping glance, then walked into the bushy area.

As he passed the second house, he stepped on an ant's nest. The biting ants crawled up his pants, and even got into his sneaker. They bit him everywhere, forcing Miguel to shake out his pants. He took off his sneaker and shook it as well. He brushed off the ants and then put his sneaker back on.

"Stupid ants."

He continued to walk, even though his foot and leg scratched and burned, and finally got to the back of Kingpin's six-foot-high wall. Kingpin's dogs, sensing him, began barking and trying to jump over the wall.

Miguel knew that Kingpin had two Rottweilers in his yard, so he had come prepared. Forgetting about the ants, he took some sandwiches from the plastic bag he had brought and threw them into the yard.

He had inserted tablets into the sandwiches. The dogs sniffed, then ate them. Miguel waited for ten more minutes, and then he pulled himself up onto the wall's edge.

Why is it so much harder to catch a wealthy man than a poor one?

For a long while, his men had been monitoring Kingpin's activities, but they hadn't been able find anything that could incriminate him. The last time port authorities had found drugs in one of his containers, he had been able to get away; his brother had taken the blame and had been jailed instead.

If only I had a little evidence, I could put him away for good.

Miguel believed that Kingpin was one of the culprits behind his wife's kidnaping and killing. On sleepless nights, Miguel caught himself thinking about his wife's gruesome death, and imagining Kingpin choking his wife and then dousing her with gasoline. At those moments he had a strong desire to throttle Kingpin with his bare hands or to beat him until he bled to death. But he wasn't sure if Kingpin had killed her himself or had hired someone else to do his dirty work.

Not having answers, and the need for closure, had pushed him to Kingpin's house.

Miguel jumped over the wall and landed on both feet, right in front of one of Kingpin's Rottweilers. He moved backwards with caution, but the dog lay there barely keeping its eyes open. Miguel looked at one of the other dogs. It was also motionless, its saliva puddling on the grass.

Miguel grinned.

I'm so damn good at this!

He found himself directly behind Kingpin's mansion. It was a massive one-story cream-colored building, with bars on the windows.

He shook his head.

How am I going to get in? I should have brought some tools.

On the wall by the door he noticed a camera. He tried to avoid its direction and crept to a window.

He peered in and saw an aged woman. She stood by the sink washing dishes; her head twitched involuntary, and Miguel recognized the symptoms of Tourette's syndrome.

Miguel's eyes scanned the whole kitchen suspiciously. It was painted in an orange color, and the counters were made of cream-colored granite. The wall by the counter had tiles as well. There was a stainless-steel fridge and a stove. On a burner sat a big pot, and on the counter were piles of corn and potatoes, cut into small pieces.

The lady turned off the water and threw the potatoes into the boiling water.

With an eye on the camera, Miguel walked to the kitchen door. He slowly pulled down the handle.

The door was locked. He walked along the side of the house, looking for another way to get inside. He passed by a deep, rectangular pool, flanked by a path of sandstone tiles. There was a glass door leading outside, and he headed towards it. He pulled down the handle, but it was locked as well.

He crept to the front part of the house. Two huge golden lions stood at the entrance leading down the path to the door.

There were two doors. The outside one was made of wrought iron bars, with a beautiful carving of leaves. It was painted in a bronze shade. The door behind it was a steel door, with a small glass window in the middle.

Miguel looked at the doors.

There's no way I can get in.

He heard the sound of a woman mumbling somewhere behind him. He slowly headed towards the sound and came across the same old lady. This time she stood outside with a huge net, trying to clear leaves out of the pool. Her back faced him.

He immediately returned to the front part of the house and walked to the back from the other side. He was so relieved to see the kitchen's door wide open that he dashed in without delay.

The smell of corn soup circulated in the air, making him inhale deeply. It was his favorite meal.

The lady returned to the kitchen.

"Where did Rayad go? He should be removing the leaves," she complained to herself. "Oh, Lord, can't I rest at my old age?"

Hearing her voice, Miguel tiptoed to a closed door. He opened it and slinked inside.

It was a huge bedroom, with a master bed that had a golden bed covering and golden cushions. A flat-screen TV hung opposite the bed, and a cream-brown leather sofa stood against a wall. The room also had a fridge, as well as a dressing table and a chest of drawers.

The man grew up in a ghetto and now lives like a king. Drug money for sure.

Unbeknownst to him, there was also a small camera that blended with other small light bulbs. Miguel failed to notice it.

He opened the first drawer in the chest of drawers and began checking it. There, neatly folded, lay Kingpin's underpants. Miguel looked between them, trying not to mess up the clothes.

His hand touched something. He grabbed it and pulled out his hand.

It was a pack of condoms.

He put it back. Then he checked the second drawer,

which was packed with vests and handkerchiefs. Not finding anything, Miguel moved to the third drawer, which was filled with socks.

He gazed around again and walked to the closet. He opened the door and looked into a large walk-in area. There was a shoe stand with shoes on them, and a row of suits, jeans, pants, and shirts. Miguel began checking through the suits, moving them aside as he did so.

The persistent sound of a car horn reached Miguel's ears, causing him to flinch. He came out of the closet and rushed to the window.

A car was entering the gate. The old woman stood not far from it.

Miguel quickly left the bedroom and ran into the kitchen. He opened the door and dashed to the wall.

The dogs were awake, but still woozy. They blinked at Miguel and then began barking.

Miguel ran towards the wall. He climbed over and fell on the other side, this time hurting his foot. He limped away, and as soon as he was in his car, he sped off.

PAYBACK TIME

On Saturday, two days before Carnival, loud music played on Marcello Hill at around 7 p.m. The whole hill was crowded with people. Everyone had come out dressed in fancy clothes. Many were wearing either shorts or short dresses, as well as skirts with sexy blouses. Some danced, others talked with each other, and the rest lined up either to get drinks or food.

There were a few stalls that offered an alcoholic and soft drinks. The patrons were treated to a variety of dishes such as callaloo, saltfish, mini roti, doubles, rice and peas, sautéed cassava, cornmeal dumplings, corn soup, and stewed chicken.

A white Nissan turned in and parked in the parking lot of Marcello Hill. Terrel and Candice got out of the car. Terrel wore a red short-sleeved shirt, black pants, and black shoes. This time he created an image of decency; his pants were pulled up all the way to his waist. Candice had on a shiny gold dress that stopped six inches above her knees and gold shoes with high heels.

Candice stared at the hill.

"How I hate climbing hills in these shoes," she said.

"Who told you to wear them?"

Terrel ogled two women walking ahead of them. Both wore black skirts, and red blouses that revealed their breasts. One of them in particular caught Terrel's attention.

He stared at her legs.

She legs bigger than elephant and the ass moving from side to side like a boxing bag. What dis woman has been eating?

As they passed them, Terrel gifted them with a smile.

"Good evening, ladies."

They returned his smile. "Good evening."

They continued going up. As they climbed the hill, they gazed around.

"What can I get for you?" he asked, once they'd reached the top of the hill.

"Tequila," said Candice, forgetting about her pregnancy.

"Are you trying to kill my child?"

"Oh, sorry. I kind of forgot. I still can't get accustomed to the idea of being pregnant."

"It's because your mind is always occupied with rubbish."

"Just leave it and get me any soft drink," she said in a raised voice.

He grabbed her bottom.

"I like when you get angry. It makes me horny."

She pushed his hand away.

"Stop it! People are around."

Terrel looked at the crowd gathered by the drink booth.

"Oh, boy. So many of them there. You wait here."

He walked away and joined the line. As Candice waited alone, she looked through the crowd, trying to find anyone she knew.

She noticed Nia and walked towards her.

Nia stood before a tall Caucasian man, a drink in her hand, and she smiled as they "wined." Music played loudly.

"Hi, Nia. I see you're having a good time."

Nia stopped rubbing her bottom on her man's pelvic area and gave her attention to Candice.

"Hey chick, you made it!"

She gazed behind Candice, trying to see Terrel.

"Are you alone?"

"Nope. Terrel is here."

Nia looked around. "I don't see him."

"He went for a drink."

"Oh. By the way, this is Oliver. He's from England."

Candice looked at him.

This girl melts for a white man.

"Hi, Oliver. Nice to meet you."

"Nice to meet you too."

"What brought you to the Caribbean?"

"Carnival and beautiful women." He glanced at Nia.

"You have nothing to worry about."

Candice heard a man talking behind her. The voice sounded familiar.

"No, the problem has been resolved."

Candice turned around, and before her stood Toothless himself. Candice dropped her cell phone as her heart raced and her lips lost its pinkish color.

Toothless stared into her eyes.

"I'll talk to you later," said Toothless to his friend.

He walked to Candice as he bestowed a smile at Nia and Oliver. "Blessed evening, all."

"Good evening," answered Nia, clutching the arm of her new boyfriend.

"Candice, can I talk to you privately?" he asked.

She stood motionless for a moment. With reluctance, she answered him. "Sure."

"Why don't we go and get something to drink first?" suggested Toothless.

"Nia, we'll talk later," said Candice, fixing a false smile on her face.

Toothless and Candice walked away.

"You look hot today," said Toothless, eying her figure.

"What do you want from me?" she said, as they passed a crowd of people.

Toothless looked sidelong at them.

"This isn't a good place to talk. Let's walk behind the toilet," he suggested.

Candice's legs became heavy and weak. She paused and looked hesitantly at the building. She didn't want to go anywhere with him, because she knew that he and his kind were capable of anything. But at the same time, she was afraid that Miguel might see them together.

"Why are you stopping? Keep moving."

She continued her walk. Toothless strolled behind her as they went around the corner of the toilet.

The area was dark. With every step, Candice was becoming more fearful. Her eyelid kept twitching. They stopped behind the toilet, and Toothless peered around the area. They were totally alone.

"Where's my money?" asked Toothless.

"I tried to get it. But right now, my purse is empty. You might have to wait a week or two."

Toothless pushed Candice to the wall and pinned her to it with both of his hands. He was so close that Candice could smell the mixture of alcohol and cigarettes on his breath. He gazed at her eyes for a moment and tried to kiss her lips.

She hit his groin with her knee. Then she pushed him.

"You idiot! Don't you dare touch me!" she said and spat on the ground.

He looked around and then pulled a penknife from his pocket. He pushed her to the wall again and, while keeping her pinned, he put the knife to her neck. As she looked at him, breathing heavily, they heard women's voices. He let her go and put the knife away.

"If I don't get my money by the end of Wednesday, I'll make a call to Miguel. Either that, or you might end up like the woman that I killed. By the way, I saw him here."

"What? He didn't tell me anything about coming here."

"I think he's just on duty. He was in his uniform," lied Toothless, trying to play on her nerves.

Candice looked down sharply at the tattoo. She had left it uncovered for the evening.

Oh! He might see it. First this idiot, and now Miguel. Things couldn't get any better.

"He can't see us together. Once I get your money, I'll call you. Meanwhile, don't come near me at all. You'll lead the police to me."

"Make sure I get my cash by Wednesday."

Candice began walking away.

Nine thousand is a huge amount. Where will I get it?

She noticed Terrel. He was walking away, looking for her in the crowd.

She rushed towards him.

"Terrel!"

He paused and turned around with a serious look on his face.

"I've been looking for you all over. Where the hell have you been?"

She squeezed a smile out of herself.

"I felt nauseous, so I ran to the toilet. Oh, boy, the line was so long. I almost pissed myself."

"You should wait for me and then go."

"Are you kidding? With this pregnancy, I pee often. I can't keep it in."

"Oh, sorry. I didn't think about that. Here's your drink."

She took a plastic cup from him. It was orange juice.

Couldn't he have gotten something better?

A speaker crackled into life.

"Good evening, everyone. Are you having a good time?"

"Yes, we are!" answered the crowed.

"Please welcome Andrea Parlo!"

"Let's go and see her performance," said Candice.

They walked toward the mob and found some space between other people.

Andrea Parlo walked onto the stage. She had long blond hair, and big breasts that were ready to pop out of her tight, laced black top. Her shorts were white. On her feet she wore black boots.

"Good evening! Are you enjoying yourselves?"

"Yes!" roared the crowd.

Andrea put her hand in the air.

"Good! Put your hands in the air and wave!"

The background music started playing as she sang:

I like fete and bacchanal,
I'm ready for the carnival.
I painted my long nails,
and put on a red mini dress.
I'm going out, to impress!
I'm only after a wealthy sugar papi,
to buy me house and car.
Spend lots of money on me,
and take me away far.
I like fete and bacchanal.
I'm ready for carnival!

As Andrea sang, some women moved their bottoms in circular movements, rubbing them on their partners' groins.

Candice moved to the music.

I could do with a sugar daddy. He could give me nine thousand.

As she danced on the highest part of the hill, she noticed two police officers passing. She stared intently.

"Oh, shit! It's Miguel!"

Her heart pounded so fast that for a moment she felt out of breath. As he came closer, though, she realized that it wasn't him after all, and practically fainted from relief.

She quickly turned away from the man who she had mistaken for Miguel. She hugged Terrel and kissed him on the lips. Terrel embraced her, and their lips sealed.

He paused and looked into her eyes.

"Gyul, a few days ago you were cold when I touched you. Now you're trying to seduce me--and in public?!"

She kissed him again.

"Just shut up and enjoy the moment," she said.

Then she moved away from him and looked around. The man who resembled Miguel was far away from them.

Phew. He didn't see me. I should leave before Miguel actually does show up.

She came up closer to Terrel and whispered into his ear.

"I feel horny. Why don't we book a hotel and have some wild sex?"

"Hmm. Tempting. But we paid so much to be here."

"Okay then, forget it," she said irritably.

She moved away from him and began dancing. Terrel's eyes ran from her breasts to her legs. Knowing that he was watching her, she purposely wined, moving her bottom in circular movements.

Terrel emptied his drink in one gulp. He walked towards her.

"Hell with the party. Let's go."

They walked away from the crowd and the noise.

At around 8 a.m., on Sunday, Elisa lay on her bed, chatting with a friend over the phone.

"Did you hear Nigel left his wife for some trash?" said her friend.

Elisa sat up, yawning.

"Really? I thought they were so madly in love with each other."

"Gyul, these days everyone in public act differently, hiding their issues. They tend to create a false image. The whole street knows Nigel horns she. I don't know who she tries to fool by pretending to have a happy relationship."

Elisa yawned again.

"What happened to you, gyul? Whenever we talk, you yawn as if you bored."

If you didn't call me so early, I wouldn't yawn.

"I'm too tired. Since Sheila's been gone, I've been looking after the grandchildren. It drains all my energy."

"Yes, I know the feeling. My sister-in-law leaves Sasha with me when she goes to lime with she friends. She could afford babysitter."

Nadia entered her granny's bedroom. She wore a green blouse with puffed sleeves, a green tutu skirt, and colorful leggings. All had red embroidery. She held a wig--a mixture of short, curly, red and green hair.

"Granny, I can't put on the wig. It's tight."

"I have to go," said Elisa, and she put down the phone.

This woman always macoing[76] other people's business when in she own house is bacchanal. Who knows what she says about me?

"Come closer, child."

Nadia came up to her granny. Elisa put Nadia's hair into a ponytail and made a bun. Then she helped her to put on the wig.

"What is Daddy doing?" Elisa asked her.

"He's talking on the phone."

Elisa stood up and walked to the living room with Nadia.

Ronnel sat on the sofa watching a movie. He wore a white sailor costume—long pants, a short-sleeved pullover shirt, a blue tie, and a hat.

Elisa looked at him seriously. "Turn off the TV. It's too early for it."

"Granny, I'm watching cartoons."

"I said turn it off!"

---

[76] Minding

Ronnel got off the sofa and picked up the remote control from the coffee table. He turned off the TV.

"You look like a real sailor," said Elisa.

Ronnel pouted, and his face became sullen.

Miguel came into the living room. "Hurry up, everyone, or you'll miss the parade."

"Just give us five more minutes," Elisa replied.

"I'll wait for you outside," said Miguel.

He walked out and headed to his car.

As he started the engine, the radio came on. His wedding song was playing, and a host of memories played in his mind.

He recalled how he met Sheila in the police station. Her car had been towed for parking in a no-parking area. On that day she had come to the police station to pay the fine to get her car back. He was the one who she had gone to in the station.

Miguel lit his cigarette. The song brought to mind the memory of their marriage ceremony. He could clearly see walking to the altar with his wife, who he loved dearly at that time.

We were so madly in love with each other. Why did things change? I should have never met Candice.

Regret crawled deep down his soul. He felt abhorred at his cheating behavior. He couldn't comprehend how he was able to look at another woman other than his wife.

Miguel threw away his cigarette and blew the horn. A moment later, Elisa hurried out with the grandchildren. Seeing them, Miguel got out of the car with his cellphone in his hand.

"Stand together. Let me take your picture."

Everyone stood next to each other. As Miguel regarded his children, he felt at peace.

"Give me a winning smile," he said.

They smiled, trying not to blink. Miguel took a few pictures. Then he took a selfie with both his kids. Right away he put the picture as his profile photo on Messenger.

"Okay, let's get going now."

They took their seats in the car and Miguel drove to Pedro Street.

The place was crowded with adults and their children, so Miguel parked a few blocks away. Some came to see the carnival parade, and others to take part in it.

Miguel and his family got out and walked for a bit.

Parents and carnival organizers lined up the children according to their groups and costumes. Miguel stayed in the group of children wearing clown costumes like his daughter. Elisa joined the group of sailors.

In front of the parade participants were two vehicles: a pickup truck that played loud music, and an ambulance. Both began moving, and one by one each group paraded behind them, moving to the music.

The group of clowns marched first. Children wearing Native American costumes—brown skirts with vests and feathered headpieces—walked behind them. The sailors followed after them, and then the children wearing blue leggings/ shorts, blouses or vests, and blue wings and masks.

The children and their parents both had a good time.

As Miguel was walking, he got a call from an unidentified number.

It was Candice. After Fete and her hotel adventure with Terrel, she had returned home the next day feeling exhausted. She had woken up with stomach pain and remorse.

"Hi, darling," she said.

The music played so loud that he could barely hear her.

"Who is this?" he shouted.

"It's me, Candice. I'm not feeling well."

"What happened?"

Out of the blue, Candice started crying as her pain increased. She couldn't understand why.

"Miguel, please come. I'm in a lot of pain."

Worries flooded his mind and heart.

"Just lie down and wait for me," he said, then put the cell in his pocket.

He glanced at his daughter, and looked around hoping to find his mother with his son, but they were out of his sight.

No, she has to wait till the parade is over. I can't leave them.

Miguel continued walking till the end of the parade. When it came to an end, Miguel dropped his family off at home and rushed to his lover.

As soon as he parked in front of her house, he hurried to her door and impatiently rang the doorbell.

He could hear slow footsteps, and then Candice opened the door. She was still in her black undergarment. Her hair was uncombed, and he noticed dark shadows under her eyes.

"You look like you just got out of a hell pit," he said, eying her.

"I feel as if I'm going to collapse."

She led him into the living room and lay down on the sofa.

"Please sit down next to me," she said.

Miguel sat next to her feet. She squeezed a smile and then screamed out loudly, "Ouch! It's paining!"

He looked at her worriedly.

"Where is it hurting?"

"Right here." She pointed to her stomach.

"Maybe you're losing the baby."

"Don't say dat."

Miguel put his hand on her belly and gently rubbed it. She rested her hand over his.

"Miguel, I miss you. Without you, my life isn't the same anymore."

A shiver overcame her as she sat up. Miguel hugged her and rubbed her back.

As he sat next to her, he felt warmness passing through his body. He gently kissed her shoulder. She raised her head and gazed at him. Their lips sealed.

He paused for a minute.

"But you're in pain."

"Please don't stop. I need you."

She took off her undergarment and lay back naked. He hurriedly undressed himself and leaned over her, kissing her body. All the desire and feelings for her that he had tried to suppress suddenly burst out, making him weak to her charms.

After they made love, he lay embracing her. His mind was overwhelmed with many thoughts.

Sheila isn't here anymore. It's time for me to move on. After all, she carries my child.

He kissed Candice's shoulder.

"I've been thinking about you a lot lately. Honestly, I tried to forget you. But it's a hard task."

Miguel sat up and looked around at Candice's apartment. The wooden ceiling had dark spots from getting wet over and over, and the wall by the window was rotting away.

"You should move in with me. This place isn't good for the baby or you."

Candice sat up, wide-eyed. She couldn't believe what was happening. Her plans were coming to fruition.

"Are you serious?"

He held both of her hands and looked into her eyes.

"Yes, I am. You're carrying my child. However, I need to put certain things in place before you move."

Miguel's phone rang and he answered.

"Yes, Mummy?" he said as he looked at Candice.

At that moment, Elisa was peeking outside through a little space between the curtains.

"I heard something fall by the door. When I looked outside, I saw someone jumping over our fence. Should I call the police?"

"No. I'll be there shortly. Keep the children away from the windows and don't open the door to anyone. Don't answer the phone either."

Miguel put away his phone, sweating profusely. He hurriedly put on his clothes. Candice got up and frowned at him.

"What happened?"

"I can't talk now. I have to go."

He rushed out and got in the car. Drops of sweat rolled down his temple as he started his engine.

"I shouldn't have come over here."

As he got on the highway, he turned on the siren so that he could get through the slow-moving traffic.

"Come on. Out of my way!"

He drove with speed, blowing the horn impatiently. In forty minutes, he was turning onto his street with the siren off. He passed a few houses, then parked opposite his mother's gate.

He took his gun out of the storage compartment and got out of the car. Holding it in his hand, he walked into the yard, down the walkway, and straight to the door.

In front of it he found a broken, burnt doll. The doll's head was hanging down, and the neck area was painted red. It smelled like burnt rubber. On her melted leg he saw a piece of paper. Taking great care not to get his fingerprints on the doll, he carefully removed the paper and unrolled it.

It read: 'Stop digging, or a member of your family will face the same fate as Sheila.'

"How did he find out?"

He ran to his car and retrieved an empty plastic bag and a pair of pliers. He hurried back and, using the pliers, eased the doll into the bag. Then he walked back to his vehicle. He left the doll in the car and went straight into the house.

He walked into the hallway.

"Mummy, is everyone okay?"

"Yes, we are."

He heard her tell the children, "Stay upstairs."

"Why?" asked Nadia.

Elisa rushed to the hallway.

"Did you see anyone?"

Both of them walked into the living room.

"Not really, but I found a burnt doll with a broken neck. There was a note attached to it."

His mother walked to the house phone.

"I'd better call the police."

"There's no time for that. You should take the children over to Kevin's," he said.

Miguel hurried upstairs and went into the children's bedroom. Both were sitting on the bed watching cartoons.

Nadia got off the bed and rushed to her father. She hugged him.

"Daddy, Granny heard a noise. Did bad people come?"

He embraced her. "No, it was just a naughty cat. Put on your sandals. We're going to Uncle Kevin's," he said.

The three of them walked down the stairs.

"Are you coming with us?" asked Ronnel.

"No, I need to go the station."

Miguel opened the door, but then put a hand out to stop his kids.

"Wait!"

He walked outside to check out the area, and then sighed with relief.

"You can come out now."

"Daddy, you're behaving strangely today," Ronnel told him. "Did anything happen?"

"No, son. I'm just being careful. You should always check your surroundings when you leave the house."

Elisa unlocked her car, and Miguel opened the passenger door.

"Get in. You'll stay with your uncle today, and I'll see you tomorrow."

They settled into the back seat. He buckled them in and kissed their foreheads.

Miguel closed the door and Elisa drove away. He went back into the house and dialed his friend's number.

Sameer's shift had just finished, and he was preparing to leave.

"What's up boy?"

"Are you still at the station?"

Sameer shut down his computer.

"Yes, but I'm ready to leave."

"Yesterday I broke into Kingpin's house, and today I found a mangled doll on my mother's door, along with a threatening note."

"Are you crazy, man? How could you go into his house?"

"I know it was foolish of me, but I needed some answers."

Sameer shut the window in his room. "Man, you have jeopardized the whole case. I have to talk to the others."

"Please don't talk to anyone until tomorrow. I'll be in the office by 8 a.m.

Sameer pinched the bridge of his nose.

"I expected more of you. Now he knows that we're on his tail."

"My bad. I wasn't thinking straight."

Sameer stared at the clock that hung over the door.

I'm going to be late.

"I have to go. We'll talk tomorrow," he said.

Miguel put his cell phone on the table and put his head in his hands.

My family is in danger because of my stupidity.

He picked up his cell and left the living room.

The next morning, Miguel left the house and headed to the police station. As he drove, he got a call from Sameer.

"Hey man, are you on the way?" asked Sameer.

"Yes, I'm on the road driving. Will be there shortly."

He put away his cell phone and focused his attention on the road.

A yellow tractor was moving slowly in front of him, slowing down the traffic. Miguel needed to get by, so he blew the horn. He pushed up the turn indicator and glanced at the rearview mirror.

He noticed a silver Toyota behind him, followed by a black Chevrolet Suburban. He moved his car to the right lane, and saw that the SUV also changed lanes.

Miguel stared into the rearview mirror again. He felt a muscle throbbing in his left temple. The heavily tinted SUV on his tail made him suspicious.

Miguel pressed on the accelerator. His speed limit increased to 160 km/h. He glanced one more time at the rearview mirror.

The SUV was right behind him. Fixing his eyes on the road, he leaned to the left and opened a storage compartment. He pulled out a Glock 17 pistol and sat up straight. Then he swung into the left lane, leaving the tractor far behind.

The passenger in the back seat of the Chevrolet lowered the glass. Miguel could see the weapon--an AK-47 rifle—and that it was aimed at his car.

He pushed down on the accelerator, and as he sped up, so did the SUV.

Now both vehicles were side by side. Miguel glanced at the Chevrolet on his right side, and then blew his horn as he attempted to pass the car in front of him.

Bullets hit the window, causing spider-web cracks in the glass. Miguel increased his speed, and almost bumped into the car in front of him. He pressed on the brakes and slowed down. The driver in front of him glanced at the SUV and, seeing a rifle sticking out of the window, sped off without hesitation.

Miguel lowered the glass of the side door and began shooting. As he emptied his gun, he felt a numbing pain in his arm, and then his shoulder. He knew that a bullet had gone into his shoulder and exited, and he was now bleeding seriously.

Miguel raised his window.

The drivers behind him, seeing what was happening, slowed down. However, the cars in front of him sped off.

Miguel pressed the accelerator to the floor, driving at 180 km/h kilometers. As he crossed to the left side of the road, the Suburban rammed the back of his car.

Miguel's body slammed forward. Luckily, his seat belt was buckled. Although shaken by the collision, he drove to the right side, trying to get away from the SUV.

However, as soon as his car crossed to the right lane he collided with a pickup truck.

The collision pushed Miguel forward, and his head bounced against the steering wheel. The Mercedes swerved from the left lane to the right and back. Everything became blurry before Miguel's eyes. He opened them widely, trying to see the road.

The SUV got close to Miguel's car again, and the bullets flew into its sides. Miguel, his vision foggy, crashed his car into another vehicle. It spun around and skidded off the road, turning upside down.

The SUV again ran into the Mercedes-Benz. The collision mashed Miguel's bumper and broke the taillights. Miguel's car spun around and then crashed into a concrete barrier, where it came to a halt. The front bumper crumpled, and the windshield glass cracked into an illusion of a huge spider web.

Miguel's head again bounced against the steering wheel. He blacked out right away.

The black SUV slowly moved toward the Mercedes-Benz. The driver lowered his window and stared at Miguel. But when he heard the car behind him blowing its horn, he sped up.

The accident created a traffic jam. Cars slowed down, as curious drivers tried to view the accident scene.

Miguel lay unconscious. It was a few minutes before someone took action.

The driver of a blue Ford Focus stopped his car and got out. He went up to Miguel's car and looked inside. Seeing an unconscious man in the car, he pulled out his cell phone and dialed the emergency number.

As soon as the dispatcher answered he said, "I'm on Paterson's Highway. There was a shooting between two vehicles, and a collision. In total, three vehicles have been damaged."

The caller turned around and looked at the pickup truck, the driver of which got out of his car unharmed.

"How many people are in the vehicle?"

The caller looked inside Miguel's car.

"There's one—the driver. He's bleeding and appears to be unconscious."

Miguel opened his eyes and tried to turn his head.

"He's awake. Please hurry up!"

"Sameer, are you here?" Miguel murmured.

The man hung up the phone. Miguel unbuckled himself and tried to get out. The driver of the Ford walked towards the door.

"Hey, take it easy. You're hurt." He looked under his feet and noticed that there was gasoline leaking from the car.

"Your car could explode at any time. You have to get out to safety."

Miguel's whole body was in pain. Grimacing, he put his right leg out first, and then the left. He stood up, holding onto the car. When he tried to take a step, he collapsed onto the ground.

Oh, boy, I might have to take him myself to the emergency. With this traffic, the ambulance might take ages to get here.

The man took hold of Miguel under his arms and dragged him away from the car. Once Miguel was out of harm's way, he left him on the ground in order to hurry to his own car and open the back door. Then he rushed back to Miguel and dragged him over.

With his help, Miguel managed to crawl into the back seat. The man jumped into the driver's seat and drove to the hospital. While driving, he kept glancing at Miguel in the rear-view mirror.

Miguel sat up, squinting, trying to see. Everything seemed to be spinning before his eyes. He gave up and leaned his head back, closing his eyes.

"Keep your eyes open. You must stay awake," his rescuer advised. "By the way, I am Nikolai. What's your name?"

Miguel opened his eyes, grimacing with pain.

"I am Miguel. You must call my friend Sameer."

"Let's take you to the emergency first, and then we can call anyone you want."

Miguel closed his eyes and passed out again.

"Hey, man! Stay with me!"

Nikolai sped up. He didn't want to have a dead body in his car.

After what seemed like forever, he drove through the Caribbean Hospital's gate and stopped right in front of Emergency. He got out of the car and dashed through the doors. He ran to the security attendant.

"I have a bleeding man in my car. He's been shot!"

"Where did you park?"

"Right in front of the entrance."

The security spoke to his dispatcher.

"There's a wounded man in the car right outside the doors here. Please send someone for him."

In less than five minutes, two men came downstairs with a stretcher. They followed Nikolai out the doors. When they reached the car, they found Miguel staring vacantly, seemingly in a daze.

One of the nurses opened the door and touched Miguel's shoulder.

"Can you move?"

Miguel turned his head and gazed at them.

"What? Where am I?"

"You're at the hospital. Please try to get out of the car," the attendant told him.

Miguel grasped the backrest of the seat and tried to put his leg outside, but he felt too dizzy and weak. The male nurse leaned forward and pulled him out. Then he helped him to get onto the stretcher.

Miguel lay down, and the nurses pushed it into the building, leaving Nikolai behind. He looked at his back seat and shook his head. There was blood splattered on the seat and the car's floor. He closed the passenger's door and, after getting into the driver's seat, he left.

Miguel was taken to the emergency unit.

Two hours had passed since Sameer had spoken to Miguel. He waited for his friend impatiently, checking his watch every few minutes.

He should have been here an hour ago.

He dialed Miguel's number.

Why isn't he answering?

Then he called Elisa's cell number.

"Hello," she answered.

"Good morning, Mrs. Siglobeen."

"Good morning, Sameer. It's been a long time since I've heard your voice."

"Yes, yes, I've been busy." He took a steadying breath. "Did Miguel call you?"

"No. Has something happened?"

Sameer could hear the panic starting to rise in her voice.

"He was on the way to the station, but he didn't show up, and isn't answering his phone calls."

A police officer came into Sameer's office.

"Miguel's Mercedes-Benz was found on the Paterson's Highway," she told him.

He looked up sharply. "What?" Then he spoke into the phone. "Sorry, Mrs. Siglobeen. I have to go."

He ended the call.

The officer resumed her report.

"It looks like he was being chased by an armed person or persons. There are many bullets on the road. Some bullet shells were found in his car doors."

"What about Miguel?"

"He's been taken to the Caribbean Hospital."

Sameer jumped up and hurried towards the door.

"I'm going to go see how he is."

He left the police station and was at the hospital in less than a half hour.

He rushed to the medical receptionist's desk.

"Hello? Can you help me? Sergeant Miguel Siglobeen was admitted here this morning. Could you tell me where he is, please?"

The receptionist looked up at him with a smile.

"Just give me a moment."

She looked at her computer.

"Oh, yes. We admitted him about three hours ago. However, he's in the ICU unit. No one can see him until he's out of there."

"But I just want to make sure he's okay."

"He has two gunshot wounds, but his condition has been stabilized. Be assured he's in good hands."

"Can I see him for just a couple of minutes?"

"No, sorry. Rules are rules, and the same goes for everyone."

The smile had disappeared, replaced by a firm determination.

Sameer walked away.

I told him to leave the man alone. But no, he has to be stubborn.

Sameer sat in his car and dialed Elisa's cell.

"Mrs. Siglobeen, it's me again. Miguel was in a car chase accident, and has been shot."

"Oh, no! They got him," she whispered.

"Please don't panic. He's alive, and in Caribbean Hospital."

They shot him. They're going to come after us as well!

A bead of sweat rolled down her face. She slowly sat down on a chair.

"They might go to the hospital to finish the job," she said.

"That won't happen. He'll be guarded."

Sameer's other cell phone rang.

"I have to go, Mrs. Siglobeen."

However, by the time he took out his other cell phone, it had stopped ringing.

As soon as Elisa heard about the accident, she tried to get hold of Kevin. He and his wife had decided to take the children to the beach. They had left the house at 7 a.m., to avoid traffic, but they had left their youngest, Amelia, with Elisa.

Answer! I need to get to the hospital!

No one answered.

Elisa put the phone in her pocket and walked to the window.

Why won't they pick up the phone? I can't leave she alone, and I can't take she with me.

She turned on the radio and listened to the news as she dialed Ria's number.

What happened to she phone?

The announcer was reading the local news. Elisa sat on the sofa, waiting to hear about the accident.

Amelia's cries suddenly echoed in the living room. Elisa rushed to her son's bedroom and picked her up from her crib.

She sat in a rocking chair in the room, and laid Amelia on her chest. She began gently rubbing her back and rocking her grandchild.

The baby finally fell asleep, and Elisa put her back in the crib. She hurried out of the room in hopes of catching the news.

As soon as she sat on the sofa, she heard what she had been waiting for.

'There's another road accident on Paterson's Highway, involving three vehicles. According to the South North police station, Officer Miguel Siglobeen was ambushed here. He was chased and shot by gang members. Consequently, the chase and shooting between the police and unknown shooters has caused an accident.

"The drivers of the other two cars got only a few scratches. Miguel Siglobeen was shot and has been taken to the hospital."

Oh, my God! He barely escaped death!

Amelia started crying again. Elisa went to the bedroom and picked her up.

This time she rushed to the kitchen, carrying the baby. She prepared a baby bottle and returned to the bedroom, sat in a rocking chair, and put the bottle nipple into Amelia's mouth. The child began drinking hungrily.

Sad thoughts went through Elisa's mind.

Bad times have come upon my family. First, Sheila was taken from us, and now Miguel is in the hospital and I can't even see him. People don't feel safe anymore, even in their own houses.

She spent the whole afternoon waiting anxiously for Kevin's return. Towards evening, as she sank into her thoughts, she heard distant voices. She listened and realized that her family was back.

Kevin opened the door, allowing the children and his wife to enter the house first. Then he went back out, locking it after him.

"Girls, take your sandals off by the door and run to the shower," ordered Ria.

Shantel and Nadia had gotten a sunburn that had made their skin red.

"Aunty, my skin is burning!" Nadia complained.

"Get in the shower and rinse yourself. Afterwards I'll rub something on it."

The girls walked to the bathroom, giggling with each other about the day's adventures.

Ronnel took his sandals off as well.

"Ronnel, you can take a shower in my bathroom. But don't take long. We need to clean up as well," said Ria.

Ronnel rushed to Kevin's bedroom, still wrapped in his beach towel.

"Hey, Granny! We're back!" he called out loudly.

"Hush your big mouth!" Elisa had a sleeping Amelia in her arms. "You'll wake the baby!"

"Oh, sorry."

"Did you have fun?"

"Oh, yes. Uncle bought ice cream, and my favorite--shark and bake."

"Looks like you went for your belly.[77] Go and bathe now."

Elisa put Amelia back in her crib and went out to the living room. Kevin came in from outside, carrying two bags that had beach toys and other things that they had taken with them that afternoon.

Elisa looked at him without saying anything for a moment. When he glanced at her, he looked puzzled.

"Why didn't you answer your phone? I've been trying to get hold of you since this morning," Elisa said.

"Ronnel drained the phone's battery playing his game."

"What about Ria? Didn't she take her cell phone?"

---

[77] It looks like you went there for food.

Kevin put the bags on the floor and sat down on the sofa opposite his mom.

"She left her phone charging at home. You sound upset; did something happen?"

Elisa's eyes teared up.

"Miguel. He got...He..."

She broke down and cried. Kevin got up and went to his mom. He rubbed her back.

"Calm down and tell me what happened."

"He was in a car accident and...they shot him!"

"What? Is he alive?"

"Yes, he is, but he is in the intensive care unit."

Kevin called out, "Ria! Come here please!"

His wife came into the living room, still in her bathing suit.

"Miguel got shot," he told her in a low voice, in case any of the children were around.

"Stay here. Me and mummy are going to see him."

"They're not allowing anyone to visit him today. We will go tomorrow," said Elisa.

They heard Nadia shouting, "Granny, please get me a towel!"

Her voice woke Amelia up, and she started crying. Both women rushed out of the room to tend to the children.

Around 7 p.m., that evening, the Chevrolet Suburban SUV was parked in an empty field. The driver, David, sat in the driver's seat, keeping his hands on the steering wheel. His accomplice, Jonathan, slouched in the back seat, bleeding from his waist. He leaned his head on the headrest.

"Boy, I'm feeling like crap. Take me to the hospital."

David turned around and stared at Jonathan's waist. Blood had soaked through his t-shirt and pants.

"Are you kidding? The police are probably searching for us. They'll arrest you right there."

Jonathan grimaced in pain.

"But I'm going to bleed to death."

David's attention returned to the road beside the field, and he noticed headlights. The car was slowed as it drove up, and then it came to a halt. David picked up the AK-47 rifle from his lap and sat waiting.

Someone got out of the car, a pistol in his hand. He spat on the grass and stared at the Chevy.

David flashed the headlights.

The light fell on Cyclops. Recognizing him, David got out of the car.

"Why did you ask me to come here?" asked Cyclops.

"Jonathan was wounded. There's blood in the car. Can you take him to Dr. Ragbir?"

"Does he know about all of this?"

"Yes. Bossman spoke to him."

Cyclops walked to the Chevrolet. He opened the back door and stared at Jonathan.

"Hey boy, you look like shit. Try to get up. We have to get going."

There was no response. Cyclops shook Jonathan by his shoulder.

"Man, get up nah. We have to leave before the police find us."

Jonathan was totally silent. Cyclops put two fingers on his neck for a long moment, then stood up and looked at David.

"He's dead."

"Oh, shit. He was alive just now. What am I going to with his body?"

"If you had taken him to Ragbir earlier, he wouldn't have bled to death. Leave him in the car and let's go."

"The police will find my fingerprints all over the car. If we had a canister of gasoline, we could burn this thing."

Cyclops walked back to his car. He opened the trunk and removed a canister from the trunk. He brought it over and said,

"Here it is."

David took it from him and opened the front door. He checked the inside of the car, then picked up the firearms and passed them to Cyclops. Once he'd made sure the interior was empty of valuables, he doused the inside of the car with the gasoline, including Jonathan. Using a lighter, he ignited small spots of fire in various places. Then he closed the doors and watched as the seats of the car began burning.

"He was more than a brother to me. I can't even bury him," David said, spitting on the grass.

"I will avenge his death. That idiot will regret that he'd ever been born."

"Let's go, man, before the car explodes," said Cyclops.

Both men hurried to Cyclops's car. He turned the key and the car jolted forward.

On [78]Jouvert, in the early morning, the revelers of Extreme Masquerade gathered on Wince Street. The women wore t-shirts, tank tops, or sports bras. Shirtless men enjoyed the company of scantily clad women. Loud music and the voices of revelers polluted the air, breaking the usual silence.

Christian, the carnival leader of Extreme Masquerade, and his wife, were giving out buckets filled with paint or mud. Those who got the buckets smeared the paint and mud on themselves and their friends. In an hour, almost everyone was covered with either colored paint or mud.

Candice stood silently, wearing a sports bra and shorts, as Terrel rubbed mud on her face, neck, and chest A tall, muscular man bit his bottom lip as he eyed her. She noticed his attention and gave him a smile.

"Hey gyul, rub some mud on my back," Terrel said.

---

[78] J'ouvert is a large street party held annually as part of Carnival.

He put the bucket on the ground. Candice lifted the sponge and began spreading mud on his back. As she did so, she stared at the other man's six-pack abs, his wide chest, and his hands. She loved muscular men. She saw muscularity as a man's beauty and strength.

Once she'd finished, she passed the sponge to Terrel, and he covered the rest of his body with the mud.

Christian climbed onto a trunk and picked up a mic.

"We have to start moving to Harvey Stadium. If you've finished with the paint and the rest, please put your buckets in this trunk."

He put away the mic and got off the trunk in order to let the revelers return his buckets.

The lead pickup truck began to move as the music became louder.

Candice and Terrel walked along with the crowd. Candice's admirer strolled behind them.

The mob danced as it moved along the street. Some women wined by themselves, and others on men. Then the band stopped by the bar, where soft drinks and rum were bought out in plastic cups.

Terrel rushed to the bar and lined up to get a drink for himself and Candice.

The tall man who had been eying Candice approached her. He stood behind her and began rubbing his groin area on her bottom. Candice moved to the beat of music, rotating her bottom on his pelvic area.

"You look sexy. What's your name?"

She stopped winning and faced him.

"Candice. And yours?"

"Jacob."

Candice couldn't take her eyes off his broad chest. She put her hand on his abs.

"I love your six-pack abs. You must have trained a lot to develop them."

"I spend two hours in the gym every day."

Terrel turned around right then, and noticed the two of them, and her hands on him. He squeezed his plastic cup, and the drink splashed everywhere.

Jacob leaned forward and whispered into her ear.

"You look too hot. I would like to see you again sometime."

"Damn it!" Terrel muttered to himself. "What the hell is she doing with that guy?"

Terrel stormed towards them. *If I had a gun, I'd shoot that idiot.*

He stormed up to Jacob from behind and grabbed his hand. As soon as Jacob turned around, Terrel punched him in the face.

"Hey you! Don't touch my woman with your dirty hands!"

Jacob curled his hands into fists and threw punches at Terrel. Candice's boyfriend was suddenly hammered by blows to his face and head, and he reeled back in pain. He pressed his feet to the ground, trying not to lose his balance, then tried to kick Jacob. But Jacob caught his leg and pulled it to himself.

The crowd encircled the men. They now had a new entertainment—watching a fight. Their eyes flicked from Terrel to Jacob. Some even took photos and posted them right away on social media.

Terrel fell to the ground. Jacob sat on him and punched him nonstop. Jacob's fist collided with Terrell's nose, which immediately spouted blood.

Candice was alarmed at how badly Terrel was getting beaten. She came up and tried to get between them.

"Hey, stop it! You're going to kill him!" she shouted.

"Leave them alone!" said a spectator.

Candice looked around and noticed a bucket of mud. She ran and picked it up, then came back and emptied the contents of the bucket on Jacob's head. The mud spilled all over him, and also on Terrel.

Jacob got up and stormed towards her. He raised his fist, ready to hit her. However, another man got between him and Candice.

"All right, enough! Everyone is watching you," he said.

Jacob looked at the others and then at Terrel, who was getting up and spitting blood.

"I'll deal with you later," said Jacob. Then his attention turned to Candice.

"You could do with a better man."

He spat and walked away.

Candice went over to her boyfriend. "Are you okay?"

He looked at her through narrowed eyes.

"If you weren't acting like a whore with that loser, none of this would have happened."

"What did I do? We were just talking about his exercise. He was advising me how to get abs like his."

"You feel I dunce [79]? You were all over him."

"That's not true."

"I'm not in a mood for this walk and talk anymore. I'm leaving," he said.

He began walking away.

Candice looked at him and then at the band, wondering whether she should go or stay. Then she followed him.

They passed three streets on their way to Terrel's car. Both silently got into it. Terrel turned the key and pulled out onto the street.

A song on the radio began playing:
She mudda lost she mind,
doesn't want to leave she youth behind.
So she picked up a young boy,
She likes to treat him as she toy.

---

[79] Stupid

236

Oh, oh, oh, oh
She limes and drinks every day,
all she wants to do is to play.
She takes him everywhere he is she toy.
She doesn't need a man just him for joy.
Oh, oh, oh, oh

Terrel turned off the radio. He continued driving without saying a word.

On Carnival Tuesday, the revelers lined up in the streets early in the morning. Each masquerader was part of a different band, which had different colorful costumes.

Candice stood in the middle of the crowd, wearing her full outfit. This time she was alone, because Terrel was attending a meeting in Kingpin's house.

Candice picked up her phone and dialed Miguel's number. She hadn't heard from him for two days, which made her wonder if he'd changed his mind about her move.

As before, the call went straight into voicemail.

Why can't you answer one damned phone call?!

She put her phone in a small purse that was around her waist.

The band began moving as the music played. Everyone wore feathered wings, bathing suits, and headpieces. As the women walked, they either jumped up, waved, or wined on the men's pelvic areas or on the other women.

Candice noticed two foreign blond-headed and shirtless men. They were holding bottles of beer and taking pictures of the revelers. Candice came up and wined on one of them. Then, making slow dance moves, she faced them.

"Hey guys, I'm Candice. Where are you from?"

"I'm Ben and this is my friend Jack. We're from the UK."

They kept moving while the music played.

"Have you seen the city yet?"

"Yes, we did, and we met beautiful women as well," answered Jack, looking at her breasts.

As Candice spoke to the tourists, Kingpin was holding a meeting in his living room. He sat in an armchair with a drink in his hand. Not far from him were Cyclops, Toothless, Terrel, and David.

Two security officers were also present. They were heavily built, with bulky muscles and shaved heads. Both stood behind Kingpin. Their arms were crossed over their massive chests.

Kingpin took a drag on his cigarette and looked at his watch.

"They'll empty the containers tonight. I expect all of you to be at the factory."

"What if the police show up?" asked Cyclops, his eyes darting aside.

Kingpin exhaled a cloud of smoke.

"Police is busy now looking for Miguel's attackers," Cyclops continued.

Kingpin got up and walked to his bar. He poured a whiskey for himself and walked back to his seat. As he sat down, his attention fixed on Terrel.

"I heard you had a fight on Carnival Monday because of your whore. Are you dotish? You can't attract the police to yourself!"

Damn it. Everything I do gets reported to him.

Terrel stared at Kingpin's polished black shoes. Kingpin loved wearing spotless apparel, especially shoes. He had a lot of them, of different colors and styles.

David walked to the bar and poured rum for himself. "Boss, should I go to the hospital and finish my job?"

"No, I need him alive for now."

Kingpin's phone rang and he answered with a smile on his face.

"Hi babe," he said.

He put the phone on his chest, trying to block the noise, and said to his men, "You can go for now."

One by one everyone left the room. Finally, Kingpin was alone. "I'm going to be super busy tomorrow. Can you come on Thursday instead? I have a surprise for you."

"Hmm...a surprise," purred the other voice. "I'm wondering what that could be."

"You'll know when we meet. I gotta go."

Kingpin put his cell away. He took out a small gift box from his pocket and opened it.

In it lay a huge diamond ring.

Time to bring a woman into the house. I'm getting old and have no heir at all.

He learned his head on the backrest and closed his eyes.

On Wednesday morning, Miguel's brother and his friend stood by his bed. Miguel was awake and resting comfortably.

"I don't want to scare you, but you have to be careful. They might strike again," said Sameer.

"Maybe you could provide security for my family," suggested Miguel.

Kevin glanced at his brother's bandaged arm and shoulder.

"Do you think they'll come after me and my family?" he asked.

Miguel sat up and put his feet on the floor.

"They're after my blood, and anyone affiliated with me could be in danger."

"You never listen." Sameer frowned at him.

"I warned you to leave the man alone. But instead you dared to go into his house. So, you put yourself and your family in danger."

Miguel lay down. He was cold and sweating at the same time.

"He killed my wife. I tried to prove it. You know how it is when you lose someone."

Elisa walked into the hospital room and headed towards her sons, holding two bags in her hands.

"Did I miss anything?" she said.

"No, aunty," said Sameer, hugging her.

"My hands are full. I can't even hug you."

She put the bags on the bedside table and stared at Miguel.

"How are you today, son?" she asked, all attention on him.

Miguel was getting some pain in his back and arm. Not to worry his mother, he said, "I'm feeling much better than earlier."

"'I'm so glad that you're alright," Kevin told him.

"Mummy was worried sick, trying to find out what exactly happened."

"I was driving on the highway, and someone in another car shot me. That's what caused the accident."

Elisa began emptying the bags. She put two bottles of juice, a bottle of water, and a container of soup on the bedside table, and she put various toiletries and a set of pajamas in a drawer. Then she sat down on the edge of the bed and held her son's hand.

"I brought your favorite--corn soup--and some other things."

Miguel smiled and looked toward the bedside table. "Thanks, Mummy."

She caressed his hand.

"I never liked the idea of you working for the police force. I could have lost you today."

"Mother, if something is meant to happen, it will. Doesn't make a difference if someone works as a policeman or electrician."

A stout nurse with dreadlocks came into the room.

"How is my favorite patient feeling today?"

"I'm getting some pain near my shoulder blade and in my arm."

"I'll get some pain killers for you."

"By the way, these are my mom, my brother Kevin, and my best friend Sameer."

The nurse smiled at them. "It's a pleasure to meet you."

She bustled up to Miguel's bed and put a thermometer in his mouth. Then she removed it and looked at it.

"Hmm. You still have a fever."

She looked at the monitor attached to his finger. His blood pressure was 120/89. She wrote down the findings in the report book.

"When can he go home?" asked Elisa.

"I'm not sure. You need to speak to the doctor."

Kevin glanced at his watch. "I must be going. Mother, are you coming?" he asked.

Elisa stood up and kissed Miguel's forehead.

"I'll come and see you in the evening," she said.

"Mummy, take it easy. You can come tomorrow."

"I have to leave as well. See you tomorrow," said Sameer.

The three of them headed outside, talking.

"Sameer, why are you looking so thin? Doesn't your girlfriend feed you?"

"She cooks every day, but I've been missing out on my meals lately, due to late hours at work."

"Why don't you come over for dinner when Miguel gets out of here?"

"I will gladly come. Thank you, aunty."

Sameer took out his car key, and turned towards his car. "See you later, aunty."

———◆———

A month went by, and Adrian still had not returned to the brothel. Not seeing him pushed Sheila into a state of frustration and agitation. She lost her appetite, lost weight, and became ill.

As she lay burning with fever, Daniela sat at the edge of her bed with a bowl of soup. Valeria made herself comfortable on the floor.

"Sheila, you need to eat. If your condition worsens, you'll become useless. They'll get rid of you."

Sheila turned onto her left side without answering. Her eyes were teary.

"He didn't come for us. He lied to me," she whispered.

Daniela got up from the bed and put the bowl of the soup on the bedside table.

"She's refusing to eat. I give up," said Daniela.

Valeria picked up the bowl of soup and went over to Sheila.

"Aunty, please have some. I don't want to lose you."

"No, leave me alone. I'm not hungry."

"But you'll die from hunger. Take a few spoons."

Sheila sat up, a slight smile on her face.

"Child, you are stubborn."

Valeria dipped the spoon into the bowl and put it up to Sheila's lips.

Sheila opened her mouth and the spoon went in. Slowly she ate from Valeria's hands. When she had eaten half of the chicken soup, she pushed away the bowl.

"No more."

She lay back, and Valeria put away the bowl. Then she covered Sheila with her blanket.

The door opened, and Camille stuck her head inside.

"Hey, little one. Come. Bernadette is asking for you."

Valeria caressed Sheila's hair. A frown formed on her face. "Why?"

"You have to mop the guest room."

Camille walked towards Sheila and gazed at her.

"How are you feeling?"

"Aw, not so good," groaned Sheila, stretching her left leg.

"I hope that pig calls a doctor. Let's go, Valeria, before she acts up like a wild animal."

"Aunty, I have to go, but I'll be back soon."

A little flicker of a smile appeared on Sheila's face.

"Go, and don't worry about me."

Valeria left the bedroom and went with Camille to the guest room.

In the middle of the room was a new piano, and Victor was standing next to it. She also noticed a mop and bucket that had been left by the wall.

Camille walked to the piano.

"Did you decide where to move it?" she asked.

"We should put it by the window," suggested Victor.

Valeria felt tension in her forehead as she gazed at them. *What's a piano doing here?*

Her father had been a piano teacher, and had taught her how to play. She remembered sitting at the piano together with her father, both playing a song that he had written. They had sung while playing, sometimes looking at each other with a smile.

Then an image of her ill father popped into her mind. The smile left her face as soon as she recalled seeing him lying in the bed. He had been dying from cancer.

She wet a cloth and dripped some water into his mouth. The sickness was turning him into a skeleton. His eyes were shut, and he was unresponsive. Teary, she prayed for him.

Please, God. Don't allow him to leave us. He is my joy.

Her mother had tried to raise money for chemotherapy, but her attempts had failed. Thus, he didn't last for a long time.

With the help of a relative, they were able to bury him.

After his death, everything changed. Many times, they went to sleep on hungry bellies. Her mother went from door to door looking for a job. Not finding any, she was forced to sell things from the house.

And then the house was gone as well, because they couldn't pay the mortgage. They were forced to rent an apartment from Bernadette.

Valeria's heart raced when a memory of her drunken mother entered her mind.

A few weeks after her father's death, Valeria came back home from school. Feeling hungry, she went to the kitchen and opened the fridge's door. She looked inside and sighed. The fridge held only a few onions and potatoes.

She went into the living room and gazed at her father's portrait on the wall. With a sigh, she walked to the piano and sat down on the bench. Tears poured down her cheeks as she passed her hands over the piano.

"Why did he get sick and leave us?"

She heard the door opening. Her mother was home, after an afternoon of getting drunk. Valeria began playing her father's song.

Her mother staggered into the living room.

"Stop it!" she commanded.

Valeria looked at her mother.

"Why? This is Father's favorite."

She continued playing.

Her mother left the room and came back with a hammer. She came up to Valeria and shouted, "Forget about this piano! He left us and is not coming back home. I have no money and no job to support us because he died."

Seeing the hammer in her hand, Valeria jumped up in alarm and rushed away from her.

Valeria's mother bashed the piano with the hammer. The wood splintered.

"I hate you! You're gone, and you left us with no money! No hope! How are we supposed to survive?" her mother cried.

Valeria ran towards the piano and stood before her mother.

"No, Mother! Please leave it alone!"

Her sobs echoed through the whole house.

A few of the black and white keys were smashed.

"Why did you destroy it? It was the only thing that he left for me!"

Her mother dropped the hammer and knelt, sobbing. Valeria embraced her mother.

"I'm sorry. I was frustrated. Since your father died, everything has gone wrong. If I don't pay the rent, Bernadette will put us out. I'm barely finding small change for food. I don't know what to do."

"If you hadn't broken the piano, you could have sold it."

Bernadette's voice brought Valeria back from her memories.

"Leave the piano and come to massage my shoulders," she told Victor.

Camille and Victor moved the piano to the window, and Camille left. Bernadette was plopped comfortably on the sofa and was putting red polish on her nails. When Victor started massaging her shoulders, she put away the nail polish.

"Not so hard. A little bit to the left. Oh, yes. It feels so good."

She closed her eyes. Victor licked her ear and then kissed her neck. She laughed.

"Stop it, naughty!"

He moved his hands in a circular motion, as he stared at the clock on the wall.

Bernadette opened her eyes and noticed Valeria.

"Why are you looking at me? Am I a clown in the circus?"

She gazed hatefully at Bernadette.

You took me away from my mummy. I hate you.

"Sorry, Aunty Bernadette."

Bernadette sat up. "Silly girl. Don't call me aunty. I'm not your aunty."

Victor frowned at Valeria with his cold eyes.

"Stop standing around doing nothing. Go and mop the floor!"

Valeria picked up the mop. She dipped it into the water and started moving it around the floor. She glanced at Victor, and was relieved to see that his attention had been diverted.

Bernadette stood up.

"Sit down, my pudding. Let me continue massaging," he said.

Bernadette glanced at her watch. It was 6 p.m.

"No more. I need to step out."

Her attention shifted to Valeria and then to him. "I warn you. Stay away from her."

Victor looked at her and then shook his head.

"When will you stop thinking the worst of me?"

"Your bad image makes it hard to trust you. Don't think that I don't know what's going on at nights with you and the girls."

"I have no idea what you're talking about."

"You know very well what I mean. I have ears and eyes everywhere."

"I'm not going to stand here and listen to your false accusations," he spat out.

He stormed out into the corridor, where he collided with Daniela. She moved aside.

"Oh! Sorry," she said.

He said nothing in reply and made his way to the bedroom. Bernadette also charged out.

Valeria dipped the mop into the water, and then looked at the piano, sighing. She walked towards it and lifted the lid.

A crucifix fell on the floor. She looked at the doorway entrance and then picked it up.

Where did this come from?

She put it in her pocket and put her fingers on the keyboards. The sound of the piano filled the room. She sang:

I'm in Bernadette's home,

Lord, I'm here lost and alone,

I really need some help,

My mother sold me for wealth,

Help me please, oh Victor is scaring me.

I don't want these cruel men to see

the tears all over my face,

I want to escape from this nasty place.

Hearing the piano Luciana, one of the residents, came into the room. She sat on the sofa without saying anything and listened to Valeria's singing. Luciana's eyes became moist, and she began clapping.

"Bravo."

Valeria got up quickly. She turned around and stood motionless, staring fearfully at Luciana.

"I...I...I wanted to see how well the piano worked," she stammered.

Luciana came up to her and embraced her.

"Valeria, you are such a gem. I never knew you had such a beautiful voice and could play the piano. Come and take a seat."

They sat down on the sofa. Luciana took out a tissue from a pocket and patted it over her eyes.

"So, tell me—where did you learn to play that thing?" She pointed at the piano.

All in smiles, Valeria answered, "My daddy taught me."

"He must be proud of you."

Valeria looked down. "He went to heaven."

"Oh, sorry. I didn't know."

Luciana caressed Valeria's cheek. "I have a daughter, and she's very beautiful and smart. You remind me of her."

Valeria's eyes sparkled with curiosity as she looked at Luciana's face.

"Where is she?"

"She's with her daddy."

Luciana's eyes became sad. She became lost in her thoughts for a while, thinking about her daughter and her husband, Santiago.

They had had a good life until he lost his job as an electrician. Right away, they both had begun searching for employment while their eight-year-old daughter was in school. Unable to find a job, Luciana had asked her distant relative, Bernadette, for help.

Bernadette had refused to give her money but offered her work as a prostitute. Luciana had been disgusted by the offer and had refused. However, a few weeks later, unable to get a job, she had taken the offer and had told her husband that she had gotten a job as a cleaner in a hotel. This way she was able to fool her husband and put bread on the table.

Victor entered the room. He glared at Valeria.

"I wasn't even gone for five minutes, and you're chilling out on the sofa!" he shouted.

Then he looked over at the piano. The lid was still up.

"Who dared to touch the piano?" he demanded.

Valeria's hands began to shake as she gripped Luciana's.

"I played," answered Luciana with a smile. She got up from the sofa.

"No, it was me." Valeria hid behind Luciana, avoiding Victor's eyes.

He came up to Luciana and raised his hand to hit her. But, upon recalling Bernadette's warning, he put his hand down.

"Out of my way!" he said, pushing Luciana.

He grabbed Valeria's top.

"If you touch it again, I'll smack your fingers with a hammer. Do you understand?"

"Victor, she's only a little child. Please don't get mad at her."

Victor ignored her words.

"Do you understand?" he demanded again.

"Yes, I do."

Valeria's heart seemed to be ready to jump out. Her knees shook, and she wet herself.

He stared at the puddle under her legs.

"Nasty girl. This isn't a toilet."

He let go of her blouse, picked the mop up, and thrust it at her.

"Take it and get back to work."

She took it and began mopping.

His attention shifted to Luciana.

"You leave this room. You have a bad influence on her!"

"She plays and sings so well that she could entertain customers with it."

"Don't you understand? Men come here to f--- women, not to hear some stupid music!?"

Victor stared into her eyes, sending cold spikes into Luciana's heart. She walked away without saying anything.

Victor glanced at Valeria and then headed to Sheila's bedroom.

Sheila trembled like a leaf, despite the room being so hot. She closed her eyes, feeling unbearable pain in her stomach. Tears kept falling from the corners of her eyes.

"Ouch! It hurts so much!" she mumbled. "Adrian, you told me that you would come back soon. Why are you taking so long?"

Victor stepped in. Sheila opened her eyes and looked towards the door.

As soon as she noticed Victor, she sat up. Her heartbeat sped up, and stabbing pain attacked her temples. Everything seemed to be spinning before her eyes.

"So, so. Here you are. Weak and hopeless."

He grinned and clapped slowly.

Sheila stared into his eyes. "What do you want?"

He walked to her and grabbed her hair, pulling it back. He put his nose in it.

"Hmm. Good question. What do I want?"

She held onto the edge of mattress.

"Please let go of my hair."

He passed his hand over her face, touching her cheeks and lips.

"You're like a lurking magnet, arousing my hunger."

"Please Victor, leave me alone today. I'm unwell."

"Lie down and stop shaking. I'm not going to touch you today."

Trembling, she put her head back onto her pillow. He sat next to her legs and began caressing them.

"Smooth and soft skin."

She moved her legs away from his hands. Drops of sweat formed on her forehead.

He learned over her, putting his face closer to hers.

"Stop resisting. You know you can't win this battle."

She spat in his face, staring at him coldly and breathing heavily.

One day victory will be mine.

He slapped her.

"Ow!" she shouted.

Upon hearing Sheila's voice, Valeria threw the mop on the floor and rushed to her bedroom. She opened the door and stood there wide-eyed.

Victor pulled out the belt from his pants and hit Sheila. She tried to sit up but he pushed her. The hitting started over.

"Please stop it!" Sheila cried.

Valeria looked around to see what she could get to stop him. With every lash, she flinched as if she herself was getting hit.

Thinking quickly, she ran to the kitchen. She grabbed a knife from the counter and ran to her room.

She rushed over to Victor, the knife raised.

"Stop beating her! You monster!"

Victor dropped his hand and faced Valeria.

"You shouldn't be playing with knives. You could get hurt!"

Valeria thrust the knife towards him.

"Move away from her!"

Victor made a few steps backwards.

Sheila got up, shaking.

"Valeria, leave the room please."

The girl ran to Sheila. "No, aunty! He deserves to die."

Victor put out his hand. "Give me the damned knife."

He stepped forward, forcing Valeria to step back. Her hands trembled.

"No!" She shook her head.

Sheila grasped Valeria's hand and took the knife from her. Valeria hid behind Sheila.

"Victor!" shouted Bernadette from the front door.

"Come and help me with the bags!"

Victor glanced at the door, then at Sheila and Valeria.

"You are lucky today."

He walked away, putting his belt back on.

Sheila took a step and grimaced in pain.

"Child, violence and knives are not a solution. Please never pick up a knife to hurt anyone. Crime is punishable by law and by God."

Valeria embraced Sheila, crying.

"But I couldn't just stand there and watch him hurting you. I hate him. He is an ugly man."

"My head is spinning. I need to lie down."

Sheila made a few steps towards the bed, but collapsed.

Valeria bent over her and shook her shoulder. "Aunty, please get up!" She cried.

Turning toward the door, she called out, "Help! Aunty Sheila is dead!"

She put her head on Sheila's chest and cried bitterly.

"Why have you gone? Who is going to love me and protect me from all these men?"

She pulled out the crucifix from her pocket and laid it on Sheila's chest. Then she turned her head up and stared at the ceiling.

"Jesus, I've been a good girl. Please bring her back. I already lost my daddy. I can't lose her as well."

She put her head on Sheila's chest again.

"Please don't let her die."

She sat up and shook Sheila again.

"Aunty! Aunty? Why have you gone, leaving me? Mummy sold me out, Daddy's gone, and now so are you."

Bernadette ran into the bedroom. She took one look at Sheila and Valeria, and then rushed to them. She pushed Valeria aside and put her ear on Sheila's chest.

"Why did she die, leaving me alone?"

"Shut up! Silly girl. She's alive," she said.

Bernadette shook Sheila.

"Wake up, you troublemaker!"

Camille, Debra, and Luciana entered the room. Sheila opened her eyes and saw Bernadette bent over her.

"What happened?" she asked.

"How would I know?" Bernadette replied.

"Get up and get back in the bed."

Bernadette moved away from Sheila and looked at the other dwellers.

"Don't congest the room. Shoo away!"

Debra ignored her words. She grasped Sheila's hand and helped her to stand up. Holding her hand, Sheila managed to stagger over to her bed and lie down. Debra covered her with a blanket as Valeria sat down on the edge of the bed.

"All of you leave the room now, except Valeria."

The women left, and Bernadette walked over to the bed.

"You've only caused confusion since you've come here. Now I have to spend money on you as well."

Bernadette took out her cell phone and made a call.

"Good day, Thiago. This is Bernadette."

"Hi, Bernadette. It's always nice to hear your voice."

"One of my girls is sick. Can you come and check her please, as soon as possible?"

"I'll be there in two hours, if that's okay with you."

"That's fine. Thank you."

Bernadette put the cell phone back in her pocket.

"Stay with her until the doctor comes," she told Valeria.

Then she left the room.

Valeria picked the crucifix up from the floor where it had fallen and sat down not far from the bed. She bent her knees and wrapped her arms around them. Her sobs echoed in the room as she held the small crucifix.

Suddenly she felt coldness because of her wet clothes. The shock of the day's events had wiped the feeling completely from her mind.

Her heart filled with sorrow and anger. She began singing a song that she had written with Sheila.

Anger is crawling out of my heart,
Polluting, a plague of poison deep into my soul.
How many times must I be hurt and harmed by others.
I keep asking the Lord for help and intervention,
All the time wanting to scream out to the whole world
The ruinous punctures of this excruciating pain.
Nonetheless, I resist the urge by staying strong.
I'm tired, weary, and exhausted from keeping back my tears,

When I'm crying inside like a rushing waterfall,
All the time feeling so lonely.

Sheila sat up. Valeria blinked in disbelief when she saw her awake. She rose, went to the bed, and sat down on it. Together they continued,

Yet, I manage to turn to God but still wonder,
When my endless suffering will cease.
A cunning and malicious demon peers at me and laughs.
This devil's job remains incomplete
Since such a gremlin wants to see me no less
And no more than dead.
However, with God in my life,
I will find my freedom

When they finished, Sheila hugged her young friend.

"Yes, we'll find a way out," she told her.

Valeria changed her clothes and then got into the top bunk. Both lay quietly until they fell asleep.

Two hours later, Sheila was awakened by voices next to her. Bernadette was shaking Valeria's arm.

"Get up, you lazy one."

Valeria sat up. "What happened?"

"Doctor Thiago is here. He has to examine Sheila. So fly away!"

Valeria stared at Dr. Thiago with a serious face. She jumped off the bed and left the room.

The gynecologist approached Sheila's bed as Camille and Debra came in. Valeria stood by the door, peeking inside.

"Please sit up and take off your top," he told her.

Sheila sat up and removed her top.

"Breathe in. Now breathe out."

Thiago listened to her breathing with a stethoscope.

"Your lungs are clear. Please lie down. I need to perform a pelvic exam."

Sheila looked over at the girls and then lay down.

"I feel uncomfortable being checked with so many people around," she whispered.

Thiago looked at the ladies. "*Senoras,* please wait outside. The patient needs some privacy."

Valeria dashed away from the door. The brothel dwellers left also, except Bernadette.

Thiago gazed at her. "Would you mind leaving us alone, please?"

"Okay. I'll give you some space."

Bernadette walked out, meeting the girls by the door.

"What do you think she has?" asked Camille.

"She might have picked up some disease from one of the clients," answered Bernadette.

"Could it be HIV? It's very contagious," said Debra.

"I don't know. I've been asking you to use condoms. But you ignore my words."

"Theodore had strange blisters on his legs. Maybe he passed something to her."

"Enough talking. Clients will be coming soon. Go and fix yourselves!"

Debra and Camille left.

Doctor Thiago removed some gloves from his bag.

"Please take off your panties and bend your knees."

Sheila followed his instructions as he bent over to take out the speculum from his bag.

He stood up with his tool.

"I'm going to insert this into your vagina. It might hurt, but the pain is bearable."

Feeling uncomfortable, Sheila closed her eyes. As he inserted the speculum, Sheila felt its coldness, and a much sharper pain than she would have thought.

"Ouch! That really hurts!"

He leaned forward and inserted his finger as a part of the

procedure. When he removed it, Thiago noticed a yellowish and greenish substance on it. He wiped off the finger. Then he took a sample of discharge from her with a brush. He put the brush into a plastic bag and then removed the speculum.

"You can get dressed now."

Sheila slipped into her clothes.

"Dr. Thiago, what's your prognoses?" she asked him.

"Your chest is clear, and your throat and ears are fine. Yet there is yellowish, bloody vaginal discharge. Have you been vomiting or getting abdominal pain?"

"I've thrown up a few times since I got sick. My stomach is hurting right here."

She pointed at the lower part of her abdomen.

"With these symptoms, I would suggest that you have gonorrhea. It has progressed into a pelvic inflammatory disease. It's transmittable, and you should abstain from sex till it's cured. But I will wait on the swab results to be certain."

Sheila grinned. "You should mention this to Bernadette. She thinks we're sex machines made to please men at any cost."

"That's what happens when you choose this kind of field." He looked at her accusingly.

"But it wasn't my choice."

Dr. Thiago dug in his bag, and removed a new set of gloves, a syringe, and a vial.

"I'll need to draw some blood from you. Make a fist with your right hand," he told her as he donned the gloves.

Sheila followed his instruction, and he took blood samples from her. Then he wrote a prescription for her.

"I have to leave now, but I'll be back," he said after removing the gloves.

Sheila stood up and clutched his hand.

"Please wait. I didn't choose to become a prostitute. They kidnapped me from Trinidad and brought me here. Can you please notify the police?"

"This is a serious accusation. To my awareness, all the girls here are hired prostitutes."

"No, Dr. Thiago. Daniela was also kidnapped and shipped here from Romania. Please help us get out!"

Dr. Thiago picked up his bag from the floor and threw his gloves into the bin.

"I'll see what I can do. Meanwhile, lie down and rest."

He left the bedroom, and nearly collided with Bernadette and Valeria.

"Can I talk to you in private?" he said to the madam.

Bernadette looked over at Valeria.

"Why are you standing here as if you have nothing to do?"

Valeria walked away slowly, looking back over her shoulder.

Bernadette rolled her eyes and turned back to the doctor. "What's wrong with her?"

"She's contracted gonorrhea. Here is her prescription." He passed it to her.

"It's so hard to find medicine here. Where am I going to get it?"

"Come to my clinic and I will get it for you. She has to take them. It might take up to two weeks to go away, with treatment. Without it, who knows? You should insist that your girls use condoms. They could get infected with HIV or catch other diseases and pass them to their clients."

"They have been using them. I don't know how she ended up with this. Maybe the condoms were defective."

The doctor glanced at Sheila's door and lowered his voice. "I must warn you. Sheila asked me to help her get out. You have to be watchful of her. She talks a lot."

Bernadette nodded, and glared at the door. She took money from her pocket and put it in his hand.

"This is for you."

He put the cash away.

"Thank you, Bernadette."

They walked towards the door, and Bernadette began opening the locks.

"Quite a lot of locks you got here."

"This is to make sure that our girls are safe."

"Ah. Okay, see you tomorrow," said Dr. Thiago, and he left the brothel.

* * *

Two weeks after Carnival, at 4 a.m., Terrel was sitting in the driver's seat of a rented Toyota. He and his gang friends Nico and Jaren were waiting for a man by the name of Kin Chin. Outside, the streets were still dark and empty.

The men wore sunglasses and black caps. Nico was in the front passenger's seat and Jaren sat in the back. Silently, they scanned the empty streets. They held guns on their laps, and each had a balaclava ready to slip on.

A silver Skyline parked behind the building they were staking out—the Food-Market Supermarket. Kin, an owner of the supermarket, got out of the car. He always came early to complete his projects before the day got busy.

"Boys, he's here," said Terrel. They put the balaclavas over their heads, covering their faces.

Holding a briefcase, Kin headed to the huge gate of the supermarket. He unlocked the padlock on it and slid the gate open. Then he put a key into the keyhole of the glass door and unlocked it. He went inside and turned on the lights.

Jaren and Nico ran towards the Food-Market. At the same time, Kin went to the door and turned the "CLOSED" sign the other way. Upon seeing the men running towards him, Kin tried to get another bunch of keys from his pocket. His hands shook, and the keys fell.

As he tried to pick them up, Jaren pushed the glass door open, banging it into him. As soon as Kin stood up straight,

Jaren pointed a gun at him.

"Stay still or I'll shoot you."

Kin slowly turned around as Nico came in with a pistol in his hand.

Terrel drove up closer to the entrance.

Nico put a sack over Kin's head and caught his arms behind his back. The two men, gripping his arms, pulled him out to the car, where they shoved him in. Nico sat in the back seat and Jaren got in the front seat. Then they uncovered their heads.

"Let me go!" Kin demanded, trying to free his hands.

"You're not going to get away with this. My cousin is a policeman!"

"Drive quickly, man," Jaren told Terrel.

"Make him lie down. Someone might see him."

Nico pointed a gun at Kin's groin area.

"Lie down or I'll shoot your balls."

Kin complied. Outside, it was getting lighter. Terrel drove the car through the quiet streets.

"Where are you taking me?"

Jaren pressed his gun to Kin's stomach.

"Ask one more question and see what happens!"

Terrel drove to Keets Street and toward the house of another accomplice, Brandon. He turned in at the driveway and stopped the car. Then he faced the passengers in the back seat.

"Put the balaclavas back on."

Everyone followed his instruction.

"Take him inside now. Make sure he doesn't see your faces."

Jaren and Nico hurried to the house, pulling Kin with them. Terrel followed, his eyes scanning the neighborhood. Jaren rang the bell and Brandon, wearing a balaclava, opened the door.

"What took you so long?"

"Move aside, boy, and then talk," said Jaren.

The men entered Brandon's house and followed him into a bedroom. It had its own bathroom, a bed, and a small folding table with two chairs around it.

Jaren pulled the sack off of Kin's head and, aiming his gun at Kin's back, ordered, "Sit in that chair."

Kin didn't move. He stood defiantly and glared at him.

"Don't play deaf with me," said Jaren, pushing his hostage.

Kin sat in the chair.

"Please let me go. There's a debit card in my pocket. You can take out all the money you want from my account."

Terrel dug in Kin's pockets and took out a small wallet and his cell phone. From the wallet he took out his credit cards and debit card, as well as his money. He put it all in his pocket and passed the cell phone to Jaren.

"Keep this phone. We'll use it to call his wife."

Then he faced Kin.

"What's your debit card PIN?"

Kin kept his mouth shut.

Without hesitation, Terrel punched him in the mouth.

"Hey! Easy!" said Jaren. He took a step toward Terrel.

"Seven, eight, six, two." A few drops of blood ran down from Kin's lips.

"Now we're talking. What type is your account?"

"Savings."

Terrel looked around at his partners in crime.

"I need to step out. Watch him!"

Terrel left the house and drove to the nearest bank. He parked a block away and walked towards the ATM booth.

It was empty. He went over to the ATM machine and inserted Kin's debit card. He was overjoyed to find that he was able to take out two thousand. With the cash in his hands, he practically danced back to his car. Then he got in and headed to Candice's.

While Terrel was away, the others got busy. Jaren put a gun to Kin's temple, as Brandon held Kin's cell phone.

"What's your wife's number?" asked Jaren.

"She has no working phone."

Jaren glanced at Brandon.

"Make sure he can't get up from the chair."

Brandon wrapped his hand around Kin's neck and held his head with the other hand. Jaren pushed a gun into Kin's mouth.

"Her number! Don't play games with me."

Kin attempted to move his head and gargled something. Jaren took the gun out of his mouth, and Kin told him the number. Jaren dialed it.

At the other end, a woman sat up in bed and answered.

"What happened, Kin?" she asked.

"Hey bitch, listen to me carefully. We have your husband. If you want him alive, give us 400,000," came the answer.

There was silence on the line. Then: "Is this some kind of joke?"

"I'm damn serious."

Kin's wife jumped out of bed and began pacing.

"I need to hear his voice." Her voice trembled.

Jaren put the phone to Kin's ear. "Talk to your bitch."

"Honey, please do what they say."

She slowly sat down on the floor.

"Did they hurt you?" Tears formed in her eyes as she trembled.

"No, but if you don't follow their instructions, they will."

Jaren took the phone away.

"I'll give you two days to get the money. When you get it, call your husband's cell number. No police, or you will see his head by your doorstep!"

He clicked the "end call" button. Then the three of them left the bedroom, locking the door and leaving Kin alone.

Two days went by, and Kin's wife still hadn't called his kidnappers.

In the morning Nico, Brandon, Jaren, and Terrel sat at the table in the living room playing poker. In the middle of the table lay four hundred dollars and several bottles of beers.

Terrel looked at his watch.

"She's taking too long to call us."

"No one keeps that kind of cash in their house. She might have gone to the bank," Jaren told him.

Brandon fanned out his cards: the Ace, King, Queen, Jack, and ten of hearts.

"How you so lucky, man?" Jaren asked with the cigarette in his mouth.

Brandon picked up the cash and put it in his pocket.

"When it comes to money, luck is always on my side," he said.

"That's why you always beg everyone for cash," said Terrel mockingly.

"Hush your mouth." Brandon poked his friend.

"Hey! Untie my hands! I need to pee!" shouted Kin.

Jaren put his cards on the table and got up. He put on his balaclava, then he walked to the sofa and pulled up a cushion. He lifted a piece of wood and put his hand in the hole. From it he removed a pistol, then he walked to the bedroom. He unlocked the door and went inside.

"Hurry up!" Kin was squirming madly.

Jaren untied him, and Kin dashed to the toilet.

While in there, he looked at the small window that was above the urinal. He put the cover of the toilet seat down and climbed onto it. Then he grabbed onto the windowsill and lifted himself up.

Unfortunately, his leg hit against a small ceramic flower pot that was sitting on the top of the toilet tank. It fell and smashed on the floor.

Jaren opened the door and rushed in. He pulled Kin

down and began kicking and punching him.

"Stop it!" shouted Kin.

Terrel came in and stood by the toilet's door.

"What's going on, boy? He's making too much noise!"

"He tried to escape through the window."

"Leave him alone. His wife just called, and we have to take him to the drop point. Put this sack over his head and tie it around his neck."

Terrel passed the sack to Jaren and left.

"Stand up and go back to the room!" Jaren told his hostage.

"But I didn't pee yet."

"Go ahead!"

Kin lifted the toilet seat and unzipped his pants. He looked at Jaren.

"Can you at least turn away? I feel weird when someone is watching my dick."

"I'm not a gay."

Kin emptied his bladder. After washing his hands, he went back to the bedroom. Jaren handcuffed Kin's hands behind his back and put the sack on his head.

He prodded Kin. "Move!"

Kin and Jaren went out into the living room. Nico was sitting on the sofa listing to Terrel, who was on the phone. Brandon sat at the table.

"Listen to me carefully. If the police catch any of us, your husband's body will be cut off into small pieces. We'll be happy to drop his head off at your door and throw his body in the river."

Terrel hung up and looked over at Kin and Jaren.

"Keep him quiet and down all the time. Let's go."

All of them walked outside, except Brandon. Nico sat in the back seat with Kin. Jaren got into the front with Terrel.

Nico put the gun to Kin's side. "Hunch down and stay quiet. If everything goes smoothly, you'll be free."

Terrel pulled out of the driveway. As he drove, his eyes wandered from the road to the rear-view mirror. He tapped his fingers on the steering wheel.

After a while the tires hit the highway. Kin raised his head, but Nico pushed him down.

Jaren looked over at the other side of the highway.

"Oh, shit! Policemen on the road!" he said.

Terrel moved his car to the left lane and increased his speed.

"Hey, make sure you don't speed," said Nico, with his eyes on the police cars.

At the first opportunity, Terrel got off the highway and drove to the Pureto Forest on the back roads.

Soon they noticed a white Prado in the distance. Terrel's car came to a halt.

"Cover your faces!" he said.

The men put on their balaclavas. Terrel made a call to Kin's wife's phone.

"We're here," said Terrel.

"I can see you," answered a man's voice.

"Where's Kin's wife?"

"Did you expect I would allow my sister to come here? Free Kin."

"First, pass the money to us. Then we'll let him go."

"I want to hear his voice first," said the man.

Terrel passed the phone to the back. Nico held it to Kin's ear.

"Kin, are you okay?" asked the voice at the other end.

"Yes, I am. Do as they say."

Nico gave the phone back to Terrel.

A man got out of the Prado with a sports bag in his hand. Jaren, with a pistol in his hand, got out of the car and walked towards him.

He took the bag from him and opened it. After a quick glance, he signaled with his hand and then walked back to the vehicle.

Nico opened the car's door. He untied Kin's hands and removed the sack from his face.

"Get out and don't look back!"

Kin ran towards the Prado as Jaren opened the trunk and put the sports bag in the trunk.

Then he got into in the car. "Wow, we did it! One hundred thousand each!"

Terrel turned the radio and music filled the air. He drove away, leaving the forest behind.

As the days passed, the guilt that had been eating Miguel from the inside was wearing off. He kept thinking about moving on with Candice. After all, they were going to have a baby together.

However, he didn't know how to approach his mother and children about Candice. He didn't like the fact that the mother of his unborn child was living in a wooden house that could collapse, either from a landslide or rotten wood. He needed to move her out of there.

An opportunity to open up finally presented itself. Late at night, while sitting with his mother in front of the TV, he saw a chance.

"Mother, I need to discuss something with you."

Elisa turned down the TV volume, and her attention moved to him.

"What is it?"

Miguel exhaled loudly, and his body tensed.

"There's a woman in my life, and she carries my child."

Elisa's eyes narrowed. She dropped the remote control and stared at him in bewilderment.

"You just recently buried your wife. When did you manage to meet someone, and impregnate her as well?"

"Sheila isn't here anymore. I can't keep grieving. I need to move on."

"Did you think about your children? How do you think they'll react, seeing you replacing their mother, and so soon?"

Miguel wiped his forehead with his hand.

"Mother, don't you understand? She carries your grandchild, and her current place is unhealthy. The children will just have to accept her."

The house phone rang, and she rushed to the hallway and picked up the receiver.

Miguel looked at the clock on his wall.

A good opportunity to leave and run.

He got up and walked to the door.

"Mother, I'm leaving. We'll talk later."

Elisa put her hand over the receiver.

"Where are you going?"

"By she."

Elisa went back to talking on the phone.

He picked up his keys and rushed to the car, then drove straight to Candice's house.

As he was driving to her place, Candice was sitting on the sofa with Terrel, counting money. As she laid it out, she laughed as Terrel kissed her shoulder.

"One hundred thousand! We could fly over to the Bahamas!"

"No, I plan to buy land, and then build a house for my baby."

He rubbed her tummy.

"Hey, little man, do you hear? I'm going to give us a better life."

She spread herself on the money and he covered her with kisses as he threw bills on top of her. She laughed joyfully, feeling on top of the world.

"Money is power. I love it."

However, her ecstasy was short-lived. She heard a car horn, and her heart sank.

She got up and walked to the window. Her heart raced when she saw that it was Miguel's car. She ran to the sofa and picked up the black sports bag.

"Help me to put the money away. Miguel is here!"

They hurriedly threw the cash into the bag, as Miguel walked up to the door and rang the bell.

Terrel picked his gun up from the table and walked towards the door.

She clutched his hand. "Please leave from the back window."

"No. I'm going to blow out his brains."

Candice gave the bag to Terrel and put her arms around his neck.

"Please leave him alone."

The hatred left his eyes, and Terrel sighed.

"All right. You're lucky that I love you."

They walked to her bedroom.

"You need to break up with that idiot."

"I was going to leave him, but Kingpin wants me to stay with him so I can spy on him," she lied.

"I'm kind of getting fed up with following Kingpin's instructions, like I'm his puppet. I want out."

"But you have no choice, If you try to leave, they'll cut your throat or come after me," said Candice.

Miguel rang the bell again.

"Go now!"

Terrel went over to the window, as Candice made her way towards the door.

"Who is it?"

"Hey, Candice. It's me."

"I'm just finishing my shower. Wait."

She wet her hair under the faucet and wrapped her head with a towel. Then she opened the door.

Her lover entered inside, and playfully hit her bottom.

"Girl, you took so long in the shower."

"I'm sorry. I didn't expect anyone."

He sniffed the air, and smelled cigarette smoke.

"Have you been smoking?"

"No. My stupid neighbor always smokes as he stands outside my house."

She sat on the sofa and crossed her legs.

"Come sit next to me."

He sat next to her, and she began rubbing his manhood's treasure. He pushed her hand away.

His eyes noticed something on the floor by the sofa, and he picked it up.

"You're careless with money."

"Oh! It must have fallen out when I was looking for something in my bag."

He gave her the money. Her hand again ended up on his groin. He pushed it away but couldn't help feeling an erection.

"Not now."

Candice sat back. "What's the matter with you?"

"I spoke to Mummy about us. She didn't take the news so well."

"So, what are you planning to do?"

"Maybe I should give her some time."

"You're not your mother's little boy anymore. Why can't you make your own decisions?"

He got up and walked to the window and stared outside, then gazed around the living room.

There in the corner stood a bucket filled with water from the morning's rain.

She's right. She can't control my life.

"Look at this place! You can't stay here anymore. Start packing, and in a few days, you'll move to my house!"

She ran over to him and showered him with kisses.

"Oh, I love you Miguel!"

He rubbed her belly.

"I love you too, and this one as well."

As they spoke, Terrel left Candice's yard, his hands balled into fists. It was his dearest wish to be able to burst open the door and break all of Miguel's teeth.

He stared at the window.

If she doesn't leave him, I will kill them both.

At that moment, his phone rang. He answered it as he walked away.

Miguel sat down on the sofa with Candice on his lap. She began playing with his hair.

"Are your children going to stay with us?"

"Yes, they are. I can't leave them with my mother."

Hmm. Those bastards better not give me any trouble.

"Will they accept me?"

"Why not? You're kind and loving, and they need a mother."

They kissed gently.

Candice's phone suddenly rang. At first, she ignored it. Then she sighed and picked it up from the table.

"Candice here."

"Chase that idiot away. Or I will do it myself," said Terrel, as he sat in his car.

Candice glanced at Miguel, feeling awkward.

"Mummy, I can't come now," she said.

"If I don't see him leave, I'll be on your doorstep."

"Alright. I'll try."

She put down her cell phone, feeling faint.

"Who was that?" Miguel asked.

"Mummy." She gave Miguel an apologetic look. "I totally forgot. I need to drop the medication that I bought for her earlier over to her place. I guess that means that you have to leave now."

Miguel got up. "I can take you over there."

"I prefer to walk. She lives nearby."

They walked to the door, where Miguel faced her.

"I'll come for you the day after tomorrow."

"Why don't you give me a week? I need to sort out something with my mom," she said, wrapping her arms around his neck.

He smiled and touched her chin.

"Anything for you. I adore you, my little dolly."

As he left Candice's house, Terrel drove away.

Miguel turned and watched it leave. Then his attention fixed on her.

"I'll see you in a week," he said, and walked away. But his mind was questioning what had just happened.

Whose car was that?

Candice went inside and lay down on the sofa, pondering about what she should do.

Oh, boy. So hard to decide. Terrel promised to build a house for us. But Miguel already has a house, a car, and a good job. What should I do? If I choose Miguel, Terrel will kill both of us. If I stay with Terrel, I might have nothing. Then again, Kingpin is another threat.

Candice knew that she was in a tangled situation. Any wrong decision could drastically affect her life. However, she chose to take the risks, move in with Miguel, and get rid of Terrel. With Miguel she could get stability and certainty.

After Gail's traumatic experience, there was a lot of tension and distrust between Gail and her mother--especially when Anil made Chelsea think that her own daughter was a liar.

As Chelsea put the food on the table, she called out, "Dinner is ready!"

Anil came in and kissed his wife.

Suddenly he farted loudly. His face reddened, and he grinned sheepishly.

"Oh gyul, I couldn't keep it in. The gas was killing me."

She began fanning with her hand.

"Boy! Not by my food!"

He glanced at the table and rubbed his hands together. There before him was his favorite: curried duck, roti, and curried *channa* with potato.

"It's not my fault. You took too long to cook. Where's the coconut water?"

"We don't have any."

He sat at the table and she joined him. He dished out some *channa*.

"Don't eat that!" Chelsea warned him. "You'll be farting all day!"

She called out into the hall. "Gail, come here right now!"

"I'm not hungry," Gail answered.

Anil looked up from his plate. "Leave she alone and eat your food, woman."

"No. She can't do whatever she please to do."

Chelsea got up and walked out. She went straight into Gail's bedroom.

Her daughter was sitting on the bed and texting to her friend.

"Listen! Move your lazy ass and come out to dine with us!"

"No! I'm not going to sit at the same table as that rapist."

Chelsea marched over and slapped her.

"Whore and a liar! You slept with some dotish boy and got pregnant from him. And now you want to accuse my husband?"

Gail got up, and tears sparkled in her eyes.

"How can you not believe your own daughter? I'm sure the police will believe me."

"Listen to me! If you go to the police with your blah blah lies, I will be dead for you!"

Chelsea looked at her daughter's phone. "Give me that phone!"

Gail handed the phone to her and lay back in her bed. She covered her head with a blanket.

Chelsea looked at her for a moment, and then left. She went back to the living room and sat at the table. She dropped the phone on it.

Anil was already halfway done with his meal.

"I heard you quarrelling. What happened now?"

"She keeps saying the same dirt about you. I can't come to terms how my own child can come up with these lies."

"You know how teenagers are when their hormones are acting up. They behave weird."

"I never acted like she. It's just doltishness. I might send her to her father. He left we for some young gyul. Let him now take some responsibility and put some sense into Gail's brain."

As the two of them ate, Gail lay crying on her bed.

"How could she betray me? I'm telling her the truth, but she refuses to hear me!"

She sat up and retrieved her second cell phone. She texted to her friend.

'I'm not feeling so good.'

'Why?' came the response.

'My life in a mess and I feel so lonely.'

'You're not lonely. You have me, and other friends.'

'There's something I have to tell you.'

'What is it?'

'Anil drugged me and then raped me.'

'What? Are you sure? Did you tell anyone?'

'Only Mother, but she refuses to believe me. She treats me as if I'm some kind of jerk. I just don't know what to do.'

'Why don't you go see Pastor Drake. He might be able to help you'.

'I don't want to go alone.'

'Go outside and wait for me tomorrow at 9 a.m. We'll go together.'

'Okay. Thank you, gyul. You're my real friend.'

Gail put away the cell phone.

Anil felt relieved, knowing that Chelsea was on his side. At the same time, his cravings for Gail kept growing. Day by day, he kept visualizing playing with her body and seeing her naked.

Now he felt guilty and tried to chase away the lust for her. He needed to talk to someone about this, but who could he trust? He had two options--either visit a psychologist or go to Father Piero. Going to a psychologist was too risky. Someone could notice him there and spread gossip.

Would a psychologist keep a rape situation a secret?

The only person who could keep his secret was Father Piero.

His decision made, he called him and asked about an urgent appointment. Father Piero agreed to meet him and hear his confession.

After dinner, he helped Chelsea clean up and then sat in front of the TV watching the news.

Should I tell him? What if he talks to the police? No, priests swear not to break the seal of confession.

Chelsea went into the bathroom and began brushing her teeth. Worries swirled through her mind.

Why is this happening to my family? First, Gail got pregnant. Then she got rid of it. If Anil didn't take her for the abortion, who took her then? What a shame I can't even tell anyone about it. They would say I brought up a whore.

She spat out the toothpaste and rinsed her mouth. Then she went into her bedroom. She slid into her pajamas and lay down.

Why does Anil come to bed after I fall asleep?

Anil looked at his watch and turned off the TV.

"Hey Chelsea, I'll be back in an hour!" he said loudly.

He picked up his keys from the table and left the house, then drove to the priest's house.

Upon reaching it, he parked the car in front. He sat debating whether he should open up to Father or leave. Then he got out of the car and rang the priest's doorbell.

Father Piero opened the door.

"Good evening, Father."

"Good evening. Please come in."

Anil went into the living room. The TV was still on.

Father turned it off and gestured toward the furniture. "Please have a seat."

Anil looked around and then sat down in a chair.

"Would you like anything to drink?"

"No, Father, thank you. I just need to confess something horrible that I've done."

Father Piero sat down on another chair.

"I'm listening."

"Hmm. I don't even know how to start." He stayed quiet a moment, then blurted, "She got pregnant by me and I took her for an abortion. She almost died because of me."

"I'm not getting it. Who got pregnant?"

Anil didn't dare to raise his eyes.

"My 14-year-old stepdaughter."

Father Piero froze for a moment, speechless.

"How could you lay your hands on a teenage girl? She's still a child! What you did is very malicious and sinful. There will be consequences for your actions."

Anil stood up, unbuttoning his top shirt button.

"But Father, I didn't do it purposely. I can't get rid of this strong attraction to her."

"Please sit back down. You are in control of your mind. You had free will to fight it off. Yet, instead, you chose to be a prisoner of your evil desires and lust."

"Do you think it's easy? Many times, I said no to myself, and still I went into her bedroom and watched her sleeping."

"Then you shouldn't have been living in the same house with her."

Anil wiped his forehead with a handkerchief.

"That's not easy to do. Can you please accept my confession?"

"A child should never be touched or hurt. You should turn yourself in to the police and face the legal consequences of your evil actions. Unless you do that, your sins will never be forgiven. You won't be able to receive holy communion."

"No, Father Piero! I can't do that. My whole life will be ruined."

Father looked at his watch. He was late for his appointment to see a dying parishioner. He stood up.

"I'm sorry, but I must cut our conversation short. I have to visit a dying person."

"Oh, sorry. I didn't know."

Father walked Anil to the door and opened it.

"Remember, you are in control of your actions. Do what's right. If you don't change and repent, you'll be sent to the burning furnace of Hell."

Anil shook Father's hand.

"Thank you, Father Piero, for listening to me."

"Welcome."

Anil walked to his car, feeling worried. He started the engine and looked at himself in the rearview mirror.

He wants me to turn myself in to the police. Is he crazy? Once she moves in with she father, things will get back to normal.

He drove back home.

However, after Anil's visit Father Piero couldn't find peace. He left his house and headed toward his appointment. While driving, his mind was in turmoil, and he felt hot and agitated.

So many children are being sexually or physically abused. They're not safe anymore. Please Lord, protect them.

What he had heard was a horrible crime against the teenage girl, and it had to be reported to the police. But he had given an oath not to break the sacred seal of confession.

"Oh, Lord please show me a way. If I report him, I will break my oath. But If I keep silent, he might hurt her again or someone else."

As he neared the police station, he slowed down and looked at it as he passed. At that moment, his cell phone rang.

"Father Piero here."

"Father, his condition is deteriorating. He might die before you get here.

"I'm on my way," said the priest, and put his cell on his lap.

Selfish man. He only thinks about not ruining his own life, but has ruined the poor child's life and her future marriage, and he has also stolen her innocence.

He sped up and passed the station.

<hr>

In the morning Gail, dressed in a green blouse and a black skirt, left the house without notifying her mother. She stood on the road waiting for her friend Darla.

A private taxi stopped, and a young driver popped his head out.

"Where are you going? I can take you."

She looked at his number plate and then at his smiling face. She'd heard stories of women getting raped by taxi drivers. He could be one of them.

"No, thank you."

He drove away. Another taxi stopped next to her. She looked inside and felt relief upon seeing her neighbor Inshan in the driver's seat and her friend Darla in the back.

"Hi, uncle," she said, opening the door of the car.

"Good morning, Gail."

"Hey Darla. What's up?"

"Nothing much, other than boring schoolwork."

Gail got into the back seat.

"Where are you going, girls?"

"Can you please take us to Pastor Drake's house on Rosan Street?"

The driver headed to the stated address.

Darla looked sadly at her friend. Gail's eyes were sunken, and her chin seemed to have become longer.

"You look horrible. Your face is so thin."

"Did we make this trip so that you could discuss my face?"

"No, it's just I haven't seen you in school for a few days. It seems ages."

"You know I couldn't come."

"How is your mummy doing?" Inshan asked. "I haven't spoken to her for a few weeks."

"She's fine."

"What about Anil?"

She kept silent, then in a near-whisper she said, "I don't want to talk about him."

Inshan looked surprised. "What happen, gyul? Did you have a fight with him?"

"No. I'm just not in the mood."

"Why? Something happen at home?"

"No, uncle."

Gail's blood rushed to her temples, and she broke out in a sweat. She looked outside.

Why is he minding my business? I want to be left alone!

Inshan stared at Gail through the rear-view mirror. Knowing Gail from childhood, he could say that something was happening in her life that was not good.

After a while, the driver stopped at Pastor Drake's office. It was a two-story house painted in white.

Gail got out and waited for Darla. When she didn't move, Gail stuck her head back inside.

"Are you coming?"

"I need to drop something off at my aunty's. I'll come to pick you up in a while."

Gail paid the driver and closed the door.

She walked into the yard. When she reached the pastor's door, she rang the doorbell. A man in his sixties, with short, gray, curly hair, opened the door.

"How can I help you?"

"Are you Pastor Drake?"

Pastor looked around and then at her. "Yes I am."

"I have to get some solution to my issues, and I need your help."

"Come in and I'll see what I can do."

He led her to a small cream-colored room that had a sofa and a coffee table in the middle. The aroma of lavender hit her nose. She looked around, uncertain.

"Take a seat and let's talk," he said.

She made herself comfortable on the sofa. He brought a chair close to her and sat on it.

"I'm having problems at home and don't know how to deal with them. It seems as if I'm attracting bad things to myself."

Pastor put his hand over his mouth and stared at her for a few moments.

"Your aura is dark, and your energy vibes are low. It seems that you have been attracting evil spirits to yourself. Have you been having issues with your boyfriend?"

"No. I have none."

His staring and questioning were making her feel awkward. She didn't dare to look into his eyes.

"Are your parents divorcing?" He flicked his gaze at her boobs.

"They're already divorced." Sweat dripped down her face.

"Would you like something to drink?" he offered.

"Yes, please," she answered, hoping that he would stop eying her.

"I'll be back," he said.

As he left, a feeling of restlessness or as if something wasn't right overpowered Gail's mind. Her face became moist with sweat.

What am I doing here? He can't solve my problems. He's only a pastor, who has no clue to anything.

Drake returned with a glass in his hand, which he passed to her. She looked at it and hesitated.

"Have a drink, and let's see what is the root of your problems."

She drank the juice, which had an unfamiliar sweet taste. He took the glass away from her and sat on the chair.

"Give me your hand," he said.

He grasped her hand and stared somewhere above her head.

"You have dark spots in your aura. In some places, it's broken. We need to clear and restore it, or you will continue attracting bad luck to yourself, along with the spirits from the lower levels. They feed on your anger and bitterness. As long as you sin, you act like a magnet to those spirits."

She found the courage to raise her eyes.

"But I didn't do anything wrong!"

"Anger and unforgiveness is your failure. Get rid of them or your soul will be destroyed."

Trembling took over Gail's fragile body.

"Can you fix me up?"

"I'll perform a cleansing aura ceremony. But you have to purify your own soul, with good thoughts directed toward positiveness and toward God."

She pulled her hand out from his.

"I'm feeling a little bit sleepy."

The pastor got up and left the room. He came back with a white sheet.

"Take off your clothes and wrap yourself in this sheet, then lie down on the sofa. Then we will start the ceremony."

She took the sheet, and he was gone again. She stood up and looked toward the doorway leading to the other room.

Why would a man of God talk about auras? It's not a Christian notion. Shouldn't he just be praying?

She took off her clothes and sat on the sofa. Then she wrapped herself in the sheet and lay down.

The pastor came back with a pot of strong-smelling incense in his hand. It burned and smoked, making Gail cough.

He held out some more of the odd juice.

"You need to relax. Drink this."

She sat up and peered at the green liquid, and then drank it.

"Lie down now."

She lay back, yawning, as the pastor walked around her with incense in his hand. Her eyes followed his every movement. Her mind and body relaxed, and a smile flickered on her face.

He put the incense on the coffee table. Then he went over to her and looked at her face.

"How are you feeling?"

She just stared blankly at him.

He smiled, then took off his clothes. Seeing him naked, Gail tried to get up, but was unable to. It was as if her strength had left her body. Her eyes felt heavy.

"Why are you undressing?"

"The evil spirits refuse to leave. I have to face them without any material attachments."

She put her head back on the cushion. Everything spun around her eyes. She suddenly started sweating and feeling cold shivers.

And then she blacked out.

He came up to her and gently unwrapped the sheet. His eyes ran hungrily across her body as he sat on the sofa beside her.

Foolish, but pretty girl.

He gently caressed her legs.

She so fresh and young.

He positioned himself over her.

Just then, the doorbell began ringing, once, twice, then incessantly. He got off her and hastily put on his clothes. Then he quickly wrapped her back in the sheet and rushed to the door.

He opened the door slightly and peered out at Darla.

"I'm kind of busy. Can you come later, please?"

He tried to close the door, but she pushed it towards him.

"I came for my friend."

"What friend?"

Darla tried to take a glimpse down the corridor.

"I dropped my friend Gail off here and have now come back for her."

"Oh, that girl. Come in, please."

He let her in.

"You stay here and I'll get her."

He walked into the other room and closed the door. He approached Gail and shook her shoulder.

"Get up. It's over."

She opened her eyes.

"Where am I?" She stared around.

"You're in Pastor Drake's office."

"Oh. When will you perform the ceremony?"

"I did it. Your friend is here. Please dress and leave."

"Were you able to clean my aura?"

He came up closer and eyed her cautiously.

"You will need to come one more time. Then you will be free of all negativity."

He went to the corridor. "She's coming."

Gail slowly stood up and dressed.

Pastor's phone rang and he answered. Darla could hear him joking and laughing,

Gail weaved dizzily out of the room and came out to the corridor.

"We can go now. Thank you, Pastor Drake," said Gail.

"Just a minute," said the pastor into the phone. He took the cell from his ear, and Gail put money into his hand.

"Don't be anxious. I will chase away all evil spirits. Just go home and rest."

The girls left his office and then got into the taxi.

"So, how was the session?" Darla asked her.

"I don't know. I think I fell asleep, but I'm at peace now."

"He was able to relax you. He's so good with people. They call him charmer and doctor."

I still can't get it why he undressed.

Gail leaned back and yawned.

"I feel so sleepy. Wake me up if I fall asleep."

She closed her eyes and dozed off.

A week after their conversation, Candice moved into Miguel's house. To her joy, his children were still with their granny.

Once she was settled in, Candice removed Sheila's underwear from the bedroom drawers and put them in a garbage bag. She packed the chest of drawers with her own undergarments. A portrait of her wearing a red dress went up on the wall right above the bed's headboard.

However, her joy wasn't going to last long, because Miguel's children were coming back home. She didn't like the idea of looking after children that weren't hers. They required too much time and were noisy.

On a late Monday afternoon, when the sun shone brightly, Miguel was at his mother's. He carried two bags of clothes out to his car and returned to the living room.

Ronnel sat on the floor, playing with his toy soldiers.

"Son, go tell Granny that we're ready to leave."

Ronnel picked his soldiers up and put them on the table. Then he went to the bedroom.

Elisa was packing her grandchildren's clothes in a garbage bag. Nadia came up to Elisa and gave her a fluffy rabbit and a pink bear.

"Granny, please put them in the bag."

Elisa did so. Miguel's son came in.

"Granny, Daddy is ready to take us home!"

She looked at him. "Come here, big boy." She looked at Nadia. "And you too."

They ran to her. She embraced him and Nadia tightly.

"Granny, you're choking me!" said Nadia.

Elisa eased up on her hug.

"I'm going to miss you so much. Please behave and don't give Daddy any trouble. If anything happens, please call me."

"What can happen to us?" Ronnel stared at Elisa.

"Nothing. I'm just saying. Let's not keep your father waiting."

She picked up the two garbage bags and carried them into the living room.

As soon as the children came in, Miguel stood up.

"Time to go."

His mother looked at him.

"I hope you know what you're doing," she said.

Miguel smiled.

"Mother you're worrying unnecessarily. Everything is going to be fine."

"I hope so. If you need any help with the children, call me any time."

Miguel took the bags from his mother.

"Me and Candice will manage well."

They walked to the door.

"Bye, Granny!" her grandchildren called as they went to the car.

As soon as the car began moving, Ronnel asked, "Who is Candice?"

"Hmm. She's my girlfriend. She's going to live with us."

"But why?" asked Ronnel.

"I love her, and she's going to help me to look after you."

"But Granny was looking after us. I don't want a stranger in our house," said Nadia.

"She's not a stranger. She is a woman who I plan to marry."

The children looked at each other wide-eyed.

"But she's not our mother," said Ronnel.

A few cars passed Miguel. He glanced in the rear-view mirror, trying to see his children.

"You know I love your mummy, and no one can take her place. But Mummy has gone to heaven, and we have to move on."

"Sometimes I see Mummy in my dreams, as if she's never left us," said Ronnel.

Miguel looked at Ronnel in the mirror.

"She's with us because her memory lives in our hearts."

Miguel turned the car to the left. After passing a few houses, he parked the car in his driveway, and they got out. He took the bags out of the car and opened the door to the house.

The children slowly entered the house. Loud laughter accosted their ears. They stood in the hallway, both staring upstairs.

Ronnel recalled standing at the top of the staircase, seeing his father being hurt. His body flinched, and he glanced at his father.

"Daddy, who is upstairs?"

"Candice. Go and meet her."

Ronnel did not move.

"Walk up, boy," said Miguel.

Ronnel slowly climbed upstairs, followed by Nadia. They stood by the closed door, hesitating.

"Are you kidding? Children only bring trouble," they heard her say.

"I'm going to my room," said Nadia. She walked away.

He grasped the handle and slowly opened the door. His heart raced as he walked in.

Candice was lying on the bed using her cell phone. She sat up and looked at Ronnel.

"I will call you back," she said, ending the call.

"Hi," mumbled Ronnel. He started to back out.

"Hey, you. Come here," she said.

He slowly walked towards her.

"I don't bite," she said.

Her voice seemed familiar to him. He came up closer to her.

"So, you're Miguel's baby boy."

"I'm not a baby."

"Hmm, you don't even resemble him."

"I look like my mummy. Daddy used to say she was the prettiest woman in the world."

"Really?"

"Can I go now?"

"Yes, you can leave."

Ronnel walked to his bedroom. Nadia was on his bed, playing with her doll.

"Did you see her?"

"Yes."

"Is she a nice lady?"

"I don't know."

Miguel called to them from downstairs.

"Ronnel, get your sister and come downstairs."

"Let's go, Nadia."

They left the bedroom, and ran into Candice at the top of the stairs.

"Oh, sorry," said Nadia, moving back.

Candice looked at her with curiosity.

"And you're his daughter. Probably look like Sheila as well."

"Why are you playing slow turtles?" came Miguel's voice again.

"They're coming," said Candice.

The three of them walked downstairs and into the dining room. Miguel was putting food on the table.

"Sit down, and let's have some dinner."

They took their seats. Miguel gazed around at his children.

"This is our first dinner in this house since... Anyway, I'm glad that we're in our home now. You probably already met Candice."

The children gazed at her.

"She's beautiful," said Nadia.

"Oh, thank you," answered Candice.

"She looks like a rat," thought Candice.

Nadia looked at the food on the table. There stood her favorite pasta.

"Daddy, could you please give me some pasta?"

He dished it out for her. She ate some.

"Tastes like Mummy's." She put down her fork and peered up at her father. "I miss her. Why did bad people kill her?"

"Honey, you focus on eating. We'll talk about Mummy later," said Miguel.

Nadia stared at Sheila's photo on the wall.

"I want Mummy to be here with us. She used to take care of us good and loved us."

Can't she shut up? 'Mummy' this and 'Mummy' that. I wish Sheila actually was dead.

"Nadia, stop talking about Mummy," said Ronnel.

He looked at Candice. "How long are you going to stay in our house?"

Candice glanced at Miguel with a smile. "Maybe you should answer," she said.

"I'm not sure. However, she can stay as long as she wants. Now please have your dinner."

Candice picked up a bowl of potato salad not far from Ronnel. The movement exposed her hands. His mother's gold bracelet on her wrist caught his attention.

Why is she wearing Mummy's bracelet?

Then his attention moved to her chest, and he tensed up.

His mother's gold chain and pendant were around Candace's neck.

Then he glanced at her hand and noticed a tattoo of a snakelike head.

Seeing him staring at her, Candice glanced at her hand. The make-up had worn off a little bit, exposing the snake's head.

She got up. "I'll be back," she said.

I have to be twice as careful now, with these little demons around.

She rushed to the washroom to apply some concealer. Ronnel stared after her.

What was that on her hand?

Candice came back, and the rest of the dinner went quietly.

Later on, after putting his kids to bed, Miguel came into his bedroom. Candice was in the bed wearing a red nightie.

"Hey, I thought you would never come back."

"You know how it is with children around. They want all your attention. They also talk your ear off!"

He pulled off all of his clothes except his underpants and sat down on the bed. Then he lay down next to Candace and started kissing her. He patted her belly.

"Hey, little one. I can't wait till I see you."

A smile sparkled on her face.

"You are really built amazingly," he said. "Some women at this stage already have big belly bumps. But looking at you, one would never guess that you're pregnant."

"It's hereditary. When my mom was carrying me, no one knew she was pregnant until she reached five months."

Miguel lay on his left side, facing her.

"Sheila also had a small build. I don't really remember her having a huge belly."

What the hell is he recalling her for? She's gone for good.

As they spoke, they heard a knock at the door. Then the door opened slightly. Nadia came inside, her eyes wet.

"Daddy, I saw bad people taking Mummy away. Can I stay with you, please?"

Miguel jumped off the bed. He put on a robe and picked his daughter up. He caressed her back.

"The bad people are not here anymore, and Mother's now with Jesus."

"They're going to come for us!"

"No, honey, they won't."

He put her gently on the bed. Candice was forced to move to the edge.

Miguel brought out a book from a drawer.

"Let's read some stories," he said, sitting on the bed beside her.

Candice looked at them silently. Jealousy was eating her from the inside.

First, they messed up my dinner, and now this caterpillar is stuck to my bed.

Miguel began reading. As he read, Nadia kept closing her eyes and yawning. Candice turned away on her other side.

Nadia fell asleep in the middle of the story. When he looked down at her, Miguel couldn't help but see Sheila, and then recalled the last events of her life.

He put aside the book and opened a drawer, from which he took out matches and a pack of cigarette. He walked down the steps and then outside.

He stood by the door, smoking and gazing at the bright stars.

She looks exactly like her mother. Will always remind me of her.

The neighbor's dogs began barking. He threw the butt on the ground and checked his surroundings. Then he went in.

———◆———

At Toothless' house, under a starlit sky, a few men and women sat in his yard on plastic chairs, smoking and drinking. They were celebrating Toothless' birthday.

Loud music filled the air. On a plastic table stood a big pot of corn soup and plastic plates, cups, and cutlery with napkins. A curried chicken, roti, pumpkin, and bodi[80] were also on the table, covered with aluminum foil. His friend, Darion, who had long dreadlocks and wore a gold chain, smoked marijuana as he watched Toothless.

A woman wearing a blouse and shorts was making herself too comfortable on Toothless' lap.

After a lengthy make-out session, he pushed her away.

"Enough. Go get your own chair."

She sat down on the one next to him.

"Boy, I can't believe it. You made it to 40! All those escapes from death you've had!" said Darion.

"The last one was a narrow escape. I could have ended up with a bullet in my head," said Toothless.

"Yeh, man Jah is with you," said his Jamaican friend, sipping rum.

Another woman, Trianna, came up to Darion.

"I'm tired of sitting. Let's dance."

Darion got up and went with his girlfriend. He held onto her waist and she put her arms around his neck. They moved slowly to the music.

---

[80] Long beans

At the same time, a white car stopped in front of Toothless' house. A man got out of the car, holding a newspaper over his hand.

He stood by the gate and called out, "Where's Toothless?"

Toothless got up and walked to the gate.

"I'm here. Why are you looking for me?"

The man whipped a pistol out from under the newspaper and shot Toothless in the belly.

Toothless fell to the ground. His guests ran inside the house and dropped to the floor, afraid of further shooting.

The man looked at Toothless' bleeding body and then walked away.

Trianna stood up and looked outside through the window.

"He killed him! Oh, God. He's dead!"

"Hush, woman!" someone admonished her. "Lie down before he kills you as well."

Instead, Trianna ran outside. She dashed to the body, screaming, "Bastards! They hurt him!"

Toothless lay on the grass, his hand on his stomach. He breathed heavily as his blood colored the grass red. His eyes were fixed on dark shadows in the sky. Those shadows were coming closer.

"He's bleeding to death. Someone call the police!"

The other guests slowly came out and surrounded Toothless as Darion called an ambulance.

Onlookers poured onto the street, wanting to see what had happened. Some were taking pictures.

Darion rushed towards them.

"Have some respect for the man. Stop taking pictures!" he shouted.

The ambulance arrived, and Toothless was lifted into it. The EMTs bandaged his wounds, trying to stop the bleeding, and connected him to some oxygen.

"Hey man, try to stay awake," said one of the EMTs.

Toothless' vision became blurry, and he gasped for every breath.

However, he didn't make it to the hospital. Halfway there, his heartbeat stopped.

ESCAPE

It was late in the evening, and Adrian was in his office, which was on the second floor of a five-story building.

On his desk was an open briefcase, in which Adrian was packing his passport and a ticket to Venezuela.

He walked to a wall and removed the painting that hung there. Behind it was a safe.

He turned the knob and it clicked a few times. Then he opened the door and took out some US dollars from the safe, and put the money into the briefcase.

He went to his window and gazed out on the street. A bright round moon captured his attention for a second. It seemed to be so close to the earth, as if he could reach out and touch it.

Then he looked at his watch. It was 7 p.m. His plane was leaving in four hours, and he needed to stop by his apartment to pick up his luggage.

I must hurry if I'm going to catch my plane.

He picked up his briefcase and rushed to the door. As he was about to open it, his office phone rang, making him walk back to the desk.

He put the receiver to his ear.

"Adrian's Detective Agency," he said, as he unbuttoned the top button of his shirt.

He listened but no one answered. Yet he could hear heavy breathing.

"Did you swallow your tongue?" he asked.

Adrian put down the phone. He pulled open a drawer, took out a pistol, and put it on his desk. Then he waited.

Through the tiny spaces on his door's blinds he caught a glimpse of human shadows. He went over and peered through the slats.

Two men had entered his secretary's room. Both held guns in their hands. One of them pointed to Adrian's office door.

Without delay, Adrian picked up his gun and briefcase. He rushed toward the window, which gave out onto a fire escape.

Unfortunately, he bumped into a metal suit of armor that was part of his office's décor. The knight clattered to the floor.

Adrian could hear the two men run towards the door. One of them kicked the door open.

Jumping over the scattered armor, Adrian crossed over the windowsill and ran down the staircase. The men ran to the window and began shooting. The bullets barely missed him.

One of them, a man called Florin, spoke on a walkie-talkie. "He's coming down. Get him!"

Then they crossed over the windowsill and chased after Adrian.

He jumped from the last platform to the ground, dropping his briefcase. He picked it up and ran towards his car. The door wasn't even closed before he'd started the engine and had driven away.

He stole a look into the rearview mirror and smiled grimly.

They think they can stop me.

He noticed his chasers getting into another car. It was a white Hyundai, and it was now giving chase.

It didn't take too long for the Hyundai to drive up closer to Adrian's car. Florin lowered the front window and began shooting at Adrian's car. Adrian increased his speed, trying to reach the railroad tracks.

There was a cracking sound as the bullets shattered his window.

The distance between him and the railroad tracks was closing. From afar, he could see a fast-moving train. He approached the railroad, pressed down hard on the accelerator, and drove over the railroad tracks. As soon as he crossed them, the train passed behind him.

The Hyundai stopped at the railroad crossing. Stephan, the driver, glared at the train and hit the steering wheel.

"We've lost him. Doesn't make sense to continue chasing after him," he said.

Florin opened the window and spat outside.

"What are we going to tell Corneliu?"

"I have no idea."

Stephan turned his car to the left and drove in the other direction.

Adrian headed straight to the train station, where he parked his car and then caught a taxi.

"Please take me to the airport," he said, taking his seat.

"What terminal?" asked the driver.

"International, please."

The driver pressed on the gas, and the taxi started out.

Adrian dialed his secretary.

"Hi, Elena. Sorry for calling so late. But I need a huge favor from you."

"What can I do for you?" He could hear the smile in her voice.

"Someone wants me dead. Two men came into my office, trying to shoot me. Luckily I was able to get away."

"Were you hurt?"

"No, but the car was damaged. I left it in the train station and am now heading to the airport."

Adrian scanned his surroundings outside a few times, making sure that he wasn't being followed.

"Please take my spare car key and drive my car to the garage. Let them fix it."

"In which station did you park it?"

"They might be tapping my cellphone. A place where your bag was snatched."

"Anything else?"

"Stay away from my office until I get back. It might not be safe."

The taxi stopped at the international terminal.

"I have to go now."

"Have a safe trip."

Adrian paid his fees and headed to the boarding counter. A few people with luggage were waiting ahead of him. He looked at their bags.

I didn't even get a chance to pick up my luggage. Now I have to shop in Venezuela.

He sighed. *I should bill the client for this. After all, I'm going for his daughter.*

He came up to the ticket counter.

"Good evening," he said, presenting his online reservation and passport to the agent.

"Good evening," she said, taking them.

She looked at his printed reservation and began typing on her computer. Then she printed a boarding pass.

"How many pieces of luggage are you checking in?"

He couldn't help but smile.

"None."

Her eyebrows went up in surprise, but she maintained her professional demeanor.

"Here is your boarding pass. The boarding time is at 10 p.m., at gate A 12."

Adrian took the boarding pass, along with his passport and reservation.

"Thank you."

Briefcase in hand, he walked towards his gate.

After arriving in Venezuela, Adrian checked into the hotel and started working on his plan to free Daniela, Sheila, and Violeta. It was formulated quickly, and he set out as soon as he could.

For a week he spied on the brothel's activities. He stood not far from it for hours, watching and writing the times when people came and went. He also met up with some people who would help him to carry out his plan.

One afternoon, as he stood in his usual spot, he noticed Luciana walking towards the brothel. She wore a huge hat and sunglasses. It looked like she was being followed by a man.

Luciana hurried to the brothel and put her hand on the doorbell.

"Luciana!" shouted the man from a distance.

She was too frightened to turn around. A certain paralysis hit her like a hammer. With a shaky hand, she rang the bell a few times, refusing to turn towards the voice.

It was her husband.

"Luciana! I know it's you!" he shouted.

The man strode up to her and gripped her shoulder. She turned around, pale as a ghost. She wished she was invisible.

"So, it's true. You have been selling your body in the brothel."

"No! It's not what you think!"

He slapped her and spat in her face.

"You're a cheapish whore. You can't be around our daughter anymore. Don't come back home!"

Adrian felt like he should go over, but he didn't want to blow his cover.

The man began walking away. Adrian could hear him mumbling, "I married a damned whore. What an embarrassment!"

Luciana rushed toward her husband. She caught his hand as she sobbed. A few women passing by looked at them.

"Please wait! You don't understand. I did this for us, so we could have food on the table."

He pulled his hand away.

"Don't touch me with your dirty hands. Yuck! I don't even want to imagine how many men you've slept with. You could have given us a disease!"

"Please don't turn your back on me. You couldn't find a job. We had bills to pay and a child to feed."

He pushed her towards the brothel.

"Go back to your whorehouse, and don't come near our daughter again!"

Crying, Luciana ran towards the brothel.

The door was open. Victor, who had been standing in the doorway, saw everything.

"Come inside. You're attracting the attention of the passersby," he said with a frown.

She dashed inside, still crying.

Adrian breathed a sigh of relief and walked to the hotel. He liked where he was staying, despite problems with water and not having toilet paper in the lobby restrooms.

Feeling sweaty, he decided to take a shower. But when he turned on the tap, there was no water.

"No water again."

He sat on the bed and made a call. Bernadette answered.

"Bernadette's residence. How can I help you?"

"Good afternoon, Bernadette. This is Adrian. I was here a month ago."

"Hmm. Your voice sounds familiar. Are you the one from Romania?"

"Yes, it's me. I came back again. I would like to visit your place again with a couple of my friends."

"My doors are always open to you."

"Can I book the girls for tomorrow?"

"How many girls?"

"Last time I saw a pretty teenage girl, and I had a good time with Sheila. I would like to spend time with both. For my friends you can get anyone. How much will it cost?"

"Sheila and Daniela both will cost 500 US. I'll take one hundred each for the other girls."

"No problem. We'll come tomorrow at midday."

"See you then." Bernadette hung up the phone.

After talking to Bernadette, Adrian made one more phone call, to notify his colleague Carlos about the arrangements for tomorrow. They agreed to meet at 12 p.m., in front of the brothel.

The next day, at 11.30 a.m., Adrian left the hotel with two bottles of whisky, carrying them in a plastic bag. Before leaving his room, he had added a powerful drug to both bottles and had mixed them well.

He headed towards the brothel. As he walked, he regarded various walls with paintings of the Venezuelan leader. Then he passed through the park and turned left. At the corner of the street, he met Carlos with three men.

"Amigos! How's it going?"

"Not too bad," said Carlos. "Let me introduce my friends to you."

He pointed to a broad-shouldered man. "This is Eduardo."

Carlos gestured toward the other man. "And this is Gonzalo. He's the one who will take Sheila back home. However, he wants a quarter of his payment beforehand."

Adrian shook Gonzalo's hand.

"This is Lautaro. He's a man of action. He would fight till the death if necessary. No fear in him."

Lautaro was short and had bulky muscles.

"Nice to meet you guys," said Adrian, shaking his hand.

Then his attention turned to the subject of the brothel.

"Did you get a car?" he asked.

"Yes. It's parked on the other street," answered Carlos.

"Let's go into action then."

Adrian walked towards the brothel, followed by the men. He rang the bell, and the door was opened by a tall fat man who Adrian had not seen before.

"Adrian?" he asked, looking at each of them inquiringly.

"Yes, I am, and these are my friends."

They went inside. The man, Pablo, locked the door and led them to the guest room.

"Please have a seat," he said.

Adrian noticed the piano. His eyebrows flew up in surprise.

"Where's Victor?" he asked Pablo.

"He's gone somewhere."

Adrian frowned. "What about Bernadette?"

"Oh, she's here. She'll join you shortly."

Adrian took the whisky bottles from his bag.

"Do a favor for me, please. Put these in the kitchen. We'll have it later."

Pablo took the bottles and left.

"It looks like he's the only man here. It'll be an easy job for us," said Adrian.

Carlos looked around, assessing the room.

"I agree," he said.

Violeta entered the living room. As soon as she saw the men, she turned around to leave.

"Are you Violeta?" asked Adrian, getting up.

She paused and stared at him.

"How do you know my name?"

Adrian smiled. "Sheila told me. Come closer. I'm not going to hurt you."

Violeta nodded her head. Then she looked at the piano and walked towards it. She sat on the chair that was near the piano.

"Do you play piano?" asked Adrian.

She didn't dare raise her eyes. "Yes, I do."

"Can you play for us please?" asked Adrian.

"I'm not allowed to touch it."

Adrian got up from the sofa and walked to the piano. He began playing a song that was familiar to the girl.

Violeta's face lit up. She put her hands on the keys and played together with Adrian.

Luciana, Sheila, Camille, and Daniela came into the room, together with Pablo and Bernadette.

Adrian turned around and looked directly at Sheila.

Upon seeing Bernadette, Violeta moved quickly away from the piano.

Sheila's heart raced as soon as she recognized Adrian. She began feeling happy again, but also tense.

He kept his promise.

Her hands trembled. The rest of the women walked towards the men. Luciana walked over to Carlos.

"Hi, I'm Luciana."

He got up. "I'm Carlos. Please have a seat."

She sat on the sofa and he made himself comfortable next to her.

"Violeta, you can leave now," said Bernadette.

Violeta made a step to leave.

"Bernadette, please let her play. I'll add another fifty to the fees."

Her eyes lit up. "Anything for a paying customer."

Bernadette had felt ill since early that morning. She had a fever and body pain, so she decided to go to her bedroom.

Once she left, Sheila went over to Adrian.

"I thought I would never see you again," she said.

He eyed her from head to toe.

"A man never breaks his promises. By the way, you look as if you haven't been eating enough."

"I was ill."

"I came to rescue you."

"What about me?" asked Violeta, who stood behind them.

"You too. That's why you should stay close to us."

Carlos and Eduardo stood up.

"We need to neutralize Pablo and Victor," said Carlos.

They walked out of the living room and headed downstairs. They found Pablo in the kitchen, along with his friend Sebastian. Both were smoking cigars and playing poker.

As soon as they came in, Pablo asked, "How can I help you?"

"We needed something to parch our dry throats."

Pablo stood up. He took a bottle of Adrian's drugged whisky and poured it into glasses, then passed them to Eduardo and Carlos.

Sebastian, a short, muscular man, blew smoke towards the guests.

"Fill a glass for me."

"Do you mind?" Sebastian asked Carlos.

"You can have as much as you wish."

Pablo poured a drink for himself and Sebastian.

"Thank you," said Carlos. "Now we'd better go. The girls are waiting for us." He nodded to Pablo and Sebastian, and they walked away.

Pablo sat at the table and picked up his cards.

"These men so stupid. They pay money to sleep with a prostitute when they can get women for free," said Pablo.

Sebastian picked up his glass and drank the whiskey.

"You know, with a prostitute they can do whatever they want. But other women won't agree to certain things. They're too self-conscious for me."

Pablo coughed. "My throat is itching today. I hope I'm not getting the flu," he said, taking a drink.

After a while they both started feeling hot. They took off their t-shirts and again filled their glasses with whiskey.

Carlos and his partner went upstairs and rejoined the others. He took the glass from Eduardo.

"It's time to go after the hostess. Violeta, come here please," said Carlos.

She looked at Carlos and then at Sheila.

"Go and see what he wants," said Sheila.

Violeta walked towards Carlos. "Yes, *señor*?"

"Can you please show me where Bernadette's room is?" he asked.

"Follow me, *señor*."

She led him to Bernadette's bedroom.

"Here it is," she said, pointing at the door.

"Thanks. You can go back now."

As she walked away, he knocked on the door.

"Who is it?"

"This is Carlos. I brought a drink for you."

"Come in."

Carlos opened the door and entered a pink bedroom. Bernadette lay on the bed under a purple silk sheet.

"*Señor*a, I hope I didn't disturb you."

She eyed him, stopping on his biceps.

"Not at all. Shouldn't you be having fun with the women?"

Carlos approached her. "No, *señora,* those women are not my type."

Bernadette sat up, and he gave her the drink.

"Don't call me *señora*. Please sit down."

He sat on the edge of the bed. Bernadette took a few sips.

"What kind of women are your type?"

He eyed her with a smile.

"I love strong-willed, tough women with big breasts."

Bernadette fixed her top and straightened up, exposing her chest.

"Would someone like me fit that description?"

"Why don't you drink? And then we'll talk."

She took a few sips of whisky and giggled.

"Are you trying to make me drunk?"

"I don't use alcohol for that. I have my natural tools, which are very effective on women."

"Show me."

He stood up and took off his pants. He was wearing tight underpants, and there was a huge lump in it. Then he took off his t-shirt.

She gazed hungrily at his muscular body, especially the lump, and in no time was feeling aroused.

"Wow! I want to see what is inside those underpants!" she said.

Victor was nothing compared to him. She drank her whiskey, which seemed to have some bitterness in it.

He pulled down little bit on his underpants, which aroused her. Her eyes enlarged as she hungrily looked at his manhood.

"I never saw as huge a d..."

He quickly pulled up his underpants and took the glass from her. "Good girl."

She took off her top, bra, and red panties. Then she threw them on him. He caught them and sat down on the edge of the bed.

"I want that treasure of yours inside of me," Bernadette told him.

"You're playing dirty. What would Victor say?"

"Victor is my puppy. He has no right to dictate anything to me."

"Good for you."

Bernadette squeezed her breasts with her hands.

"Come to Mummy, baby," she said in a little-girl voice. "I need that toy."

Carlos looked at her with a strained grin.

Oh, Lord I shouldn't have taken off my clothes. She's getting on crazy.

"Why don't you lie down and wait for me? I have an automatic, soft toy for you. Let me get it from the car. I promise that it'll make you cry for more."

She lay back, showing her teeth.

"I prefer the real thing, not something automatic. There's a fire inside me that needs to be extinguished," she said. Then she passed her hands over her face, and Carlos knew that the drug was working. She was obviously feeling dizzy.

He put his clothes back on and walked to the guest room. Adrian was standing not far from the piano, talking to Sheila and Daniela. Violeta wasn't far from them. They came to attention when he walked in.

Adrian quirked an eyebrow at Carlos.

"Done," said Carlos.

"Cool."

Then Adrian looked at Daniela.

"Your father hired me to find you and bring you back home. I'm going to take you back to Romania."

Daniela gasped in happy surprise and had to be reminded to keep her voice down so that she wouldn't attract unwanted attention.

"What about me?" asked Violeta.

His eyes looked from Violeta to Sheila.

"You'll come with us. Then we'll think about what we should do with you."

Eduardo and Lautaro were talking to the other girls. At a signal from Adrian, both got up and gave the girls some money.

"Thank you for your company, ladies. We must leave," said Eduardo.

"Go and get the car," Adrian told Carlos.

Camille looked worriedly at the men.

"Why are you leaving so soon without even getting what you paid for?"

"We didn't come here for sex or women."

A frown appeared on her face. "Why then?"

"I came here for Sheila, Daniela, and Violeta. I'm taking them out of this brothel. I would advise you to leave this kind of life behind as well."

Camille shook her head.

"No, I can't. I have family to support. Without money they will die from hunger."

"Why don't you get a decent job?" asked Adrian.

Camille shook her head again. "Don't you watch the news? Things here just get worse and worse. Poverty is everywhere. It's hard to find food, medication, and jobs."

"My apologies. I didn't mean to offend you."

Carlos walked toward the door, and found it locked.

"Pablo must have the keys."

They suddenly heard coughing by the door.

"Tish!" Carlos said, looking at Adrian.

Victor opened the door. Carlos flung his arm around Victor's neck and jabbed a penknife into the surface of his skin. He forced Victor into the guest room.

The women stopped talking and stared at them.

"What you gonna do about him?" asked Luciana.

"Ladies, please leave," said Adrian.

Camille looked over at Sheila, Violeta, and Daniela.

"I guess this is goodbye. Run away from here, and never look back."

"What about you?" asked Sheila.

"I will stay here till I get a decent job." Teary-eyed, she walked away.

"Who are you? What do you need?" Victor's eyes ran from the men to Sheila.

"Nothing. We're here to free these ladies."

Carlos forced Victor onto the sofa. Eduardo tied his hands behind his back with an extension cord that he found nearby.

"You're not going to get away with it!" Victor spat out. "My people will find you and kill you all!"

Sheila marched up to him and spat in his face.

"You will burn in hell for eternity."

He returned her glare. "I'll deal with you. You piece of garbage! You think you can get away from us?"

She slapped him. He sneered and stared into her eyes.

"The whore is acting up."

Carlos yanked his head back and put a knife to his neck. "Apologize!"

A little drop of blood rolled down Victor's neck.

"I'm not going to apologize to a whore."

Carols brought the knife closer to his eye.

"I said apologize," he growled.

Victor relented. "Okay, I'm sorry."

"The only whore in this room is you," Sheila spat at him. "You have chained your soul to demons for the love of money."

Victor glanced at Sheila and frowned. Then he broke into laughter.

"Don't worry about my soul! What I took from you can't be changed. You're a whore, and will remain one."

Sheila slapped him again. Adrian gently pulled her away.

"Leave him. He'll get what's due to him."

One more time she spat into his face. "Didn't I tell you that the victory would be mine?"

She moved away. Luciana came up to Violeta and hugged her, tears in her eyes.

"I'm so happy for you. I hope they'll take you to a better place."

"Let's move on," said Adrian.

"Bye Luciana," Violeta said, embracing her.

The women walked away to freedom beside their saviors.

Outside, Sheila, Violeta, and Daniela got into the car.

Adrian patted Carlos' shoulder.

"Thanks for helping me out. I'll call you when she's ready to go home."

"No problem."

Carlos' friends walked away, but Carlos got in the driver's seat of the rented car. He took Adrian and the women to the hotel. After getting the portion of money he'd requested, he drove away.

It was 1 a.m., and Anil was in a sweat as he slept next to his wife. He was dreaming about Gail. She was taking a shower. She gently soaped her skin as the water ran down her body in rivulets. She gazed at him with a smile.

"Come and take a shower with me," she said.

He took off his clothes, leaving them on the floor, and got into the shower. She rubbed his back with a sponge. Then she dropped the sponge, and they came together in a passionate embrace.

Anil woke up, feeling aroused. He looked at Chelsea, who was sleeping soundly. He slowly got up and tiptoed out of the room. He went to the fridge and took out a beer. Then he sat in the living room and emptied the whole bottle.

I must see her.

He left the bottle on the floor. Wearing only underpants, he walked towards Gail's bedroom. He opened the door and peeked inside. The light from the moon fell on Gail's bed. She was uncovered and wore only a bra and panties.

He tiptoed towards her. The desire to have sex with her overpowered him. He cautiously lay down on her bed and began masturbating. He inhaled the smell of Gail's hair.

Chelsea suddenly woke up, needing to empty her bladder. She went to the toilet, then she came out and noticed the lack of a body in her bed.

Where is he?

She walked out of the bedroom. When she got into the hall, she noticed Gail's door open.

Chelsea walked towards the door and looked inside. What she saw enraged her. She grabbed onto the wall and couldn't move for a moment. Nausea rose in her stomach, and she felt like she was going to puke.

She marched quickly to the tool cupboard and picked up a cutlass. Then she ran like the wind to the bedroom, slamming the door into the wall.

Anil jumped off the bed. His underpants were down.

"Hey, put dat away!" he said, his eyes riveted on the cutlass.

She ran towards him, holding the cutlass in the air. Anil jumped onto the bed.

"Hey, keep away from me!"

"You freaking man! You couldn't find someone your age?"

Gail awoke and raised her head, blinking sleepily at her mother. Seeing where her mother was staring, she sat up and turned around. She jumped out of bed when she saw Anil standing on it.

"What's going on?"

Chelsea walked towards the bed.

"I found him lying in your bed with his underpants down."

Gail shielded her eyes in disgust.

"Yuck! Pull your underpants up!"

Chelsea bore down on him, her eyes ablaze.

"You impregnated my child, and because of you she almost died!"

Anil barely managed to pull his underpants up. Chelsea raised the cutlass and slashed it at him. He jumped off the bed and ran out, pushing Gail aside. He took the car key that hung by the door and dashed to the car.

Chelsea ran after him. She hit his car with everything she could get her hands on.

"Get out, child molester!" she shouted.

Shaking, Anil started the engine. He opened the gate with the remote control and reversed outside.

Gail came to the door. "Mother, come inside," she said.

Chelsea went back into the house and sat on the floor in the living room. She dropped the cutlass on the floor, her whole body trembling, and began crying.

"I'm so sorry for not listening to you. Please forgive me."

Gail knelt next to her mother and embraced her.

"I felt so hurt when you refused to believe me. If my own mother refused to accept the truth, who would believe me?"

"Please forgive me. I just couldn't comprehend that my husband could do these nasty things."

"It's okay. Calm down."

Chelsea quieted down and sat for a while without saying anything. Finally, she stood up.

"Get out of your pajamas. We're going to the police station. These things can't go unreported. Men like him will go after any child. He has to face the consequences of his evil behavior, and he must be stopped."

The two women went into their bedrooms. They changed into some daytime clothes and left the house.

The news about Toothless' death spread through the country. It was highlighted in the local newspapers and the TV news.

Candice found out about his death unexpectedly. When the children left for school with Miguel, she sat at the table eating doubles [81] for breakfast. She had the newspaper laid out in front of her.

She turned the front page and began reading.

---

[81] Doubles is a street food used as a breakfast or snack. It is made with two baras filled with curry channa

'A few friends were liming together when an unknown gunman came up to one of the men and shot him. The victim was rushed to the hospital, but on the way succumbed to his wounds. He was identified as Caleb, nicknamed Toothless.'

Candice spat out the drink in her mouth.

Toothless is dead? Finally!

She continued reading.

'Toothless was a gang member and had many enemies. However, at this point the motive behind his killing is unknown.'

One is out, but the next one is still in my way.

She got up and washed her plate. Then she went to take a shower.

Ever since she had moved to Miguel's house, Terrel had called her nonstop. He was asking her to leave Miguel and come back to him. His blackmailing was putting her in a corner.

Her phone was ringing when she came out of the shower. It was Terrel.

She answered, wrapped in a towel.

"Yes, Terrel?"

"I called you yesterday, but you didn't bother to answer."

"Miguel was standing right next to me."

"Did you hear Toothless got killed?" asked Terrel.

Candice sat on the bed.

"Yes. It's in the newspaper. He was celebrating his birthday, and someone shot him. Who would want him dead?"

"He was kind of crazy. He raped a few women. Maybe one of those killed him," suggested Terrel.

"I was suspecting Kingpin. I heard Kingpin was worried that Toothless' behavior with women would attract the police to the gang."

Candice's voice took on a serious tone.

"If we don't leave this life of crime, we might face the same fate."

"That's doesn't bother me. When are you planning to

leave that idiot?" asked Terrel.

"Why are you pressuring me? I have no feelings for you anymore. Get another woman."

"I can't. You belong to me, not him. When am I going to see you?"

She stood up, shaking. "I'm not your woman anymore. So leave me alone."

She hung up the phone. But he kept calling. Eventually the phone calls stopped, but then a message notification came up.

"So, this how you are ending things? I have no choice other than to call Miguel. He'll not only find out that his wife was kidnapped by you, but also that she's alive."

She dropped the cell phone. But then a new idea entered her mind, and she picked it up again.

I must get rid of him. I am so fed up with his threats.

She knew that he wouldn't leave her alone, and she needed to devise some sort of plan. If Toothless was alive, she would ask him to silence Terrel. But this time she was on her own.

How am I going to silence him?

Then she remembered that she had a key to her friend's beach house. She decided to take him there and find some solution.

She called him back.

"It looks like you won't leave me in peace. We really need to figure this out. Why don't we go to a quiet place and discuss this?"

"You can come over to my house," he answered back.

"No. I have a key for Sunny's beach house. We could stay there."

"Now you sound like my old gyul. What are you going to say to Miguel?"

Candice heard the gate opening. She walked to the window and looked outside.

"Miguel's home with his bastards. Meet me tomorrow at 5 p.m., at my house," she said, and ended the call.

She quickly ran downstairs into the kitchen and began washing the dishes that had been in the sink since morning. Miguel came inside with his children, where they took off their shoes.

Miguel walked into the kitchen.

"Hey babe, I'm back," he said.

He came up to her and embraced her from the back. She turned around, leaving the water running.

But they were not alone. Both of his children stared at them. She returned their stare and asked, "Where are your manners?"

Ronnel frowned. "What did we do?"

"When you come home, you should say good afternoon."

"Good afternoon," said Ronnel.

Candice glanced at Nadia.

"What about you?"

"Good afternoon, Aunty."

"Now go and change your clothes."

The children left. She put her arms around his neck and they kissed. Out of the corner of her eye, she noticed that her tattoo was exposed.

I shouldn't wet my hand.

She pulled away and gave him a smile.

"Did you catch anyone today?"

"Yes, I did."

"Who?"

"You," he said, grabbing Candice around her waist. She laughed but kept an eye on her hand.

After another prolonged kiss, she pulled away.

"My mother's blood pressure is very high. I might have to stay with her tomorrow," she said.

Suddenly Nadia shouted, "Daddy! Daddy!"

"What's happened now?" he asked.

"Daddy, come quickly!"

Miguel removed his hands from Candice and rushed upstairs. She went back to rinsing plates.

When he entered Nadia's bedroom, both were on top of the bed.

"What's wrong?" he asked.

"We saw a mouse!" said Ronnel.

"Get off the bed. There are no mice in the house."

"Please check under the bed," said Nadia.

Miguel bent down and looked under the bed. All he saw was a small lizard. He stood up.

"There are no mice. Change your clothes and go downstairs."

Shaking his head, he left the room.

Candice rinsed the last plate and rushed upstairs, straight into the bathroom. She turned on the light and got out her make-up bag. Then she began concealing her tattoo.

I can't keep hiding it forever. He'll find out one day. Maybe I should color it over. He would think that I got a new tattoo.

Miguel went into the bedroom and noticed that the light was on in the bathroom.

"Are you there?"

"Yes, I am."

"I have to go back to the station."

"Why?"

"We're having a meeting with the commissioner."

Miguel took off his shirt and put on another one.

"Please make something for the children to eat."

"Sure," she answered absentmindedly.

Candice inspected her hand closely. The tattoo was now totally hidden.

"I'm going now," said Miguel, and he walked out.

Candice put away her make-up bag and headed to the living room. She turned on the TV and then lay down on the sofa.

Just as she was getting interested in a movie, Nadia entered the living room.

"Aunty Candice, I'm hungry. Can I get some snacks, please?"

Candice looked at her, irritated, "Go and get it yourself."

Nadia went into the kitchen and opened the fridge. She looked the shelves over and saw some chocolate.

She stretched out her hand, trying to get the chocolate. In the attempt, her elbow hit a glass bottle of ketchup. It fell and broke, and the ketchup splattered on the floor.

Nadia moved away from the fridge.

"Aunty Candice! Aunty!"

Candice sat up.

"What does she want now? I can't even watch TV in peace."

She went into the kitchen and stopped, staring motionlessly at the mess.

"Yuh dotish gyul! Get some paper towel and clean up your mess!"

"No! The glass will cut me."

Candice left Nadia in the kitchen for a moment and came back with a broom and dustpan. She began sweeping.

I didn't sign up to clean and look after his children. He should leave them with his mother. But no, he has to bring them here.

"You go now. There's no use for you."

Nadia went upstairs. After sweeping, Candice mopped the floor to get rid of the ketchup. Then she went back to watch TV.

The next day, Candice stopped at the pharmacy and bought some white tablets. She then drove to her own house, where she packed some gloves, wet wipers, and a small bottle of bleach into her large handbag.

What else do I need?

She gazed around the living room and, satisfied, zipped up the handbag.

Terrel arrived a little later and rang the doorbell. She picked up her purse and went outside.

"Let's go," she said as she started walking toward his car.

He grabbed her around waist.

"I missed having you in my bed."

She pushed his hand away.

"Wait nah till we get to the house!"

They got into his car and headed to the beach.

Terrel put his hand on her knee.

"I've paid off my debt to Kingpin, and even bought some land."

She looked over at him. "So, you used up all the money. Your pockets must be empty now."

"Nope, my pockets will always have cash. Me and the guys are planning something big."

"To rob or kidnap? Boy, one day you'll get killed, just like Toothless."

"Meh get killed? You must be kidding."

"I'm leaving the gang. This life only leads us to destruction. I don't want to have the same fate as Toothless or spend the rest of my life locked up in a cage," she said.

He looked at her, a wide grin on his face.

"Kingpin won't allow you to leave. He gonna kill you."

"I don't care."

Candace glanced through the windshield. They were nearly on another car's bumper.

"Boy, watch the road nah, not me."

Terrel shook his head. "Living with Miguel has made you cuckoo."

"Shut up and drive nah."

Terrel's car drove onto the highway. From there they drove for about an hour.

When they reached Malbrew Street, Candice said, "Take a left turn."

He followed her instructions, and drove down a street that had houses on both sides. Then Terrel turned right again, and they ended up on a street with only a few houses on the right side.

"Which house?" he asked.

"Keep driving until you see a two-story yellow house."

He continued driving. Then he found the house and parked.

Candice got out, holding her handbag tightly. She glanced around and walked towards the gate. Terrel locked the car and followed her.

Candice opened the gate and entered the yard. As she passed by the pool, she slowed down and considered it.

No. Better if taken care of at the beach.

Then she walked to the door. As she opened it, Terrel grabbed her ass.

Candace flinched, and he reared back in surprise.

She laughed. "You frightened me, boy!"

She opened the door and they went in.

They entered a living room that was furnished with a leather sofa, coffee table, and a TV. Candice dropped her handbag on the sofa and went into the kitchen. She took out a soft drink from the fridge and went back to the living room.

Upon her return, Terrel took off his t-shirt.

"Let's go for a swim before the day ends," he suggested.

"I need to pee. You go ahead. I'll join you in a while."

Terrel walked out to the pool and jumped into the water. Then he swam from one side of the pool to the other.

Candice stared at him through the window for a while. Then she opened her purse and took out the white tablets and a vial of clear liquid from her bag. She looked from one to the other.

Which one?

Then she went to the kitchen and got a cold bottle of beer. She broke off the tip of the vial and emptied it in the bottle. Then she took out a spoon from the drawer and began mashing the white tablets. She emptied the crushed pills into the bottle and shook it until everything was dissolved.

She took out another bottle from the fridge and went back into the guest room, where she took off her top and shorts. Wearing only her underwear, she walked outside with the bottles of beer.

She tested the water with her foot, and then went down the steps.

"I got a beer for you," she said with a smile.

He swam to her and took the bottle she held out to him. Then he held onto her hand and pulled her into a hug. She wrapped her legs around him and they kissed.

Then she removed her legs from him.

"Let's drink to our reunion," she suggested.

He gently hit her beer bottle with his.

"Cheers."

"Finish up, boy. I'm ready for some fun."

He drank the beer in one go.

She took the bottle from him and got out of the pool. After putting the bottles on the porch, she came back.

As she stood on the lowest step, he grabbed her hand and pulled her into the water. Her head went under, and she came up to the surface, coughing.

"Are you nuts?" she demanded. She tried to hit him, but he swam away.

"Come and get me."

She swam after him. When she finally caught his wrist, he pulled her closer to him and began pulling down her panties.

"I want you so much," he said, touching her private parts.

She pushed him off and pulled up her panties. Then she swam away.

"You're not going to have my pussy so easy."

He swam towards her. As he got close, she began splashing water on him, and then she dove under and got away. He swam in circles, trying to catch her.

"Shark is coming for you. I'm going to gobble you up by kissing every inch of your body."

"No way! You're too slow!"

As he swam after her, he began to feel nauseous, and his vision became blurry. He paused to rub his eyes.

When he tried to focus on Candace, he was surprised to realize that he was seeing two of her.

"Give me a hand. I'm kinda feeling sick."

She got out of the pool.

"Help yourself out," she said, walking away.

"Candy, come back! What did you put in my drink?"

She turned around and looked at him. A wicked grin decorated her face.

"Your death."

Terrel splashed around, shaking, trying to stay above the water. Finally, he passed out, and floated face down in the water.

Candice looked around and saw a long-poled net that was used to remove leaves from the pool. She picked it up and pushed Terrel under the water with it.

"Come on! Go down!"

After some time, his body sank into the water. She put the net back and stood watching bubbles floating to the surface. When the bubbles stopped, she jumped back into the pool.

She dragged him to the stairs and then out of the water, leaving him at the edge of the pool. As the realization of what she'd done hit her, she ran away from the body, back inside the house.

She didn't stop until she'd reached the kitchen. Her whole body trembled

"I need a drink," she gasped, and took out another bottle of beer. Her hand wouldn't obey her, and the bottle fell from her nerveless grasp, shattering splinters of glass all over the floor.

"I killed him! I'm a murderer!"

Her mind started to go into shock, and she knew that she had to do something. Otherwise she would be standing there all night.

She left the kitchen and came back with a broom and dustpan. She swept the floor, and then emptied the dustpan into the garbage bin.

No one should know I was here.

She took out the garbage bag from the dust bin and put in another one. Then she dried the floor.

I told him to leave me alone but he kept pushing and pushing. It's not my fault. He caused it.

After putting away everything that she had used, she went into the living room with the garbage bag. She put on her clothes and sat on the sofa, thinking.

She looked at her watch. It was 6:30 p.m.

What to do with the body? I can't leave him here.

Her phone rang, making her jump. She looked at the number. It was Miguel.

Why is he calling me now?

She answered her phone.

"Hi darling," she said, her eyes fixed on the pool just outside the window.

"Hi, babe. You haven't called me since you left."

"I got busy with my mom."

"How is she doing?"

"She's burning with fever and covered with rashes."

"I hope she gets better soon. The house feels empty without you."

"I'll be back tomorrow. Oops-- she's calling me. I have to go."

She put away the phone.

The day turned into night as Candice sat on the sofa and thought.

I can't sit here and just look at him lying there. I need to get rid of him.

She went outside and opened the gate. For just a moment she stood there, gazing into the distance. Then she got to work.

She drove the car into the yard, as close to the pool as she could get. Then, dragging Terrel by his legs, she managed to pull him into the back seat.

She then closed the door and drove to the beach. After parking right next to the sea, she dragged his body from the car and rolled him into the water. The waves slowly washed his body away.

Then she drove back to the house and, using the wipes she had brought, cleaned off everything she had touched, including the doors. She threw Terrel's beer bottle away in the garbage bag, along with his clothes. Then she left the property and headed back to her own old home.

As she drove, she kept seeing Terrel's body lying by the pool.

Forget him and focus on the road. Nothing stands in your way now.

Upon reaching home, she turned on the shower. After undressing, she stood under the water and washed repeatedly.

He asked for it, she reasoned. *If he had moved on, nothing would have happened. But no. He never let me just leave--as if I was his property.*

She got out of the shower and wrapped herself in a towel. Then she lay on the bed, feeling exhausted. Her hands and arms ached. She rubbed them gently.

Damn it! He was too heavy for me.

She fell asleep, planning to go back to Miguel's the next afternoon.

***

After escaping captivity Sheila, Violeta, and Daniela stayed for a few days in the hotel. Adrian had booked another room for the girls and had bought new clothes for them.

They were all sitting in the hotel's restaurant having dinner one evening. Violeta was silent as Daniela spoke nonstop.

"It's so unbelievable. I'm going to see my parents and sister! I haven't seen them in two years! It seems ages!"

"Please try to forget what happened here," said Sheila.

Daniela gave her a serious look.

"We went through a horrible nightmare together. I thought there would be no end to it. How can I forget?"

Sheila scooped up a spoonful of soup.

"Yes, it was a horrible experience for all of us." She looked intently into Daniela's eyes. "But please listen to what I have to say.

"Growing up, I was taught to pray and have faith, but at the same time to make every effort to make things happen. If it wasn't for my faith in God and a positive outlook, I might not have survived all of this."

Daniela looked back at Sheila with the same intensity.

"I know what you mean."

"When I get back home, I will visit my church and give to the poor as thanks to God for answering our prayers. Many pray, asking Him for many things, but their prayers are not answered. Yet, He answered mine," Sheila told her.

All this time, Adrian had been listening carefully, unable to stop smiling.

"The problem is, people tend to ask God for all kinds of rubbish, giving Him orders as if He was some kind of waiter," he added.

"They approach prayer with the wrong set of mind and heart. Before going to God, they should forgive, and get rid of any anger or bitterness. They must repent and ask first for the forgiveness of their own sins--and then pray. Also, they should make sure that their thoughts are not scattered around. Focus is important."

"Many times," Sheila told them, "when I ask God for something, I tell Him 'Heavenly Father I know you are loving, and I believe in you. Lord, you know what I need. Let it be according to Your will. Have mercy on me, a sinner'."

Violeta touched Adrian's hand, and finally spoke.

"Uncle, where are you going to take me?"

He looked at Sheila, then back to the girl.

"I don't know. I'm trying to locate your relatives."

"I want to go to my granny's," she said.

"Do you remember where she lives?"

"Yes, I do."

Adrian patted her shoulder, a huge smile on his face. He took in a relieved breath.

"This is so amazing. Yes, of course I'll be able to take you to her."

He looked over at Sheila. "I've arranged everything for your safe trip home. In a few days, you will be reunited with your family."

Warm joy surrounded Sheila's heart. She looked around at her surroundings and smiled.

"It feels so good to be free. I can't wait till I hug my children. When are you planning to leave for Romania?"

"I'm not sure. I still have to get travel papers for Daniela. As soon as you leave, I'll take her to the embassy," said Adrian.

Sheila nodded. "Oh, yes, the embassy will help you."

She gazed at him silently for a moment. Then she spoke.

"Will I ever see you again?"

He stared thoughtfully at her, silent in his turn.

"Surely we will keep in touch," he finally said.

They continued their dinner, each of them thinking about the future that awaited them. Smiles covered their faces.

When dinner was over, Sheila took the girls to their bedroom. She waited for them to fall asleep, then she went to Adrian's room and knocked on the door.

At that moment, Adrian was in the shower. He came out

and wrapped himself in a towel, leaving his upper body exposed.

He looked through the peephole, then opened the door and let her in. She walked into the room and stared at his upper body.

"Six-pack abs and muscled arms. You must spend a lot of time in the gym," she said.

"With the kind of job I do, I have to stay fit and strong." He blushed and looked slightly uncomfortable.

"Please turn around," he said.

She turned away, and he picked his underwear and undershirt up off the bed. He put them on.

"I hope you don't mind seeing me in underwear. I didn't expect anyone."

"It's fine. I'll pretend that you're wearing shorts." She smiled widely.

"Deal. You can look now."

She turned back around and looked for a place to sit. The armchair was not an option; it was covered with new clothes.

So, she sat on the bed.

He gazed down at her and folded his arms.

"What can I do for you?"

"I'm worried about the boat sailing. Our local fishermen have been kidnapped by Venezuelans. What if I get snatched again? I won't be able to take it."

Adrian sat next to her and grasped her hand.

"You have nothing to worry about. I've organized everything, and you'll have someone with you."

"These two months were hellish for me. I can't get rid of the feeling of being dirty." Her eyes filled with tears.

He hugged her and rubbed her back.

"You're free now. Leave all that behind."

She put her head on his shoulder, and for the first time since she was kidnapped, she felt at ease.

"Look into my eyes."

She looked at him.

"You are the most beautiful woman that I've ever met. Never think that you are unclean."

Sheila's heartbeat sped up. She slowly moved herself to him, and her lips touched his. They kissed passionately.

Suddenly she gave a cry and jumped up.

"No! I can't!"

She ran to the door, and he followed her.

"Sheila, it's fine."

However, she ignored him. She bolted out the door and rushed back to her room.

Adrian closed the door, shaking his head.

"I should handle my feelings better."

He took out a notebook from his briefcase and began writing.

The next morning, everyone got up early. Violeta was strangely quiet than usual. She didn't want to be separated from Sheila.

After having breakfast, they walked through the lobby and stood by the door.

Violeta hugged Sheila. "Aunty, can I stay with you?"

"I wish I could keep you. But it would be illegal to do so without the permission of your guardians."

"Can't you talk to Granny? She might let me go with you."

"It's not that easy. You must stay with her. I'll come to visit you."

Sheila caressed her head.

"Let's go, Violeta," said Adrian.

Violeta walked to Daniela and hugged her as well. "I'm going to miss you."

Daniela sniffed, and her eyes filled. "I'll miss you too. Don't give your granny any trouble!"

"The taxi is waiting," Adrian said. "Let's go."

They silently walked out and got into the taxi. As it drove away from the hotel, Adrian noticed a crowd with posters. Some posters said, 'Traitors! Sellout!' Others had words such as 'New Election,' and 'We need food and medicine!' The driver turned to the left to avoid the crowd.

In about an hour, the taxi parked in front of a wooden house.

"Wait for me," said Adrian.

He and Violeta got out of the car. They went up to the gate, and Adrian pressed the doorbell.

After what seemed a long time, a lady in her sixties came out. She looked at the gate with a frown on her face, but seeing Violeta she ran towards them.

She opened the gate and pulled Violeta to herself. "I thought I would never see you again!"

Tears welled in her eyes as Violeta buried her head into her granny's chest. Then the woman looked at Adrian, suspicious of the stranger standing before her.

"Who are you, and what are you doing with this child?"

"My name is Adrian. I'm a detective from Romania. I found your granddaughter in a brothel."

"Oh, my God! How did she end up in there?"

Granny began shaking, and dizziness came over her. She swayed slightly, looking as if she was about to faint.

Adrian caught her arm.

"We should go inside before you fall," he advised.

He walked with her into the house. As they stepped into the front hallway, the walls caught his attention.

The paint was peeling off. He noticed that the old wooden floor was termite-infested. They walked into the living room, which held an old torn-up sofa and a small table.

He helped her to sit down.

"Go and get your granny some water."

Violeta ran to the kitchen and filled a glass with tap water. She came back and held it out to her. Granny drank the water gratefully, and then looked at Adrian.

"I can't understand how my little Violeta got into a brothel."

Violeta sat next to her granny. "Mummy sold me out to some people."

The old woman rose slightly, still trembling.

"You're mistaken. She said that robbers came into the house and snatched you."

Violeta stood up, her hands now curled into defiant fists.

"No, Granny! I heard everything. They wanted the money that she owed to them for rent, but she told them to take me instead."

Her granny leaned back, disbelief and shock etched on her face.

"I can't believe it! How could she do this to you?"

"I advise you to get custody of the child," Adrian advised her. "She can't go back to her mother. There's no guarantee that woman won't sell her again to pay off her debts."

"Yes, I'll do that."

Adrian got up and pulled his wallet out of his pocket. He took out $300 US.

"Pardon me, but I must leave."

Granny got back up and tottered towards him. She embraced him tightly.

"Thank you for saving my grandchild. You're an angel!"

"I was doing what anyone would do."

She let him go. He took her hand and put the money in it.

"This is for Violeta."

She looked at her hand, and then put the money into her pocket.

"Thank you very much. May the Lord bless you for your kindness."

A smile ran across his face. "Thank you, *señora*."

They walked towards the door, where Adrian embraced Violeta.

"You're very brave for a little girl. Try to leave all those bad things that happened to you behind and go back to school. You should continue playing piano. One day you might become a famous pianist."

Violeta looked into his eyes, her vision blurry with tears.

"I want to be a piano teacher like my daddy."

"Why not? You're smart and talented. If you believe in yourself and keep working hard, you can become whoever you want to be."

"Thank you, Adrian, for saving me. I will never forget you."

"You're welcome." He smiled at the granny, who was enfolding her granddaughter in her arms.

"Adiós, *señora*," said Adrian.

"Adiós, Adrián."

She opened the door and let him out. Adrian waved good-bye as he walked to the taxi.

The next evening, Eduardo picked up Adrian, Daniela, and Sheila from the hotel and drove them to the port. Adrian sat in the front seat.

"It's unbelievable. We're going back to our lives!" said Daniela, glee in her voice.

"Yes, we are. It's a miracle!" responded Sheila.

Yet we will always carry the burden of what happened to us.

"As soon I reach home, I'm going to fill a tub with warm water and stay in it," said Daniela.

"I'm going to hug my children and tell them how much I love them."

"I'm glad to hear that both of you are in good spirits," said Adrian as he turned and looked at them. "I hope this nightmare won't follow you anymore."

"You should call your husband or relatives and tell them that you're coming back home," Daniela suggested.

"No. I want to surprise them."

They headed toward the port, and Eduardo drove over the sand. They could see a pirogue, and two men standing by it. Eduardo stopped not far from the pirogue.

"Eduardo, thank you for helping us out," said Adrian as he gave him some money.

Adrian and the other passengers got out. Adrian held a sack filled with water, apples, and other snacks. He gave it to Sheila.

"These are basic food necessities."

He took out some TT currency from his pocket and put it into Sheila's hand.

"You'll need it to catch a taxi to go home."

Sheila touched his face. "You're so sweet. You took care of everything."

"You're a special woman. It was my pleasure to put events in place for your safe return."

"Oh, thank you."

They walked towards the two men—Carlos, and a man by the name of Gonzales. Sheila noticed that he was carrying a pistol, and felt relieved knowing that she would be safe.

"Hey, *señora*! Happy to see you again," said Carlos.

"Oh, thanks Carlos."

He noticed a smile on her face.

"Is everything ready?" asked Adrian.

"Yes. Did you bring cash?" asked Carlos.

Adrian gave him four hundred US dollars. He counted the money.

"This is only four hundred. You promised to pay one thousand and five hundred."

"You'll get the rest after you deliver her safely back to Trinidad."

"No problem."

Carlos gave one hundred US to Gonzales and put away the rest.

"Sheila, please get into the pirogue," said Gonzales.

"One moment."

Sheila went over to Daniela and hugged her.

"Ever since we met, you have proven to be a strong young lady. Stay this way, and please keep in touch with me."

"I will, for sure."

Tears formed in their eyes.

Then Sheila went to Adrian and held his hands.

"You're a very noble man. You have given my children their mother back. Thank you."

She embraced him and then ran to the pirogue, followed by Gonzales. As she sat down in the boat, he pushed it further into the water and then climbed in.

"Bye, Adrian!" shouted Sheila.

"Call me when you get home."

"I will!" she responded. She found herself trembling like a leaf.

Gonzales started the engine, and the pirogue sailed away. Sheila watched, teary, as Adrian's figure became smaller and smaller. Then she turned around and gazed ahead into the darkness.

Home, sweet home. Here I come! Strong and unbeaten!

The sky was filled with stars. She looked up at it.

Thank you, Lord, for answering my prayers.

The waves beat the boat as the moon lit up the sky, showing them the path back home. Sheila's heart raced with a mixture of sadness and joy. The journey seemed ages to her.

To her relief, the pirogue finally reached the shore of Trinidad. It was still dark.

Gonzales put down the pistol and helped Sheila get off.

"*Señora*, you have to be careful. It's not safe for a woman to roam the beach in the dark."

"Thank you, Gonzales. I'll be fine."

She began wading towards the sand.

"Good-bye, *Señora*," Gonzales called after her.

She turned around and gave him a big smile.

"'Bye, Gonzales! Gracias!"

She ran splashing through the water. Upon reaching dry sand, she fell on her knees and cried profusely.

Gonzales peered at her, confused. "Are you okay?"

She raised her head and looked at him.

"Yes, I am. Thank you."

He started the engine, and the pirogue began its voyage back to Venezuela.

"Oh, my God! I've been counting the days, waiting to come back home!"

Crying, she kissed the sand. "I'm free. Yes, I'm free!"

Sheila lay on the sand and rolled over and over, unable to stop laughing. After a while she lay motionless, staring at the night sky. Then she fell asleep.

In the morning, Sheila woke up to the feeling of something wet touching her cheek. It was a dog's nose.

As she sat up, the dog moved away from her. She picked up her bag and took out a biscuit.

"Hey, doggy. Come here," she said.

The dog slowly approached Sheila. She gave him the biscuit and then patted his back.

"Good doggy."

She got up and looked around but didn't see a single soul.

Slowly she began taking steps toward the road. The sun burned her face and was bothering her eyes. A few times she put her hand over her eyes to block the sun's rays.

Drops of sweat rolled down her face. Her legs were hurting, and in addition she now had a stabbing pain behind her rib.

I can't walk anymore.

She sat down on the ground and drank a bottle of juice.

After a moment's rest, she got up and continued towards home. There seemed to be no end to her walking.

Why are there no cars on the road? I won't be able to make it.

When she reached the junction, she turned left. She could see a few houses.

From afar she noticed a car coming toward her. She began waving her hands.

"Hey! Stop!"

However, the driver passed her. She continued walking, and soon she heard a car horn behind her.

Sheila turned around and saw an old white car slowing down behind her. The elderly driver wound down his window.

"What are you doing in this area alone?"

"I'm trying to reach home."

"Where do you live?"

"Pentecost Street. It's not far from the Lystra police station."

The driver stopped. "Get in. I'll take you home."

She sat in the car, and he took off again.

"Thank you very much."

"You're welcome. What are you doing walking on the road so early?"

"I got in an argument with my boyfriend and he kicked me out of the car," lied Sheila.

"Men can be jerks at times."

"Totally agree."

Not in the mood to continue conversation, Sheila rested her head on the seat back and closed her eyes.

I need a shower, rest and a peace of mind. But will I be able to live peacefully, knowing that they might come for me again?

She tried to quiet her mind by avoiding any thoughts about it.

In an hour, they arrived at the Lystra police station.

"Where to now?"

She opened her eyes and sat up, looking at the road. She could feel her heart thumping. As she looked at the road, her whole body began trembling.

"As soon as you pass a traffic light, turn right."

The driver drove forward and then turned right.

"Turn left, and then drive straight."

Sheila's heartrate sped up when she saw her street and then own house.

"Please stop by that yellow house."

He parked in front.

Sheila took out the money Adrian had given her. "How much can I give you?"

"Nothing. I couldn't leave you alone on the street."

Sheila regarded him gratefully. Such a nice person—it brought a feeling that maybe the world wasn't all evil after all.

"Thank you."

She got out of the car and went up to the smallest gate. Sheila took a small key out from underneath a rock that sat under the tree. She unlocked the small gate and walked in.

She headed to the door and rang the bell impatiently.

When there was no answer, she walked around the house, trying to open the windows. But all of them were locked.

Frustrated, Sheila lifted a big rock from the grass and pounded the stone on the door handle over and over.

"Nadia! Ronnel! Where are you? Why is no one at home?"

At that moment, Candice was in a deep sleep upstairs. Miguel was at his desk at the police station, going over reports.

The children were playing a game on TV in their bedroom. Because of the closed door and the noise of the air conditioner, they didn't hear anything.

Candice was having a dream. She saw herself in a cemetery, standing by Terrel's grave. The earth over his grave began moving apart, and two hands popped out. Then slowly

Terrel's head emerged, and he looked at Candice. His flesh was rotten and covered with worms. His lifeless eyes were dull.

"Candice! Candice!" he screamed. His voice echoed in the far distance. He pulled himself out and began walking after her.

"Murderer! Murderer! Your punishment is near!"

As he grabbed her hand with his bloody one, she woke up.

She sat up covered with sweat. Then she heard noises coming from downstairs. Not knowing what to expect, she slid the door of the closet open and took a box from the top shelf. She removed a pistol from the box and slowly went down to the door.

Outside, Sheila threw the rock away in frustration and rang the bell.

Candice looked through the peephole. She was utterly shocked when she recognized Sheila.

She dropped the gun on the floor.

That can't be! How did she manage to run away?

She picked up the gun and opened the door.

Sheila froze with fear upon seeing her kidnapper. Candice pointed the gun at her.

"You again!" Sheila gasped, recognizing her. "What are you doing in my house?"

Candice blocked the door, not removing her eyes from Sheila.

"I live here. Miguel invited me to live with him."

"You lie. Why would he invite you to live with him?"

"Long before you were gone, we used to date secretly. When everyone thought you were dead, he asked me to move in with him."

The news of her husband cheating on her with her kidnapper made her light-headed.

How could he bring a criminal into the house with our kids?

"Move now to the living room!" Candice commanded.

Sheila slowly walked to the living room. Candice put a chair in the middle of the floor.

"Sit down."

Sheila followed her instructions.

"Why would everyone think that I'm dead?"

"I hired someone to kill a woman. When her burnt body was found, everyone thought it was yours."

Sheila's eyes widened. "Why are you doing this?"

Candice put a gun to Sheila's temple.

"Good question. At first, I was hired to spy on Miguel, but then I fell in love with him. We're going to marry."

"If you think he'll marry you after finding out what you did, you're an idiot."

"Shut up. I need to think of what to do."

The doorbell rang, making Candice turn around. There was a door-to-door evangelist by the gate, and she was pressing on the bell.

Sheila quickly ran at Candice and pushed her. Candice fell face down, accidentally pulling the trigger. The gunshot echoed through the house.

Hearing the gunshot, the visitor ran away, dropping her booklets on the ground.

Ronnel and Nadia jumped off the bed. Both ran out of the room.

"Daddy, is that you?" shouted Ronnel.

"Son, stay upstairs!" Sheila called out.

Ronnel broke out in a cold sweat upon hearing his mother's voice. He swayed, uncomprehending.

Nadia ran downstairs shouting, "Mummy! Where are you?"

She ran into the kitchen but stopped short when she saw the two women.

Sheila lay over Candice, trying to wrest the gun from her hand. Candice aimed the gun towards Nadia and pulled the trigger. Fortunately, the shot was wide, and the bullet went into the door frame.

"Mummy!" Nadia screamed. She sat down on the floor, crying.

"Go upstairs! Now!" Sheila told her, but Nadia refused to move.

Her cries echoed in her brother's ears. Ronnel came down the stairs and ran to his sister.

Sheila grabbed onto the gun. Candice beat her hand and then pulled the gun out of her hand. She scrambled to her feet and pointed the pistol at Sheila.

"You bastards get over by your mother," she ordered.

The children ran to Sheila. She embraced them and kissed them.

"I missed you so much! I thought I would never see you again!" said Sheila.

"Stop with the drama! Your kids are little demons," said Candice.

"If, you want me dead, just kill me. But please don't hurt them."

"Shut up! I need to think."

"Mummy, she's going to hurt us," said Nadia.

"Hush your stupid mouth, you little bastard!"

Ronnel stared at Candace's hand and saw the tattoo. He recalled seeing the same tattoo on the kidnapper's hand.

"I know her. She's the one who hurt Daddy and came upstairs," he whispered.

At that moment, Miguel had just parked his car in the yard. He was now opening the door.

He heard a voice: "Please let the children go. Do whatever you want with me."

"Sheila?" Miguel called, disbelief in his voice.

"They didn't do anything wrong," he heard her say.

Candice walked to Ronnel and put the gun to his temple.

"Mummy, she's going to kill me!" whispered Ronnel, trembling. He clung to his mother and squeezed his eyes shut.

Sensing danger, Miguel brought out his pistol and crept to the living room. What he saw made his blood run cold.

His lover was holding his family hostage, and pointing a gun at his son!

"Put down the gun," he told her in a low voice.

Candice turned around and stared at him. She then smiled, shrugged, and lowered the gun.

"What is going on in here?"

Sheila pointed at Candice. "She's one of my kidnappers!"

Ronnel stared at his lover.

"Daddy, look at her hand! She has a snake on it."

Still pointing a gun at her, he came up closer to her and tried to see the snake. His hands started shaking, and he lowered the gun.

She sauntered slowly away. Then she spun around and aimed at his wife.

"Sheila must go!"

She pulled the trigger. It made a clicking sound, but no bullets came out of it.

Miguel shot at Candice, and the bullet went into her leg. She dropped the gun on the floor. Blood spurted from her leg.

Sheila marched up to her and slapped her in the face.

"This is for scaring my kids!"

She hit her again.

"This is for shooting my husband!"

Then she pushed her backwards.

"This is for slapping me on the beach!"

Sheila's children clung to each other, crying and shivering.

Sheila began kicking Candice. "Don't you dare come near my family again!"

Miguel rushed over to his wife and pulled her away from Candice.

"Enough!" he said.

She pushed him away.

"You're a traitor. Both of you deserve each other."

Sheila's children ran towards her, and they hugged each other.

Miguel helped Candice sit up.

"You shot me!" she screeched. "How could you?"

"You threatened my family. I had no choice."

He left the room and came back with a first-aid kit. When he stooped down to help her, she clutched his hand.

"Please let me go. I'll leave the country and never come back."

He removed her hand from his.

"No. You'll be going to jail."

He bandaged her leg and stood up. "Don't do anything stupid. I don't want to kill you."

Miguel walked towards his family and embraced them.

"Oh, Sheila, I searched for you everywhere. Up until they found a body that was identified as yours. I attended your funeral. If I had known that you were alive, I would have never brought another woman to the house."

Sheila looked at him and then at Candice.

"Call the police, and make sure she doesn't run away," she said.

Then she smiled with love at her children. "Let's go upstairs."

They walked out.

Candice gave him a victorious look.

"It looks like your marriage is falling apart. You and me could still have a future."

Miguel shook his head and left the room without saying anything. He went to get some handcuffs from his car.

Candice slowly got up and began making small steps towards the door. As she reached it, she came face to face with Miguel.

He grasped her hand. "Where do you think you're going?"

He made her walk to the wall and cuffed her hands. Then he called the police and an ambulance.

He stooped down and regarded her, pain beyond belief in his eyes.

"I had feelings for you. I was going to leave Sheila for you. Why did you do this to my family?"

She looked into his eyes.

"Kingpin threatened me. I had no choice other than taking part in his plan. But then I fell in love with you."

Miguel stood up again.

"You took away the mother of my children. All the time I was looking for her, grieving, but you knew she was alive."

"I'm sorry, Miguel. Can you forgive me, please?"

Tears filled her eyes.

Miguel glanced at her belly. "Now that poor child that you carry might be born in jail."

A smile formed on her face. "I have another surprise for you. I have never been pregnant."

Miguel didn't think he could take another shock to his system. He sat on the floor and stared silently at nothing.

Just then, Sameer and another police officer burst into the house.

"Miguel, are you here?" asked Sameer.

"Come to the living room," Miguel called as he stood up.

The policemen came into the living room and stared at Candice.

"What happened here?" asked Sameer.

"All this time my wife was alive. As soon as Sheila entered the house, she was taken hostage by Candice. When I saw her pointing a gun at my family and threating to kill them, I had no choice other than to shoot."

The other police officer took notes.

"What? Your wife is back, and your lover is shot!" Sameer exclaimed. "You have a hell of a mess to clear up."

Some curious neighbors came out of their houses to see what was happening. They stood near Miguel's house, talking to each other. As an ambulance came closer to the house, the onlookers moved to the pavement.

The ambulance parked in front of the house. Two attendants took out a stretcher and ran inside the house. They went into the living room and put Candice on the stretcher, at which time Miguel freed her hands.

She caught his hand and stared into his eyes.

"Will you be able to forgive me?"

He pulled his hand away. The nurses carried her to the ambulance.

Sameer approached him and put his hand on Miguel's shoulder.

"Oh, boy. I don't know how you're going to explain this to Sheila."

Father Piero came in at that moment. "I heard the news. Is it true?"

"Yes, Father Piero, she's back."

"This is a miracle. God heard our prayers. But where has she been?"

"I don't know. I didn't get a chance to talk to her. Forgive me Father, but I need to go upstairs to check on my family."

"Please ask Sheila to come see me once things have settled down."

Together they walked to the door.

"I'll see you later," said Father Piero, and he walked away. Miguel stared at the people outside and closed his door.

Sheila lay on her bed with both children hugging her. They didn't want to let her go.

Nadia kept sniffing her mother's hair.

"Mummy, you smell so nice. I cried a lot when you left."

"I don't understand," said Ronnel.

"Honey, what don't you understand?" she asked with a smile.

"I saw your coffin in the church. You were in it. How could you be alive?" asked Ronnel.

He raised his head up and regarded her curiously.

"That wasn't me. They've mistaken someone else for me."

"Mummy, Candice is a bad woman. She wanted me to clean the floor," said Nadia.

Sheila kissed her head. "Forget about her. She's out of our lives now."

Miguel came into the bedroom and looked at Sheila.

"Babe, I'm so sorry for this."

She looked back at him without saying anything.

He came up to them and sat on the bed. He held her hand and caressed it.

"I'm so happy to see you back home. Where have you been?"

Sheila sat up without saying a word.

You have been sleeping with a whore in my own bed. Now you are sorry?

She felt like slapping her husband for bringing a lover home. Not just a lover, but a criminal who could hurt her children. But since the children were present, she kept her urge in control.

"I've been in a Venezuelan brothel."

"What?" he gasped.

He looked into her eyes. "How did you get there?"

"I was taken by boat. Yet, I see that while I suffered, you were having a good time."

"I swear! There was a burnt body! It had your ring on its finger! If I had known that it wasn't you, I would have continued looking! Can you forgive me? Please?"

Sheila turned around and noticed Candice's portrait.

"You didn't wait too long to replace me."

He moved closer to her and caressed her face. "Babe, please try to understand me."

Sheila stood up. "Can we talk later, please? I sailed and walked today for a long distance. I would like to be alone with my children."

"Okay, babe. Take your rest."

Miguel walked away. Sheila lay back on the bed, exhaustion taking her over.

"Mummy, what's a brothel?" asked Ronnel.

"It's a bad place where people are treated inhumanely."

"Did they hurt you?" asked Nadia.

"No, child. They did not. Why don't we focus on something good?"

Nadia's eyes lit up.

"We met Santa at Christmas," she said as she snuggled next to her mother. "He gave me a nice dolly."

"No way! Santa came to our house?"

"Yes!" Nadia nodded excitedly.

Sheila recalled the gift she had received in Brothel.

Condoms for Christmas. Just sickening.

After the onlookers finally dispersed, Miguel went outside. He lit a cigarette.

I knew it. Kingpin was behind this. I shouldn't have brought Candice home. How could I know Sheila was alive? Now she knows that I lived with a liar. She wasn't even pregnant. I was so blind.

He threw the butt on the ground and went inside.

The next day, Sheila's friends and relatives found out about her return. The house phone rang nonstop. Everyone wanted to come and see her, including reporters, but Sheila had no desire to see anyone. She wanted to spend as much time with her children as she could, and to get some rest.

A reporter on the evening news announced her return, which caused a reaction in Indriani—and it wasn't a good one.

While the news was being broadcast, she was wiping a table in the living room. He husband sat in front of the TV. As she cleaned, she listened to the news.

"A few months ago, Sheila Seeglobin was kidnapped, and then a body burned to an unrecognizable state was found. The ring found on the victim's finger belonged to Sheila. Based on this, the victim's corpse was identified as hers. While everyone thought that Sheila had died, she was actually being held in captivity in Venezuela. One must wonder how Sheila's ring ended up on the victim's finger? We don't have all the details."

Hearing the reporter's words, Indriani began feeling dizzy. Her eyes became blurry, and she couldn't understand the rest of the announcer's words.

She grabbed onto a chair. "The burned woman that was buried is my child. She's dead!"

She fell, pulling the chair with her. It landed right next to her.

Her husband got up and rushed to his wife. He shook her shoulder.

"Indriani, what's wrong?"

But she was unresponsive. He put his ear to her chest.

He could hear her heartbeat, so he rushed to the phone and called an ambulance.

On the way to the hospital, he was told that his wife had a stroke.

In the morning, Miguel left with the children to drop them off at school. After they left, Sheila stood in the shower shampooing her hair. After she rinsed it, she came out of the shower.

She suddenly stopped by the toilet bowl, remembering how Victor had pushed her head into the one at the brothel.

She suddenly felt nauseous.

I hope he burns in Hell.

She took a towel from the rack and wrapped herself with it.

After she came out of the bathroom, she pulled out a drawer to get clean underwear. She couldn't find anything of hers. The whole drawer was packed with Candice's panties and bras. She pulled them out and threw them on the floor.

Miguel parked the car in the driveway and entered the house. Then he headed for the bedroom.

As he stepped in, he was shocked to see underwear scattered all over the floor. Sheila had her back to him and was sobbing.

"What's going on?" he asked.

Sheila turned around and glared at him.

"I've been disgraced, spat on, raped, and sold out as if I'm some kind of animal without human rights or feelings. They treated me like garbage. My face was pushed down into a toilet bowl. I felt disgusted, dirty, and imprisoned. My precious freedom and dignity were ripped away from me. My body wasn't mine anymore. I cried every night, begging the Lord to free me, because I wanted to come back to our kids and to you. But what have you been doing all this time?"

"I've been trying to find you."

"Really? No, you have been having a great time with an outlaw. You brought her here to live with my children. Not just any woman, but the one who kidnapped me and shot you!"

"I swear I didn't know any of this. And it's over."

"The damage is done. They took away the best of me."

He came over to her and grasped her wrists.

"Listen, we can fix all of this and move on."

She had a vivid memory of Victor grabbing her wrists. She pulled her hands out and slapped him.

"You had been cheating on me before this happened, but I kept silent, pretending as if nothing was happening only for the sake of our children. I'm not going to close my eyes anymore. I'm applying for a divorce."

Miguel fell on his knees and pulled her hand to his lips.

"I beg you to forgive me. We can work on our marriage."

Sheila glanced at Candice's portrait and pulled her hand away.

"It's too late. Go work it out with her and leave me alone."

Miguel left, heaviness in his chest. He knew nothing could change her mind.

Sheila changed into some casual clothes that she found in a garbage bag.

Can't even find anything of mine. He completely moved on and got rid of my things.

While in captivity, she grew to understand that life was too short to waste it. She went downstairs, took her car keys from the hook by the door, and left the house.

She'd caught her husband cheating on her a few times. Yet, she kept forgiving and playing dumb and deaf. However, Candice made her lose her final drop of patience. She decided to start the divorce process and move out of Miguel's house with her children.

***

Thank you for reading Caribbean Tears. Considering what is happening in the world, I cannot keep my eyes closed to it. And so I wrote Caribbean Tears to highlight the plight of the victims of human trafficking. Please leave your review of my book. Your reviews mean a lot to me. United, we can make a difference. Silence is not golden.

MESSAGE TO MY READERS

Dear readers: *CARIBBEAN TEARS* was written in order to highlight the plight of trafficked victims. Every day, unfortunate souls become victims of trafficking. There is no value for human freedom or rights as the greed for money grows.

Those who have turned away from the Lord and have followed the path of evil cannot be satisfied with what they have. Therefore, they yearn for riches, control, and power. These are destroyers of the human soul. Can money, or things that humans acquire, be taken with them when death comes? No!

However, the soul will find its permanent dwelling either in Hell or Paradise. All depends on the choices that humans make, their actions, and their chosen path. Hunger for wealth blinds one's mind and heart. Therefore, many continue running after monetary rewards.

Other humans become targets for these kinds of people. Trafficking has turned into a money-making business. Therefore, the hunters are everywhere in search of vulnerable prey. They are even on the social websites.

Some people are kidnapped forcibly, but others fall into the trap easily. Many young girls leave their families and never come back home. Others are lured into traps by promises of good employment or marriage. Even underaged girls are forced into prostitution.

Don't be fooled by appearance or sweet talk! Don't start a relationship with someone online unless you know the person very well. Do not agree to meet someone you've only met online! Keep yourself save!

So many have been forced into prostitution or free labor, including children. They need our help!

How can one recognize the victims of trafficking?

Victims often feel depressed, agitated, and scared. The traffickers are in control of their identification documents as well as their finances. Some of the captives do not speak English and are constantly accompanied by someone. They're either underpaid or used as free labor. At times, these people are unable to leave the job place or house where they are kept. The victims might exhibit signs of abuse, such as bruises and cuts, and might have an unhealthy look. Their living condition is very poor. Some are forced to live in overcrowded places.

If you see any of these symptoms, please report it to the relevant authorities. Talk to the victims and ask questions.

To those who chose a path of crime: Turn away before it is too late and build a relationship with God. Hell is a real and very scary place. Do not make it your final destination.

God helps us in many ways and brings out the good in us. However, the path of crime leads to destruction and puts one's family in danger.

BIOGRAPHY

Emiliya Ahmadova was born in the city of Baku, the capital of Azerbaijan. Emiliya is a compassionate and spiritual person, devoted to the well-being of other people. She writes in order to highlight the social issues that are happening throughout the world in hope to bring positive changes.

Emiliya has diplomas in business management, as well as a Bachelor of Arts (B.A.) in human resources management. She also has International diplomas in the advanced study of the theory and practice of management, administration and business management, communications, hotel operations management, office management and administration, and Professional English from the Cambridge International College, in addition to a certificate in novel-writing.

Emiliya likes being around people, listening to their issues, adores travel, enjoys playing soccer. Her favorite activity, along with spending her time with family, is offering voluntary services and working on her books.

BOOKS BY EMILIYA

'*A Hell For All Seasons* features seven bone-chilling short stories that span the globe, inviting you to partake in a spine-tingling supernatural adventure that you'll not soon forget.

Inside you'll discover what happens when unsuspecting schoolgirls, strait-laced physicians, a swash-buckling cowboy, selfish hypocrites, a drunkard, a female medium, and ordinary university student encounter their worst nightmares.

What have they done to spark supernatural phenomena?

Bad choices and bad timing come to haunt them in earth-shattering ways to teach them a much needed, if not ill-guided, lesson, filled with moments of terror, hours of chaos, and years of regret.

'This is a worthy collection of great stories for horror aficionados with an imaginative and clever title that accurately reflects the book's content, and I would highly recommend horror lovers go looking for it.'

Brian O'Hare, author of *Fallen Men*

'Ms. Ahmadova has done a terrific job of relating small but very meaningful stories. Every one of them is a frightening world unto itself, and all of them are very worth reading. Highly recommended for aficionados of short horror stories.'

K.R. Morrison, author of *Be Not Afraid* and *UnHoly Trinity*

My Twin Sister and Me, written by an ex-Scout leader, is a story that introduces children to Scouting in Venezuela.

Glue on the windowsill and toothpaste in the shoes. Who did the deed?

Twelve-year-old Cub Scout twins Julieta and Rafaela have to deal with their older sister's ugly tricks, which get them into trouble.

At school, Julieta is being mocked for the freckles on her face and her crooked teeth. Forgetting her own plight, however, she stands up to a bully, Claudius, in order to protect her friend Montano from being persecuted. Out of kindness she agrees to go to the movie with Montano. Due to situations beyond her control, it ends up being an embarrassment in more ways than one. However, once again, she stands up for Montano.

Another time, their Uncle David surprises the family by flying from his home in the US to Caracas for a visit. His visit causes worry; something is wrong. Julieta faces her fears in order to save her ill uncle in the middle of the night. After saving him, she becomes a hero in the uncle's eyes.

The Scouts plan to attend a Jamboree in Russia, and the girls get caught up in the planning and carrying out of various schemes to pay for the adventure.

This book not only introduces children to Scouting, but also teaches them values, morals, kindness, and faith. My Twin Sister and Me shows how to manage anger, face one's fears, the importance of self-respect, and how to deal with bullying. Above all, it helps kids learn how to show kindness to others.

Oh--and very importantly: how to have fun.

Broken Chains is a 2017 Readers' Favorite and Bookvana Awards finalist. It has also been honored as a finalist in the 2018 International Book Awards in the category of 'Fiction - Inspirational.'

Escape is only the beginning of her nightmares. The beautiful Silvana, shunned by society through no fault of her own, leaves Azerbaijan. She migrates to Kenya, where she falls in love with a man she sees as the answer to her prayers.

But her new husband, Mark, isn't the man she thought she was marrying. Silvana must make a decision which will change her life forever.

Made in the USA
Lexington, KY
15 December 2019

58602603R00197